FEMALE SEXUAL OFFENDERS

FEMALE SEXUAL OFFENDERS

Theory, Assessment and Treatment

Edited by

Theresa A. Gannon
University of Kent, Kent, UK

&

Franca Cortoni
Université de Montréal, Quebec, Canada

⊛WILEY-BLACKWELL

A John Wiley & Sons, Ltd., Publication

Registered Office
John Wiley & Sons Ltd, The Atrium, Southern Gate, Chichester, West Sussex, PO19 8SQ, UK

Editorial Offices
The Atrium, Southern Gate, Chichester, West Sussex, PO19 8SQ, UK
9600 Garsington Road, Oxford, OX4 2DQ, UK
350 Main Street, Malden, MA 02148–5020, USA

For details of our global editorial offices, for customer services, and for information about how to
apply for permission to reuse the copyright material in this book please see our website at
www.wiley.com/wiley-blackwell.

Library of Congress Cataloging-in-Publication Data

Female sexual offenders : theory, assessment, and treatment / edited by Theresa A. Gannon & Franca
Cortoni.
    p. cm.
  Includes bibliographical references and index.
    ISBN 978-0-470-68344-6 (cloth) – ISBN 978-0-470-68343-9 (pbk.)   1. Female sex offenders.
2. Female sex offenders–Mental health.   3. Female sex offenders–Psychology.   4. Female sex
offenders–Service for.   I. Gannon, Theresa A.   II. Cortoni, Franca.
  HV6557.F463 2010
  364.15′3082–dc22   2010010080

A catalogue record for this book is available from the British Library.

Typeset in 10/12pt Palatino by Aptara Inc., New Delhi, India.

1   2010

Theresa A. Gannon: For Thomas Patrick Gannon 'Uncle Pat' (1921–2009).

Franca Cortoni: For my children, Sébastien and Alexandre.

CONTENTS

About the Editors   ix

List of Contributors   xi

Preface   xv

Acknowledgements   xvii

1 Female Sexual Offenders: Theory, Assessment and Treatment –
  An Introduction   1
  Theresa A. Gannon and Franca Cortoni

2 Understanding the Prevalence of Female-Perpetrated Sexual Abuse
  and the Impact of That Abuse on Victims   9
  Jacqui Saradjian

3 Theories of Female Sexual Offending   31
  Danielle A. Harris

4 The Juvenile Female Sexual Offender: Characteristics,
  Treatment and Research   53
  Lisa L. Frey

5 The Mental Health Needs of Female Sexual Offenders   73
  Myriam-Mélanie Rousseau and Franca Cortoni

6 The Assessment of Female Sexual Offenders   87
  Franca Cortoni

7 The Treatment Needs of Female Sexual Offenders   101
  Hannah Ford

8 A Review of Treatment Initiatives for Female Sexual Offenders   119
  Kelley Blanchette and Kelly N. Taylor

9 Using the Polygraph with Female Sexual Offenders   143
   Peggy Heil, Dominique Simons, and David Burton

10 Working with Female Sexual Offenders: Therapeutic Process Issues   161
   Sherry Ashfield, Sheila Brotherston, Hilary Eldridge, and Ian Elliott

11 Developments in Female Sexual Offending and Considerations for
   Future Research and Treatment   181
   Theresa A. Gannon, Mariamne R. Rose, and Franca Cortoni

Index   199

ABOUT THE EDITORS

Theresa A. Gannon, DPhil, CPsychol (Forensic) is Director of the MSc in Forensic Psychology and Senior Lecturer in Forensic Psychology at the University of Kent, UK. Theresa also works as a Chartered Consultant Forensic Psychologist specialising in sexual offenders at the Trevor Gibbens Unit; Forensic Psychiatry Services, Kent, UK. Theresa has published widely in the areas of both male- and female-perpetrated sexual offending and is interested in research relating to both the treatment needs and overall rehabilitation of sexual offenders. Theresa is lead editor of the book *Aggressive Offenders' Cognition: Theory, Research, and Treatment* (John Wiley & Sons) along with Professor Tony Ward, Professor Anthony Beech and Dr Dawn Fisher, and co-editor of the book *Public Opinion and Criminal Justice* (Willan) along with Dr Jane Wood. Theresa is currently working on a sole authored book for Wiley-Blackwell entitled *Sexual Offenders' Cognition, Motivation, and Emotion*. She also serves on the editorial boards of *Aggression and Violent Behavior*, *British Journal of Forensic Practice*, *Sexual Abuse: A Journal of Research and Treatment*, *International Journal of Offender Therapy and Comparative Criminology*, and is Associate Editor of *Journal of Sexual Aggression*.

Franca Cortoni, PhD, CPsych, received her PhD in clinical and forensic psychology from Queen's University at Kingston, Canada. Formally with the Correctional Service of Canada, where she held positions as Director of Sexual Offender Programs, National Consultant on Women who Sexually Offend, and Director of Correctional Programs Research, Dr Cortoni is now with the School of Criminology at the Université de Montréal. She is also Associate Editor of the *Journal of Sexual Aggression*. Over the years, Dr Cortoni has worked with and conducted research on male and female offenders in a variety of Canadian and Australian penitentiaries and community settings. In addition, she has provided consultancy and training services in the assessment, treatment and management of male and female sexual offenders in Canada, Australia, the USA and England. Her audiences include parole officers, psychologists, criminologists, parole board members, police forces (including Interpol) and criminal court judges. Her research interests include factors associated with the development of sexual offending behaviour, risk assessment, treatment and management issues in both male and female sexual offenders. She has published and presented extensively in national and international forums on these topics.

LIST OF CONTRIBUTORS

Sherry Ashfield began her career in the Probation Service (UK) in 1992, holding a number of prison and community posts where she developed her interest and expertise working with women who display harmful behaviour towards children. Sherry joined the Lucy Faithfull Foundation in 1999 and works as a principal practitioner in its Female Outreach Project. This project offers assessment, intervention and consultancy services to probation and prison staff working with female sex offenders. Sherry also provides assessments for the family courts and training focused around female sexual offending for many organisations including the Probation Service, the Prison Service and the National Organisation for the Treatment of Abusers (NOTA, UK).

Kelley Blanchette began working with the Research Branch, Correctional Service of Canada, in 1993. She completed her doctorate in forensic psychology at Carleton University in January 2005. During her graduate training, Dr Blanchette worked for 6 years as a supervisor at the Ottawa Detoxification Centre, completing assessments and referrals to treatment for alcohol and drug-addicted men and women. From 2000 to 2007, she was Director of Women Offender Research; in 2007 was National Manager, Violence Prevention Programs, and in 2008 was appointed as the Senior Director, Correctional Research. The primary focus of Dr Blanchette's research has been women offenders. She has published extensively in peer-reviewed and government journals and co-authored a book entitled *The Assessment and Treatment of Women Offenders* (John Wiley & Sons). Dr Blanchette is an adjunct professor at Carleton University, and is currently working at Correctional Service of Canada as Director General in the Women Offender Sector.

Sheila Brotherston is Criminal Justice Services Director for Women and Young People with the Lucy Faithfull Foundation (LFF) in the UK. She joined LFF after working for 20 years in the probation service where she had experience in the development and delivery of sex offender programmes including a group work programme for female sex offenders at HMP Styal. She currently manages LFF's work with female sex offenders and provides consultancy to probation and prison staff in working with female sex offenders. She also manages LFF's work with young people in the secure estate including work with young women.

David Burton is a professor at Smith College School for Social Work in Northampton, MA. His current clinical work is at Northeastern Center for Youth and Families in Easthampton, MA, and with the MA Department of Youth Services. Dr Burton has worked in the field of sexual aggression for over 20 years, primarily as a clinician with adolescents and children. His research focuses on the childhood victimisation and aetiology of child, adolescent and adult sexual abusers – current research interests include trauma histories of sexual abusers, non-sexual criminality of sexual abusers, attachment, cognitive behavioural theory and treatment, pornography, substance abuse, self-cessation methods, evidenced based practice, effectiveness of treatment for adolescent sexual abusers, and racial discrimination of sexual abusers. Dr Burton has been published in several journals including *Child Abuse and Neglect, Victims and Violence, Sexual Aggression, Evidenced Based Social Work, Smith College Studies in Social Work* and *Sexual Abuse: A Journal of Research and Treatment.* Dr Burton serves on the editorial boards of *Child Abuse and Neglect* & *Sexual Abuse: A Journal of Research and Treatment* and is the Associate Editor of *Smith Studies.*

Franca Cortoni is a clinical forensic psychologist. Formally with the Correctional Service of Canada, she now works at the School of Criminology at the Université de Montréal, Canada. Her clinical and research work has focused on both male and female sexual offenders. See 'About the Editors' section for more information about this editor/author.

Hilary Eldridge is Chief Executive of the Lucy Faithfull Foundation, a child protection charity preventing and working with child sexual abuse in the UK. She has worked with sex offenders and their families since 1975. She co-authors and monitors assessment and treatment programmes for adult male offenders, female offenders, young people and their families. Specialising in developing interventions to suit the specific needs of female sex offenders, she has published book chapters and has consulted to and provided training on this subject to a wide range of agencies. She is an honorary lecturer in Forensic Psychology at the University of Birmingham.

Ian Elliott is a research psychologist with the Lucy Faithfull Foundation, where he is engaged in projects relating to both female sexual offending and child pornography offences. Ian is researching a PhD at the University of Birmingham (UK), exploring the potential application of contemporary adult sexual offence theory to child pornography offences, and is also a Course Tutor in Forensic Psychology. He has published and presented research findings at both national and international conferences.

Hannah Ford is a clinical psychologist working in the West Midlands (UK) with young people in care, including those who are involved in sexual offending. Before moving to this role, Hannah worked for the Lucy Faithfull Foundation, contributing to the assessment and treatment of perpetrators of sexual offences against children, and completing a Home Office commissioned evaluation of national need for residential treatment provision for sexual offenders. She has a particular interest in women who commit sexual offences and has written a book and contributed chapters about this topic. She also has an interest in sexual offenders with intellectual disabilities and completed her doctoral research in this area.

Lisa L. Frey is an associate professor at the University of Oklahoma (OU) and the Director of the OU Counseling Psychology Clinic (USA). Dr Frey operated a private clinical and consulting practice for many years, where she specialised in working with female and male juvenile sexual offenders and victims of violence and abuse. Her research and teaching emphases have been shaped by her extensive practice background and by her feminist orientation. Dr Frey's research interests are in the areas of delinquent youth, particularly delinquent and aggressive behaviour in girls; diversity issues; relational–cultural theory; and sociocultural influences on relational development and gender-role development.

Theresa A. Gannon is a senior lecturer in Forensic Psychology and Director of the MSc in Forensic Psychology at the University of Kent, UK. Theresa also works as a Chartered Consultant Forensic Psychologist. See 'About the Editors' section for more information about this editor/author.

Danielle A. Harris is an assistant professor in the Justice Studies Department at San Jose State University (USA). She received her doctorate in Criminology in 2008 from Griffith University, Australia. Prior to that, she completed a Masters degree in Criminology and Criminal Justice at the University of Maryland and a Bachelors Degree in Justice Studies at the Queensland University of Technology and the University of Westminster, London. She has presented at numerous conferences including ATSA, ASC and ACJS. Her research interests include many aspects of sexual offending: specialisation and versatility; the criminal career paradigm; female sexual offending; and related public policy.

Margaret 'Peggy' Heil is a licensed clinical social worker in the USA. She has over 20 years of experience developing and directing the Sex Offender Treatment and Monitoring Program at the Colorado Department of Corrections. She also provides training and consultation in the treatment and management of sexual offenders. In addition, she is a therapist representative on the Colorado Sex Offender Management Board, and is a past Executive Board Member of the Association for the Treatment of Sexual Abusers and the Colorado Coalition Against Sexual Assault. She has been involved in a number of studies and has authored professional articles and book chapters related to sexual offenders.

Mariamne R. Rose graduated with a BSc (Hons) in psychology in 2003. Following her degree she worked as an assistant psychologist in adult mental health settings and as a researcher on projects investigating prison mental health and female sexual offending. She has interviewed and conducted research with a number of female sexual offenders in the UK and is co-author of the *Descriptive Model of Female Sexual Offending* (with Theresa Gannon). She is currently working towards a Doctorate in Clinical Psychology at Royal Holloway, University of London, UK.

Myriam-Mélanie Rousseau is a licensed clinical social worker. She completed her Masters degree in social work at Laurentian University in Sudbury, Canada, and is a doctoral candidate at the School of Criminology at the Université de Montréal. Ms Rousseau works with the Sexual Abuse Centre for children and their families in Gatineau, Québec, Canada, where she provides clinical supervision to practitioners, conducts group therapy programmes, and provides family therapy to the youth and their families. She also provides consultation services to several mental health agencies and is a trainer in systemic family therapy.

Jacqui Saradjian is Consultant Clinical and Forensic Psychologist. She has conducted the UK's largest research project into the lives, experiences and beliefs of women who sexually abuse children. She has also surveyed the impact of that abuse on their victims. She is currently employed by Cambridgeshire and Peterborough Foundation Trust as Clinical Director of the Fens Unit based in HMP Whitemoor, UK. This is a unit for the assessment and treatment of severely personality disordered men who are extremely dangerous. A high percentage of these men have been sexually abused by women.

Dominique Simons has conducted research for the Colorado Department of Corrections Sex Offender Treatment and Monitoring Program for 11 years. In addition to programme and treatment evaluation, she has consulted on projects regarding juvenile sexual offender recidivism, GLM/SRM treatment, and what works with sexual offenders in Colorado. She has presented and/or co-authored journal articles and book chapters with respect to the developmental experiences of sex offenders, process issues in sex offender treatment, the influence of therapist characteristics on treatment progress, attachment and the therapeutic relationship, crossover sexual offences, utilising polygraph as a risk assessment and treatment progress tool, formulating prevention strategies from aetiological models, prevalence and treatment of multiple paraphilias, the evaluation of GLM/SRM approach to treatment, childhood victimisation of sexual offenders and the prevalence of intimate partner rape among domestic violence and sexual offenders.

Kelly N. Taylor completed her doctorate in Psychology at the University of Ottawa, Canada, in 2008. Her dissertation research examined employment assessment, vocational interests and employment intervention with federally sentenced offenders in Canada. Dr Taylor has been working with the Correctional Service of Canada since 2000, with the majority of her time dedicated to research with women offenders. To date, her research in the area of women offenders has focused on mental health needs, risk assessment, therapeutic alliance between inmates and staff, security classification, programme evaluation, hostage-taking behaviour and gender differences in aggression. She is currently the Acting Senior Director of the Correctional Research Division and the Director of Women Offender Research.

PREFACE

Our ideas and enthusiasm for this edited collection have stemmed, in part, from our attendance at the Association for the Treatment of Sexual Abusers' 27th annual conference (2008). Not only did this conference provide the forum for some interesting presentations regarding female sexual offenders (many of which were presented by some of the chapter authors in this book), but it also provided a forum for the editors of this book to discuss female sexual offending in depth. What became clear to us, over our discussions, was that although the female sexual offending field appeared to have developed enormously over the past decade, there were no books dedicated to the topic that outlined these core progressions. From this realisation, we began to approach leading professionals about whether they would be interested in writing a chapter for a book devoted to female sexual offenders. The response that we received was extremely encouraging; and as editors we feel privileged to edit a text of special interest to us, with such a group of enthusiastic and knowledgeable professionals. We hope that this book will promote further research and empirically based gender-informed assessment and treatment practices in an area that has just begun to gain momentum.

Theresa A. Gannon and Franca Cortoni
October 2009

ACKNOWLEDGEMENTS

We would like to acknowledge all of the individuals who have made this collection of chapters possible. First of all, thank you to all of the authors who took so much time and effort into writing their chapters. We would also like to thank all those at Wiley-Blackwell who gave advice and help with this piece of work from start to finish. In particular, thank you Clive Hollin for dealing positively with the initial enquiry about this book and for directions about possible avenues for publication of this book. Also, a big thank you to everyone at Wiley-Blackwell for supporting this book. In particular, thanks must go to Andrew Peart for his enthusiasm and support on this book and to Karen Shield for dealing with all our queries. Finally, thank you to Cheena Chopra for dealing with the copyediting associated with this book.

Chapter 1

FEMALE SEXUAL OFFENDERS: THEORY, ASSESSMENT AND TREATMENT – AN INTRODUCTION

Theresa A. Gannon

University of Kent, Kent, UK

Franca Cortoni

Université de Montréal, Quebec, Canada

Research and treatment efforts with female sexual offenders appear to have gained substantial momentum in recent years. This is clearly evidenced by the selection of chapters available in this book. Only 10 years ago, it would have been difficult – perhaps impossible – to develop an edited volume of works dedicated solely to the research and treatment of female sexual offenders. More recently, however, we have witnessed an outbreak of research activity associated with investigating the *treatment needs* (Beech, Parrett, Ward & Fisher, 2009; Gannon, Hoare, Rose & Parrett, in press; Gannon & Rose, 2009; Nathan & Ward, 2002; Strickland, 2008), *mental health correlates* (Christopher, Lutz-Zois & Reinhardt, 2007; Fazel, Sjöstedt, Grann & Långström, 2008), *offence styles* (Gannon, Rose & Ward, 2008, 2010), *sexual offence histories* (Simons, Heil, Burton & Gursky), *recidivism rates* (Cortoni & Hanson, 2005; Cortoni, Hanson & Coache, 2009; Freeman & Sandler, 2008) and *typologies* (Sandler & Freeman, 2007; Vandiver & Kercher, 2004) associated with female sexual offending.

Perhaps the two most prominent questions on the lips of most professionals who work with female sexual offenders and indeed laymen who hear about female-perpetrated sexual abuse are: (1) To what extent are female sexual offenders similar to, and different from, male sexual offenders?; and (2) To what extent are female sexual offenders similar to, and different from, females who offend non-sexually? Clearly, we are unlikely to discover the answers to these all-encompassing questions overnight. In fact, the literature pertaining to *male* sexual offenders – although

Female Sexual Offenders: Theory, Assessment, and Treatment   Edited by Theresa A. Gannon and Franca Cortoni
© 2010 John Wiley & Sons, Ltd

substantially more mature than that documented with female sexual offenders – still falls short of answering questions of parallel relevance to male sexual offending (see Laws & O'Donohue, 2008). Thus, professionals who work with female sexual offenders must remain patient, since it is likely to take some considerable time before the literature associated with female sexual offending reaches a level deemed to be acceptable for the convincing implementation of evidence-based practice.

Nevertheless, it is extremely heartening to witness the recent explosion of research interest in the topic of female sexual offending. It is unclear exactly what has prompted this recent and focused interest on this special population of sexual offenders. Female sexual offending has typically been reported as being relatively rare in comparison to male-perpetrated abuse (Gannon & Rose, 2008; O'Connor, 1987; Peter, 2009), and even very recent research suggests that the ratio of male to female sexual offenders is in the region of 20 : 1 (Cortoni et al., 2009). This estimate indicates that females account for around 5 per cent of all sexual abuse (Cortoni et al., 2009). Yet even at these levels, female-perpetrated abuse therefore accounts for a sizeable number of victims and offenders in need of clinical attention (see Cortoni & Gannon, in press). Furthermore, female-perpetrated abuse appears to have received more substantial recognition in recent years from professionals, the criminal justice system and the media (Cortoni et al., 2009; Gannon & Rose, 2008). It seems likely then, that this increased research attention on female sexual offenders is not coincidental. Rather, we believe that increased recognition of the phenomenon of female sexual abuse both professionally, and in the wider community, has resulted in more concerted research efforts – and associated funding – on female-perpetrated sexual abuse.

The maintenance of current research activity in female-perpetrated sexual offending is likely to result in the generation of significant knowledge that will permit improved assessment, treatment and management practices with female sexual offenders and that will guide future generations of researchers and practitioners in this area. It is pleasing to see such vigour and enthusiasm in an area of research that has, for many years, been downplayed and minimised – perhaps unintentionally – by professionals as well as the wider society. It is comforting and intuitively reassuring to believe that males are the only likely perpetrators of sexual abuse and to assume that if a female is involved in sexual abuse perpetration alongside a male, then she must have been forcefully coerced by that male. Research suggests that this is not necessarily the case (Gannon et al., in press; Simons et al., 2008) by challenging misguided preconceptions – associated with gender stereotyping – that have pervaded the topic of female-perpetrated sexual abuse for many years.

Our edited book describes the most recent research, clinical assessment and treatment techniques with female sexual offenders. While this book is not intended to be exhaustive, the chapters are chosen to provide interested readers with a single guiding text on the research, assessment and treatment associated with female sexual offenders. Each of the chapters typically focuses on females who sexually abuse children (unless specifically stated otherwise). Since children tend to be the predominant victims of female-perpetrated sexual assault (see Tewksbury, 2004), contemporary knowledge has focused almost exclusively on women who sexually abuse *children*.

ORGANISATION AND CONTENT OF THE BOOK

The book is essentially divided into two main parts. In the first part, more general contextual and background information is presented (e.g. female sexual abuse prevalence, theoretical explanations of female-perpetrated sexual abuse, information regarding juvenile female sexual offenders and mental health correlates of female sexual offending). In the second part of the book, the information becomes more practitioner-focused: chapters examine the assessment, treatment needs and services, treatment process issues and use of the polygraph with female sexual offenders. The specific chapters have been chosen to provide key guidance on a range of areas likely to be of interest to researchers, policy makers and practitioners. We sincerely hope that professionals who consult the forthcoming chapters will find the information contained within them useful for future research direction, theory generation and for the implementation of evidence-based practice. Certainly, we believe that the contributions outlined within this book draw us somewhat nearer to answering the questions outlined earlier – that is: (1) To what extent are female sexual offenders similar to, and different from, male sexual offenders?; and (2) To what extent are female sexual offenders similar to, and different from, females who offend non-sexually?

Regarding the specific content of each of the forthcoming chapters, Chapter 2 – written by Jacqui Saradjian – reviews the prevalence of female-perpetrated sexual abuse and the impact of such abuse on victims. In this chapter, Saradjian examines a whole range of formal and informal prevalence studies and the key factors limiting the conclusions drawn from such studies (e.g. societal attitudes, study design). Saradjian also examines the issue of victim harm in relation to female-perpetrated abuse and examines the possible interactions that may occur between victim harm and the attitudes of wider society towards female-perpetrated abuse. Worryingly, Saradjian argues that society's minimisation and conceptualisation of female-perpetrated abuse may well intensify the negative impact of female-perpetrated sexual abuse. In Chapter 3, Danielle Harris describes and evaluates typologies and theoretical perspectives available for explaining female-perpetrated abuse. To our knowledge, this is the first focused evaluation of current theories explaining the phenomenon of female-perpetrated sexual offences. Harris' chapter highlights that although there remains a plethora of typologies that classify female sexual offenders along basic demographic and offence characteristics, there is very little theory available to explain the range of interacting factors leading to the perpetration of sexual offences by women. In synthesising the available literature, Harris is able to document some individual or single-factor theories associated with female sexual offending (e.g. cognitive distortions, childhood victimisation), and one offence-process theory developed very recently (i.e. *The Descriptive Model of Female Sexual Offending*; Gannon et al., 2008). However, the lack of comprehensive theory is clearly visible, and Harris suggests that feminist criminology perspectives regarding *powerlessness* might well provide the context of a convincing multifactorial theory of female sexual offending. In Chapter 4, Lisa Frey provides a comprehensive summary and evaluation of the characteristics, research, assessment and treatment strategies available for juvenile female sexual offenders. Frey's chapter highlights the importance of studying this population of offenders separately from their adult female counterparts as although there remain important similarities between juvenile and adult female sexual offenders (e.g. child maltreatment), there are also some crucial differences. For example, on the basis of currently available literature, it appears that juvenile female sexual offenders are more likely to offend alone compared with their adult female counterparts. Nevertheless, because research examining and comparing juvenile sexual offenders with other relevant subgroups is so scant, Frey warns against forming too many sets of ideas about this population or their specific treatment requirements until further valid research becomes available. Chapter 5 outlines the available evidence regarding the mental health characteristics of female sexual offenders (Myriam-Mélanie Rousseau & Franca Cortoni). This is a particularly intriguing topic of enquiry that strongly relates to Chapter 2: the wider attitudes of society – including professionals – appear to support preconceived ideas that female sexual offenders must suffer from some form of psychopathology. Consequently, many researchers have focused their attention on studying the psychopathological correlates of female sexual offenders and have reported seemingly high rates for this population (e.g. Faller, 1987; Lewis & Stanley, 2000). However, Rousseau and Cortoni highlight the limitations plaguing current research of this nature. In particular, they suggest that psychopathology may be more likely recorded for this group due to societal biases in prosecution (i.e. only the most extreme offender is detected and prosecuted), methodological sampling procedures (i.e. recruiting from mental health institutions) and possible over-reporting of mental health issues (for justification purposes) by the women themselves. Thus, Rousseau and Cortoni conclude that this area of research requires substantial investigation to further improve our current assessment and treatment of female sexual offenders.

Turning to some more practically focused chapters, Franca Cortoni, in Chapter 6, provides readers with crucial information regarding the assessment of risk of recidivism among female sexual offenders. Cortoni highlights some of the core issues facing professionals in these areas (i.e. low baseline sexual recidivism for females, a lack of validated risk factors, a lack of risk assessment tools developed for use with females), and provides professionals with guidance on how to approach the assessment of female sexual offenders given these key constraints. Cortoni suggests that, because female sexual offenders are more likely to recidivate non-sexually, professionals should focus on using tools designed to assess general non-sexual offending risk in female sexual offenders (e.g. *LSI-R*; Andrews & Bonta, 1995) and supplement this approach with research-based clinical judgement around areas specific to female sexual offending. Such advice appears sound given that professionals do not have access to the wealth of assessment tools typically associated with male-perpetrated abuse. Hannah Ford (see Chapter 7) presents readers with a comprehensive evaluation of the potential treatment needs of female sexual offenders and compares each identified need with current knowledge regarding male-perpetrated sexual offending. In particular, Ford identifies *offence-supportive cognitions, deviant sexual interests, empathy, social and sexual relationships, coping skills, mental health difficulties, male dependency* and *previous victimisation* as potential treatment needs for female sexual offenders. Ford notes that although many of these needs appear to be similar to those of male sexual offenders, it is crucial that treatment providers recognise gender-specific nuances in relation to these treatment needs. Ford also warns researchers – in our view very sensibly – against trying to 'fit' female sexual offenders to existing male models and argues that we need to begin more female-specific enquiries regarding treatment needs, treatment effectiveness and treatment processes.

Directly following on from this, Kelley Blanchette and Kelly Taylor (see Chapter 8) provide what we believe to be the first focused overview of the range of international treatment initiatives available for female sexual offenders. Blanchette and Taylor describe current assessment and treatment in *Correctional Services Canada*, and the *Lucy Faithfull Foundation, UK*, as well as female sexual offender-specific services across the US (in the states of Texas, Colorado and New York). Other developing services within the *National Offender Management Service, UK*, and the *Department of Correctional Services, New South Wales*, are also described and evaluated. Blanchette and Taylor's unique review highlights the distinct lack of treatment services available – internationally – for female sexual offenders, and also highlights some key differences being implemented across some programmes. For example, some programmes use polygraph-assisted disclosure for therapeutic purposes while others do not. Furthermore, while most programmes treat only females, Blanchette and Taylor highlight some that have treated females alongside male sexual offenders. Clearly, this is an area worthy of our research attention as Blanchette and Taylor suggest that the wider research literature is generally not supportive of mixed genders in offender treatment programmes. In Chapter 9, Peggy Heil, Dominique Simons and David Burton present research findings critical for those interested in using the polygraph with female sexual offenders. In what we believe to be the first review of polygraph work with female sexual offenders, Heil, Simons and Burton provide readers with their latest research findings relating to the use of the polygraph with female sexual offenders (Simons et al., 2008). Heil, Simons and Burton show that both male and female sexual offenders self-report more extensive previous offending (over and above official records) when asked to undertake polygraph testing. Interestingly, while implementation of the polygraph appears to decrease the age at which males self-report themselves engaging in sexually abusive behaviour, the same effect does not appear to hold true for female sexual offenders (the authors suggest that perhaps women do not label early sexually offensive behaviour as abusive, or simply begin offending much later than males). Perhaps the most interesting result noted by the authors of this chapter is that the prevalence and nature of self-reported co-offending alter dramatically when female sexual offenders are polygraphed. In short, while file information often shows that females have offended only in the company of a male, they began to disclose having engaged in offending without their male co-offender (either before or following the co-perpetrator abuse) when they were polygraphed. Heil, Simons and Burton make recommendations for implementation of the polygraph with female sexual offenders and argue that such testing may be important for fully understanding these women for treatment purposes. In Chapter 10, Sherry Ashfield, Sheila Brotherston, Hilary Eldridge and Ian Elliott present some of their most valuable experiences of having worked therapeutically with female sexual offenders. A very novel and exciting aspect of this chapter is the authors' attention to therapeutic process issues with female sexual offenders. While this issue has recently gained significant attention in male sexual offending (e.g. Serran, Fernandez, Marshall &

Mann, 2003), it does not appear to have even been explicitly reviewed in relation to female sexual offending. Clearly, the absence of dialogue – and research – relating to this aspect stems from the small numbers of females who come to our clinical attention. Ashfield, Brotherston, Eldridge and Elliott discuss therapeutic process issues for female sexual offenders that they believe are both similar to and different from those identified in male sexual offenders. Again, acknowledgement of gender appears to be critical. For example, while developing a strong therapeutic alliance is essential for all therapeutic work with male sexual offenders, Ashfield, Brotherston, Eldridge and Elliott argue that issues very specific to females should also be considered. For example, given the small numbers of female sexual offenders who come to clinical attention, Ashfield, Brotherston, Eldridge and Elliott suggest that it is vital that therapists communicate to their client that they are competent and knowledgeable in the area of *female*-perpetrated offences. Clearly, female sexual offenders may experience a number of negative emotions associated with their self-view and so, therapist confidence and experience is paramount.

The final chapter of this book is written by Theresa Gannon, Mariamne Rose and Franca Cortoni. In this chapter, current knowledge outlined within this book about research and treatment with female sexual offenders is summarised. Consideration is given to the need for effective research and programming with female sexual offenders, the form and structure required to undertake future female sexual offender research and treatment, and the need to establish female-specific assessments and measures. In particular, we argue that future research efforts *must* be gender-informed if we are to make significant progress in our knowledge about the assessment and treatment of female sexual offenders. This final chapter concludes the book with a strong yet clear message: we must not be tempted to go down the somewhat easier road of adjusting male-informed models and assessments for use with female sexual offenders. To do so may jeopardise our research with female sexual offenders and our establishment of empirically based treatment with this population.

REFERENCES

Andrews, D. A., & Bonta, J. (1995). *Level of service inventory – revised*. Toronto: Multi-Health Systems.

Beech, A. R., Parrett, N., Ward, T., & Fisher, D. (2009). Assessing female sexual offenders' motivations and cognitions: An exploratory study. *Psychology, Crime and Law, 15*, 201–216.

Christopher, K., Lutz-Zois, C. J., & Reinhardt, A. R. (2007). Female sexual-offenders: Personality pathology as a mediator of the relationship between childhood sexual abuse history and sexual abuse perpetration against others. *Child Abuse & Neglect, 31*, 871–883.

Cortoni, F., & Gannon, T. A. (in press). Female sexual offenders. In A. Phenix & H.M. Hoberman (Eds.), *Sexual offenders: Diagnosis, risk assessment and management*. New York: Springer.

Cortoni, F., & Hanson, R. K. (2005). *A review of the recidivism rates of adult female sexual offenders* (R-169). Ottawa: Research Branch, Correction Service of Canada. Retrieved 4th May 2007, from http://www.cscscc.gc.ca/text/rsrch/reports/r169/r169_e.pdf.

Cortoni, F., Hanson, R. K., & Coache, M. E. (2009). *The recidivism rates of female sexual offenders: A meta-analysis*. Manuscript under review.

Faller, K. C. (1987). Women who sexually abuse children. *Violence and Victims, 2*, 263–276.

Fazel, S., Sjöstedt, G., Grann, M., & Långström, N. (2008). Sexual offending in women and psychiatric disorder: A national case-control study. *Archives of Sexual Behavior*, Online May 2008.

Freeman, N., & Sandler, J. (2008). Female and male sex offenders: A comparison of recidivism patterns and risk factors. *Journal of Interpersonal Violence, 23*, 1394–1413.

Gannon, T. A., Hoare, J., Rose, M. R., & Parrett, N. (in press). A re-examination of female child molesters' implicit theories: Evidence of female specificity? *Psychology Crime and Law*.

Gannon, T. A., & Rose, M. R. (2008). Female child sexual offenders: Towards integrating theory and practice. *Aggression and Violent Behavior, 13*(6), 442–461.

Gannon, T. A., & Rose, M. R. (2009). Offence-related interpretative bias in female child molesters: A preliminary study. *Sexual Abuse: A Journal of Research and Treatment, 21*, 194–207.

Gannon, T. A., Rose, M. R., & Ward, T. (2008). A descriptive model of the offense process for female sexual offenders. *Sexual Abuse: A Journal of Research and Treatment, 20*, 352–374.

Gannon, T. A., Rose, M. R., & Ward, T. (2010). Pathways to female sexual offending: A preliminary study. *Psychology, Crime and Law*, 1–22 (iFirst).

Laws, D. R., & O'Donohue, W. (2008). *Sexual deviance: Theory, assessment, and treatment* (2nd ed.). New York: Guilford Press.

Lewis, C. F., & Stanley, C. R. (2000). Women accused of sexual offenses. *Behavioral Sciences and the Law, 18*, 73–81.

Nathan, P., & Ward, T. (2002). Female sex offenders: Clinical and demographic features. *The Journal of Sexual Aggression, 8*, 5–21.

O'Connor, A. A. (1987). Female sex offenders. *British Journal of Psychiatry, 150*, 615–620.

Peter, T. (2009). Exploring taboos: Comparing male- and female-perpetrated child sexual abuse. *Journal of Interpersonal Violence, 24*, 1111–1128.

Sandler, J. C., & Freeman, N. J. (2007). Typology of female sex offenders: A test of Vandiver and Kercher. *Sexual Abuse: A Journal of Research and Treatment, 19*, 73–89.

Serran, G. A., Fernandez, Y., Marshall, W. L., & Mann, R. (2003). Process issues in treatment: Application to sexual offender programs. *Professional Psychology: Research and Practice, 34*, 368–374.

Simons, D., Heil, P., Burton, D., & Gursky, M. (October 2008). *Developmental and offense histories of female sexual offenders*. Symposium presented at the 27th Annual Association for the Treatment of Sexual Abusers Research and Treatment Conference, Atlanta, GA.

Strickland, S. M. (2008). Female sex offenders: Exploring issues of personality, trauma, and cognitive distortions. *Journal of Interpersonal Violence, 23*, 474–489.

Tewksbury, R. (2004). Experiences and attitudes of registered female sex offenders. *Federal Probation, 68*(3), 30–33.

Vandiver, D. M., & Kercher, G. (2004). Offender and victim characteristics of registered female sexual offenders in Texas: A proposed typology of female sexual offenders. *Sexual Abuse: A Journal of Research and Treatment, 16*, 121–137.

Chapter 2

UNDERSTANDING THE PREVALENCE OF FEMALE-PERPETRATED SEXUAL ABUSE AND THE IMPACT OF THAT ABUSE ON VICTIMS

JACQUI SARADJIAN

Cambridgeshire and Peterborough Foundation Trust, Cambridgeshire, UK

The sexual abuse of a child always takes place in secret; therefore the true prevalence of any form of sexual abuse of children will always be secret. The more unthinkable, and consequently stigmatising, the form of abuse, the greater the likelihood that it will be under-reported and, if reported, that it will *not* be recognised as abuse and therefore the secret will be kept. Sexual abuse of children, especially pre-pubertal children, instigated by women is still unthinkable in society today. Since information about the sexual abuse of children has been brought into the public domain, professionals have reported that both men and women are involved. Yet because the social construction of women has been such that this behaviour remains 'unthinkable', that knowledge is dismissed. Consequently, each time it is 'discovered', it is again greeted with surprise followed by collective cognitive distortions relating to that knowledge, ensuring that the secret is kept.

PREVALENCE OF FEMALE SEXUAL OFFENDING

Historical Evidence

Descriptions of early societies describe child sexual abuse as highly prevalent, with women involved in that abuse (De Mause, 2008). For example, De Mause (2008) cites the writings of Petronius (ca. 27–66 AD) who describes the incident of the rape of a 7-year-old girl while women stood around the bed clapping. Tardieu (1857), in the first formal text on child sexual abuse, recognised that whilst the majority of the perpetrators are men, women also committed such crimes. Bernard (1886) reported that during a 10-year period in France (1874–1884), 181 women

Female Sexual Offenders: Theory, Assessment, and Treatment   Edited by Theresa A. Gannon and Franca Cortoni
© 2010 John Wiley & Sons, Ltd

were convicted of sexually abusing children. W. Travis Gibb (1894), Examining Physician to the New York Society for the Prevention of Cruelty to Children, while reviewing the reported cases of indecent assault against children, concluded that women sexually abuse children more frequently than is generally supposed and suggested that less cases are brought to public notice than are actually occurring. Freud (1896) reported on cases of servant-girls, nurses and governesses sexually abusing children to whom they were in a caretaking role; he himself described being sexually abused in his early childhood by his nurse (Masson, 1985). Wulffen (1934), in his treatise on Woman as Sexual Criminals, described 24 cases of women who sexually abused children. Most were sole perpetrators, including cases of mother–son, mother–daughter, aunt–nephew and grandmother–grandson; only two women acted with their husbands. In his text on female perversion, Chideckel (1935) commented on women in authority who had beaten children for sexual pleasure. Bender and Blau (1937) described the case of a 6-year-old boy who had had sexual contact with his mother. However, they minimised the abuse by describing 'at least some cooperation of the child in the activity' (p. 514). Apfelberg, Sugar and Pfeffer (1944), when researching the clinical records of male sexual offenders in New York's Bellevue Hospital, drew attention to the fact that there were many known cases of female sexual offenders but very few have had any charges or indeed other sanctions for their behaviour.

Despite this information and the existence of other more formal prevalence studies, Freund and colleagues still stated, 'pedophilia. . . does not exist at all in women' (Freund, Heasman, Racansky & Glancy, 1984, p. 193). Denov also comments that the *Diagnostic and Statistical Manual of Mental Disorders* states that 'Except for sexual masochism. . . paraphilias are almost never diagnosed in females' (APA, 1994, p. 524, in Denov, 2003a, p. 303). Given the actual available data on the prevalence of sexual offending by women, it is assumed that this position reflects more on the inability of professionals to perceive these issues in women, as opposed to paraphilia being truly confined to males.

Formal Prevalence Studies

Victim Studies

Since the 1960s, numerous studies have examined the prevalence of childhood sexual abuse and have provided evidence of the involvement of women as sexual abusers of children. Examples of these studies are given in Table 2.1. Whilst the actual percentages vary greatly, the data indicate that there is a tendency for more male than female victims to report being sexually abused by a woman. This may be because women actually sexually abuse more male children. For example, Sarad-jian (1996b) found that when women sexually abused adolescents, they tended to choose victims in line with how they defined their own sexual orientation; presumably, more women would define themselves as heterosexual. When the women targeted very young children, however, the gender of the child appeared to be less important than what the child meant to the woman. The differences between the rates of male and female victims, however, may simply be a distortion: it may

Table 2.1 Prevalence of sexual offending by women according to victimisation studies

Studies	Sample	Girls Abused by Women (%)	Boys Abused by Women (%)
Etherington (1995)	25 male victims of child sexual abuse	—	52
Finkelhor (1984)	44,700 cases reported in 1979	5	20
Finkelhor, Hotaling, Lewis and Smith (1990)	169 men and 416 women victims of sexual abuse	1	17
Kendall-Tackett and Simon (1987)	365 women molested as children	3	—
Johnson and Shrier (1987)	Male adolescents attending a clinic (1982–1984) who disclosed sexual abuse – $n = 25$	—	44
Kelly, Wood, Gonzalez, MacDonald and Waterman (2002)	67 men referred to a clinic with a history of sexual abuse	—	20
NSPCC (2004) Childline	Reports of sexual abuse by children		
	Girls – $n = 6,356$	4	37
	Boys – $n = 2,184$		
NSPCC (2007) Childline	Reports of sexual abuse by children		
	Total $n = 11,976$	5	44
	82% stated gender of perpetrator (actual n by gender not reported)		
Peter, 2009	Canadian incidence study of child sexual abuse cases		
	Girls – $n = 246$	9.3	14.1
	Boys – $n = 99$		

be less stigmatising for adolescent males, in comparison to adolescent females, to report having had sexual contact with a woman, therefore making it more likely that the latter form of abuse will be hidden.

Studies of Known Offenders

The prevalence of sexual offending by women reported in victimisation studies differs significantly from the percentage of known women offenders. It is therefore important to reiterate that case-report data, in particular criminal justice statistics, only reflect those cases that have come into contact with the criminal justice or child protection systems. These figures do not take into account

Table 2.2   Percentages of known sexual offenders who are women

Study	Data Sources	Female Perpetrators (%)
Allen Consulting Group (2003)	Child protection cases, Victoria, Australia 2001–2002	8.3
Canadian Centre for Justice Statistics (2001)	Adults convicted of sexual assault against children in 2000	1.5
Cortoni and Hanson (2005, Cortoni, Hanson & Coache, 2009)	Official reports from Canada, UK, USA, Australia and New Zealand	4–5
Home Office (2002)	Convicted adult sexual offenders in 2000	2
O'Connor (1987)	Home Office Criminal Statistics from the United Kingdom 1975 and 1984	<1
Snyder (2000)	American Justice Department–study of 60,991 victims of sexual assaults	
	Victims: <age 6	12
	Victims: ages 6–12	6
	Victims: ages 12–17	3
Trocmé et al. (2001)	Canadian Incidence Study of Reported Child Abuse and Neglect	7
Ursel and Gorkoff (2001)	Winnipeg Family Violence Court (1992–1997) ($n = 1,349$)	3
USA National Incident-Based Reporting System (1997)	12 states (1991–1996)	4
Vandiver and Kercher (2004)	Registered adult sexual offenders in Texas in 2001	1.6

unreported cases or reported cases that have not proceeded for various reasons. This indicates a potential failure for these women to be identified and/or reported to criminal justice agencies (see Table 2.2). The most comprehensive study of prevalence to date is that of Cortoni and Hanson (2005) and Cortoni et al. (2009). They analysed both victimisation surveys and official reports that identified the gender of offender from Canada, UK, USA, Australia and New Zealand. They concluded that the female to male ratio of sexual offenders is approximately 1 : 20 and that female sexual offenders are responsible for 4–5% of all sexual offences.

Pereda and colleagues (Pereda, Guilera, Forns & Gómez-Benito, 2009) undertook a meta-analysis of the prevalence of child sexual abuse in 22 countries to establish an overall international figure. The analysis showed that 7.9 per cent of men and 19.7 per cent of women (19.2 per cent without outliers) had suffered some form of sexual abuse prior to the age of 18. If 4–5% of all these victims were sexually abused by women, then a large number of people that have experienced sexual abuse by women are being ignored by society.

Confounding Factors in Establishing Prevalence

The prevalence findings, regardless of the source of the information, suggest that adult women represent the minority of sexual offenders. There is still, however, a question as to whether these data are a significant underestimate of the actual prevalence. Males commit the majority of all crimes and there is little reason to believe that this would differ for the sexual abuse of children. Whilst it is likely that all prevalence data in relation to child sexual abuse are subject to methodological problems (Finkelhor, 1986), the discrepancies in the data indicate that sexual victimisation perpetrated by women is likely to be under-identified. The different percentages reported in the studies of sexual victimisation by females reflect the type of sample selected and methods employed in obtaining results. For example, self-report studies historically yield much higher rates of female-perpetrated sexual abuse than case-report studies. However, there are other factors that will also increase the likelihood of such under-identification, including the social and cultural construction of women leading to professional biases, less than adequate research methodologies and specific dynamics that impact on the likelihood that victims will disclose.

Social and Cultural Construction of Women

Current societal schema of women and femaleness is inconsistent with women as sexual offenders (Hislop, 2001). The social schema of maleness readily accommodates a lack of expectation of men to be nurturers and carers, an expectation that men's need should and will be catered for, and acceptance of overt aggression, sexual initiation and even sexual assault on the part of men. In contrast, the social schema of femaleness readily accommodates women as the nurturers, protectors and carers, often at personal expense. Women are seen as generally non-aggressive and asexual, except in response to men's desires and male construction of sexuality. Acts that are inconsistent with this schema are readily denied, minimised or reconstructed in order to fit more readily (Saradjian, 1996b; Giguere & Bumby, 2007). Within this context, Hetherton (1999) describes beliefs that serve to maintain society's schema of women when faced with any knowledge that women may perpetrate child sexual abuse. Examples of these beliefs include 'sexual abuse by women is harmless' and that women who sexually abuse children are 'psychiatrically disturbed or are somehow not in control of their behaviour' (p. 164). Sexual offending has long been viewed within society as a male-only crime. Males are perceived as controlling all sexual encounters and females as passive and submissive recipients, even when the male is a child and the female is an adult (Allen, 1991; Becker, Hall & Stinson, 2001; Denov, 2004a; Hislop, 2001). When women sexually abuse a girl, it is often construed as a confused form of love. For example, Banning (1989) showed two identical scenarios of an adult's behaviours with a child; behaviours included breeching physical boundaries and sleeping with the child. In one scenario, the adult was a father with a young daughter and in the other, the adult was a mother with a young son. The scenario with the adult male was almost universally seen as abuse whilst the identical scenario with a mother and a son was not.

Even if it is accepted that a woman has sexually abused a child, the damage that results from that abuse tends to be minimised. Despite its age, this example by Yorukoglu and Kemp's (1966) essay titled 'Children not severely damaged by incest with a parent' is typical of such minimisation and remains current. They describe a 13-year-old boy who had experienced oral sex with his mother. The authors describe him as relatively unaffected and attributed his aggression, vandalism, absconding, fire-setting and exposing himself to factors other than the incest. Finkelhor (1984) reported on 521 parents who were asked about the perceived seriousness of different experiences of sexual abuse. Acts by females, whether with male or female victims, were perceived to be *less abusive* than the same acts by males. Such beliefs are not only held by the general public but by professionals with whom these women and their victims come into contact (Denov, 2004a; Hislop, 2001).

Professional Responses

Denov (2004a) proposes that the sex role stereotypes that exist within society impact on the responses of professionals to female-perpetrated sexual crimes. In addition, research found that training for professionals tends not to include females as sexual offenders (see also Chapter 10). Consequently, police and mental health professionals were found to have an informal, yet well-established, way of perceiving sexual assault: males as perpetrators and females as victims (Denov, 2001). This is evidenced by research that revealed that police officers reacted with disbelief to allegations involving women, minimised the seriousness of the reports, viewed the female suspects as less dangerous and harmful, and were likely to judge the case as unsubstantiated (Denov, 2004a). From interview data with similar professionals, Bunting found that her interviewees lacked an acceptance that women may play an equal role in or even initiate the sexually offending behaviour, and had a general lack of awareness on issues of female-perpetrated child sexual abuse (Bunting, 2005).

Case example: A woman disclosed that she was sexually abusing her daughter to her general practitioner. The physician, worried for her mental health, referred her to a psychiatrist who diagnosed the woman as having a psychotic episode and prescribed her medication. The child was never interviewed or referred to social services. The abuse came to professional attention 2 years later when her ex-husband was being investigated for sexually abusing his daughter. The woman then admitted again that she was the perpetrator of the abuse.

This example demonstrates how, when given incontrovertible evidence of sexual abuse by women, most groups of professionals make every effort to minimise the offending, see the women as less culpable and perceive the abuse as harmless and even attribute responsibility to the victim (Denov, 2001; Kite & Tyson, 2004). These views are often supported in the literature guiding professional practice (Denov, 2003b). Denov (2004a) reports that within the Canadian Criminal Code, until 1983, a woman could not be charged with committing rape or indecent assault and a male could not be a victim of such an assault. Denov adds that 'female sexual passivity was reaffirmed in law by implying that females could not be the instigator or the aggressor in cases of incest' (p. 21). Kite and Tyson (2004) also note that in New Zealand, it is not an offence for a woman to have sex with an underage male, whereas for adult males, it is. A New Zealand press article (The Press, 2000) called for changes to a law which allows female perpetrators of child sexual abuse to be let off as only males are recognised as offenders. Legislation in the UK remains gender-specific as the majority of laws governing sexual offences continue to state that the victim must be female and the perpetrator must be male (Keenan & Maitland, 1999 cited in Denov, 2004a, p. 21).

There is also some evidence that suggests that professionals may not recognise victimisation by female sexual offenders, or if they recognise it, may not report it in the same way as they report sexual offending by males. Peter (2009) compared male and female perpetrators of child sexual abuse cases investigated by child welfare workers. An interesting finding was that while more than half of the referrals to child welfare agencies for male-perpetrated sexual abuse came from professional services, only one third of female-perpetrated sexual abuse came from professionals. The other two thirds came to the attention of child welfare from non-professional sources. Peter (2009) suggests that this warrants further investigation because it questions how well professional organisations are actively addressing female-perpetrated sexual abuse.

Victim Disclosure

Research indicates that although children perceive the sexual abuse perpetrated against them by women as very damaging, few, if any, have disclosed that abuse prior to the research study in which they took part (e.g. Johnson & Shrier, 1987). Risen and Koss (1987) found that of 216 college men with sexual abuse experiences prior to age 14 (50 per cent of the abusers were female), 81 per cent had told no one. Some victims report that when they have tried to disclose sexual abuse by women, professionals have dismissed, minimised or ignored their disclosure (Denov, 2004b; Hislop, 2001). Hetherton (1999) cites work suggesting that disclosure of abuse is less likely if the victims believe their experience is extraordinary in any way or if they believe that their claims will not be taken seriously. Consequently, the less the female sexual abuse against children is acknowledged, the more the victims of such abuse will be stigmatised and the less likely they are to disclose. As acknowledgement of sexual abuse by women gradually increases, we should observe increasing levels of disclosure of cases of sexual victimisation where the offender was a woman.

Nevertheless, there continues to be general levels of disbelief, minimisation and even victim blaming that increase the feelings of shame, guilt and fear on the part of the victim, dynamics that inhibit any form of disclosure. For example, adolescent girls may not disclose experiences of sexual abuse perpetrated by a woman for fear of questions related to her sexual orientation. Similarly, adolescent boys who are sexually abused by an adult woman may feel emasculated and may worry about how others will perceive their masculinity (Hislop, 2001) or fear that they will be blamed and even accused of sexually assaulting the woman. Some female perpetrators have been found to use such social constructions to minimise the likelihood of disclosure. For example, one woman who sexually abused an adolescent boy told the boy that he would be charged with rape as he was the male (Saradjian, 1996b). Finally, some adolescents, boys and girls, do not construe the experience as abuse and this is encouraged by the female perpetrator who often herself construes the experience as a 'love' relationship, no matter how brief that may be (Mathews, Matthews & Speltz, 1989; Saradjian, 1996b).

Another significant factor related to sexual abuse by women that impacts on the likelihood of disclosure by victims is the relationship with the abuser. Studies that examine the relationship of the perpetrator to the victim have found that it is very often the mother or a woman in a maternal role that sexually abuses that child (e.g. Kendall-Tackett & Simon, 1987; NSPCC, 2004; Saradjian, 1996b; Trocmé et al., 2001). This abuse frequently starts at a young age and can be masked under the guise of caregiving (Kaplan & Green, 1995). For example, Peter (2009) found that the victims of the women in her study ranged in age from newborn to 15 years. On average, victims were younger for female-perpetrated sexual abuse compared with male counterparts: 92 per cent ($n = 34$) of female-perpetrated sexual abuse victims were under the age of 9 years (Peter, 2009).

Pre-verbal abuse is a critical issue in many mother–child sexual abuse cases. The ability of a child to think, observe, narrate, remember and recount rise dramatically between the ages of 3 and 6. The mother constructs the child's world and although the child may experience the interactions as abusive, they may not know that these are not 'normal' experiences between mother and child. In addition, the child is highly dependent on the mother, which will also prohibit disclosure. Lawson (1993) found that male victims of mother–son incest often only disclosed while in long-term therapeutic relationships during adulthood.

Issues Related to Research Design

The prevalence rates of child sexual abuse by female perpetrators tend to be a by-product of research looking at general prevalence rates for child sexual abuse; many studies, however, do not directly enquire as to the gender of the perpetrator. All the studies suffer from the methodological difficulties that affect the determination of any prevalence data (Finkelhor, 1986). Some, however, have a greater level of significance when attempting to establish the prevalence of sexual abuse of children by women and the design of the study will have an impact on the prevalence rate (e.g. Becker et al., 2001; Johansson-Love & Fremouw, 2006). These issues are detailed below.

Data collection methods   The form of data collection will have an impact. Large-scale self-report surveys, in-depth interviews and case-file analyses taken from victims and/or offenders provide conflicting portraits of the phenomenon (Denov, 2004a). Some study designs involve in-depth interviews. In such cases, the occurrence, form and even severity of the abuse is often determined by the researcher. Given what is known of the minimisation of female sexual offending by professionals, this can lead to a significant researcher bias. An example of such a bias is evident in Russell's (1983) research. During the interview, one participant described what she deemed to be sexual abuse by a female; however, the incident was not considered to be abuse by the researcher and that participant was therefore not added to the number of women who had been sexually victimised as a child by a woman. There is also evidence that these studies will often not be a true reflection of the

Table 2.3   Percentages of sexual offenders who report sexual victimisation by a woman

Study	Sample: Offenders Who Report Sexual Victimization	Male Abuser (%)	Female Abuser (%)
Groth (1979)	119 rapist and child molesters	42	27
Petrovich and Templer (1984)	83 rapists	41	59
Rallings, Webster and Rudolph (2001)	144 rapists	61	39
	401 child molesters	81	19

prevalence of child sexual abuse due to the reluctance of victims to disclose. In particular, Peterson, Colebank and Motta (2001) reported that if a female has co-offended with a male, the victim may only report the abuse by the male. Thus, the woman's participation would not be represented in statistics. This is supported by Sgroi and Sargent (1993) and Denov (2004b) who found that victims are more willing to report abuse by males but only disclose abuse by females later in therapy, if at all. Kendall-Tackett and Simon (1987) also state that sexual abuse by a female is unlikely to be disclosed until sufficient trust is able to be established with a therapist.

Target population   Prevalence rates will be affected by the population targeted by the study. Rates of victimisation vary according to whether the population is male or female, students or prisoners, general population or those in treatment facilities. For example, when studying the gender ratio of offenders in nursery settings, a very high rate of female perpetrators is found (e.g. Finkelhor, Williams & Burns, 1989). This is not surprising given the predominance of female staff in such settings. Research also shows a very high prevalence of sexual abuse by women in the histories of male sexual offenders (see Table 2.3), and victimisation by female offenders may affect later choice of victims. For example, O'Brien (1989) found that 93.3 per cent of the male adolescent sexual offenders who had been sexually victimised by only a female perpetrator chose female victims whereas only 32.5 per cent of male adolescent sexual offenders that had been sexually abused by males targeted only female victims – the other 67.5 per cent abused by males targeted male or both male and female victims. These studies suggest that care must be taken when deriving rates from specific populations, as the prevalence of female sexual offending will be different in different populations.

Definitions of sexual abuse   How sexual abuse is defined influences the reported prevalence of sexual abuse. For example, some studies ask about sexual contact with an adult and then ask the gender of the perpetrator (Finkelhor et al., 1990). Others ask about sexual contact with a female who is 5 years or more older than the victim (e.g. Condy, Templer, Brown & Veaco, 1987). Given that some data indicate a significant percentage of adolescent female offenders (e.g. Snyder & Sickmund, 2006), the latter is likely to generate a higher prevalence, as the former would not include adolescent female offenders who were closer in age to the victim.

Investigators may also inadvertently define sexual victimisation in a manner that reflects behaviours that involve male perpetrators (Denov, 2004a). Ford (2006) describes a range of behaviours that are sexually abusive and thus damaging to the child, but that may not be defined as such in prevalence studies. These behaviours include offences such as voyeurism, exposure, seductive touching, sexualised hugging or kissing, extended nursing or flirting with a child, invasions of privacy including enemas, bathing together, washing the child beyond a reasonable age, excessive cleaning of the foreskin or asking intrusive questions about bodily functions. Additional behaviours may include inappropriate relationships created by the adult such as substituting the child for an absent husband, sleeping with him, unloading emotional problems on the child or using them as a confidant for personal or sexual matters.

Case Example: A 20-year-old man was imprisoned for rape and attempted strangulation of a 47-year-old woman. He states that he was not sexually abused in childhood despite his mother having insisted that he sleep with her from the time he was 8 years old, when his father left her. She always slept naked and insisted her son slept naked too. She would cuddle and kiss him in bed and she would stroke and inspect every part of his body including his genitals. She would laugh and tease him about his erections. He would accompany her to any event where she needed 'a partner' and she became very jealous and possessive should he talk to any females of his own age and found a way to stop any developing relationship. These behaviours were still continuing when he was arrested.

Language used   By virtue of their gender, female sexual offenders are often seen as non-threatening. Further, because of social construction of perceived power relationships, young male victims can be seen as dominant when they have sex with an adult female. Not only can this situation lead to a lack of recognition of the damage done by such relationships, it can also lead to under-reporting. Thus, particular consideration needs to be given to the language used when conducting prevalence studies, particularly when the perpetrator is a woman. This is illustrated by a study by Coxell and colleagues (Coxell, King, Mezey & Kell, 2000). They interviewed men attending a medicine service specialising in sexually transmitted diseases. When asked about their experiences of *sexual assaults* before the age of 16, 12 per cent of 205 men (i.e. 24 men) reported sexual assaults before age 16. The mean age at the time of the first (or only) assault was 9.8 years. Twenty of these 24 men (83 per cent) cited a male adult as the perpetrator while the remaining 7 men (29 per cent) cited a female adult as perpetrator. However, when asked about *perceived consenting sexual* acts before age 16, 27 per cent of the 205 men (i.e. 55 men) reported such experiences; the mean age of such experiences being 14 years old. Seventeen of those 55 men reported that the perpetrator was a male while the remaining 38 reported that the adult involved was a female. These results indicate that sexual contact for boys, particularly adolescent boys, with an adult female is less likely to be described by them as sexual assault. This finding is supported by other studies (Kelly et al., 2002). Thus, if a survey asks about sexual abuse or sexual assault rather than sexual contact, the prevalence findings for female abusers are likely to be an underestimation. It should be noted that regardless of how the sexual contact was defined by the victim, it is still likely to have a negative impact (see below for Impact on Victims of Female Abuse).

Case Study: Andy was sexually abused by his mother from infancy until he was 17 years old. He never perceived it as sexual abuse. He says '*My mother loved me the only way she knew how. She would never hurt me, she was my mother. I could have stopped it if I had wanted to but I kind of liked it really. It never did me any harm*'. Andy is now 34. He is serving a life sentence for rape and murder of a woman. He served a previous 9-year sentence for the rape of an older woman. He was in and out of juvenile facilities from the age of 12, mainly for violent acts, glue sniffing and drug-related offences. He also sexually abused two of his younger siblings.

Consequences for Women Who Sexually Abuse Children

Bunting (2005) found that gender of the alleged offender can play an important role in how allegations of child sexual abuse are taken forward by professionals working in child protection and criminal justice settings. As a result, cases of sexual abuse perpetrated by adult women were not only unlikely to be reported, but are unlikely to be aggressively pursued within child welfare or criminal justice systems (Bumby & Bumby, 2004; Denov, 2004a; Hislop, 2001). If women are seen to be involved in sexually abusive behaviour towards children alongside a co-perpetrator, then it is reasoned that the female must have been coerced by the male. She is then treated as a victim alongside with the child. For example, Hetherton and Breadsall (1998) demonstrated that police officers and social workers tended to recommend less severe measures when the offender was a female.

The societal schema of women can impact on how the criminal justice and health care systems handle female sexual offenders. Specifically, female sexual offenders are often managed through the health service rather than referred to the criminal justice system (Saradjian, 1996b). This process begins in adolescence. A male and female adolescent can commit a very similar offence but the male adolescent will typically be sent to a young offender project while the female adolescent will be assumed to be acting out issues related to prior victimisation and sent for therapy (Vizard, 2000).

Despite the perception that charges against female sexual offenders are not pursued, Cortoni and Hanson (2005) found that, in comparing victimisation survey results with official information where the offender was reported to the criminal justice services in the USA, 34 per cent of the male sexual offending resulted in police arrest, compared with 57 per cent of the female sexual offending. This may be a more recent trend as it differs from the previous reports on sentencing of female sexual offenders. Wolfe (1985) described 12 female sexual offenders, 11 of whom had sexually offended against children. Only two of these women received a sentence, one of which was a community sentence. Ramsey-Klawsnik (1990) described 83 women who had sexually abused children; only one was subject to criminal prosecution despite the fact that 56 per cent of these women committed acts such as burning, pinching, beating, biting the breasts or genitals of the children or restraining them with straps and ties during the sexual assaults. Shoop (2003) suggests that even when female sexual offenders are charged and convicted of sexual assault, they are treated far more leniently than their male counterparts.

He states that they are more likely to receive suspended sentences, whereas male offenders receive long custodial sentences. He suggests that it is difficult for the criminal justice system to accept that sentences should be the same for both sexes, even though the destructive nature of the behaviour may be the same. Similarly, Aylward, Christopher, Newell and Gordon (2002) describe differences in post-release requirements for male and female sexual offenders. Specifically, they report that 71 per cent of male offenders were required to have no contact with minors, compared with 53 per cent of the female offenders. In addition, 86 per cent of the male offenders were to have no contact with their victim or victim's family, compared with 68 per cent of the female offenders. Finally, 66 per cent of the male offenders in their study were required to undertake treatment or evaluation, compared with 24 per cent of the females.

On the other hand, Shakeshaft (2003) contends that no such distinction exists. She suggests that this idea stems from a small number of high-profile cases in which women received non-custodial sentences, but that this does not imply that all female offenders are getting off lightly. Interestingly, Saradjian (1996b) found that when women were convicted, they received either more lenient or harsher rather than equitable sentences when compared with male sexual offenders.

Summary

This review does not intend to suggest that females commit sexual offences at the same rate as males. However, it is highly likely that the prevalence of such offending is higher than what current data would indicate. Even if the best data that we have currently available indicate that 4–5% of all sexual abuse is committed by females (Cortoni & Hanson, 2005; Cortoni et al., 2009), then, considering the overall prevalence of child sexual abuse, there is a very large number of victims whose development has been affected by this form of offending.

IMPACT ON VICTIMS

There has been and continues to be a strong resistance against acknowledging sexual offending by women. In addition to the denial of the prevalence of this form of abuse, there is a tendency for society to view sexual offending perpetrated by women as less serious than that committed by males (e.g. Denov, 2001; Finkelhor, 1984). However, when comparing the actual acts carried out by male and female perpetrators, Rudin, Zalewski and Bodmer-Turner (1995) did not find any significant differences. This is supported by Peters' (2009) study where she found that there was no statistically significant association between the type of sexually offending behaviours and gender of perpetrator.

It is believed that sexual abuse of children by women is less damaging to the victims. This is not supported by research. While there have been few studies that review the victims' experiences of being sexually abused by a woman, those studies that are available emphasise the damage to victims (e.g. Denov, 2004b; Rosencrans, 1996). For example, Denov's (2004b) sample of seven men and seven women reported that their sexual abuse by women was highly damaging and difficult to recover from; only one male reported that his abuse by a female perpetrator did not damage him. Johnson and Shrier (1987) noted that 73 per cent of their sample of 11 adolescent boys reporting a history of molestation by females reported the immediate effects of such molestation to have been 'strong' or 'devastating'. Similarly, Sgroi and Sargent (1993) stated that those victims who had been abused by both male and female perpetrators all felt that the abuse by a woman was more harmful and damaging than the abuse by a male. Finally, all the victims involved in Rosencrans' (1996) survey described the sexual abuse as highly damaging. In that study, 27 per cent of the female victims ($n = 93$) and 44 per cent of the male victims ($n = 9$) reported feeling that there was hope of recovery, whereas 73 per cent of the females and 56 per cent of the males reported they felt so damaged that they had little hope of recovery.

The abuse perpetrated by female sexual offenders against children is often construed as a distorted form of love. While some women do perceive the children they sexually victimise as a 'lover', many do not; the sexual abuse of the child can involve sadistic fantasies or actual acts. Ramsey-Klawsnik (1990) described that 56 per cent of the 83 women in their study had perpetrated sadistic acts during the sexual abuse of the children. Saradjian (1996b) found that 29 of the 52 women (55 per cent) that sexually abused children admitted to becoming sexually aroused to thoughts of sadistic sexual acts on children. Similarly, Rosencrans (1996) asked the victims to rate their experience of the abuse by the female perpetrator on a scale from violence to loving. Results showed that 49 per cent experienced the abuse as violence compared to 30 per cent who experienced the abuse as loving.

This culture of denial has powerful implications for the victims of female sexual offenders. The impact of any form of sexual abuse depends less on the actual event and more upon how it is perceived and appraised by the victim (Woodward & Joseph, 2003). Society's continuing denial and minimisation of that abuse is likely to exacerbate the impact of the abuse on the child.

Finkelhor and Browne (1986) described four traumagenic dynamics that cause the myriad of symptoms that are seen in children who experience childhood sexual abuse: *traumatic sexualisation, betrayal, stigmatisation* and *powerlessness*. When these dynamics are considered in relation to a child sexually abused by a woman, it is clear that the impact of that abuse on the child becomes exacerbated by societal attitudes towards sexual abuse by females.

Traumatic Sexualisation

Traumatic sexualisation includes aversive feelings about sex, overvaluing sex, confusion of sex and nurturance, and sexual identity problems. For victims of female sexual abusers, the trauma will be greater as it is so unexpected that women will behave in this way. As women are seen as nurturers and carers, there is often a considerable confusion between sex and nurturance. This can lead the victim to be vulnerable to behaving sexually with other children and to develop a polymorphic sexuality and/or sexual promiscuity. Alternatively, as women are deemed to be asexual in this society, there is an even greater belief in the victim that it is 'something about the victim' that caused the woman to behave in such an uncharacteristic way. In such contexts, victims can develop a belief that they 'caused' the assault(s) and develop a fear of human contact. Many feel that they cannot form close intimate relationships of any kind, and may be particularly unable to engage in sexual relationships.

Many victims of sexual abuse by women struggle with issues of sexuality and sexual identity. Dimock (1988) found that 7 of 25 adult males sexually abused as children had been victimised by women (4 mothers, 2 sisters and 1 stepsister). These men all reported sexual compulsiveness, masculinity identity confusion and relationship dysfunction as long term impacts of their victimisation. All the victims in Denov's (2004b) study reported some degree of discomfort or difficulty in sexual relationships. Interestingly, in Rosencrans' (1996) study, 33 per cent of the male victims and 15 per cent of the female victims acted out sexually as children and 44 per cent of the male victims and 3 per cent of the female victims acted out sexually as adults. One of the female victims of Saradjian's (1996a) study, who had become a prostitute, describes using sex to gain feelings of being in control: 'When I get worked up, I get a punter who wants dominatrix and charge him. I feel great' (p. 7).

Other authors have also found social and relationship problems related to sexuality and intimacy among men sexually abused by females (Etherington, 1997; Kasl, 1990; Lawson, 1993). In addition, various sexual problems have also been recorded (Sarrel & Masters, 1982; Johnson & Shrier, 1987) such as sexual identity concerns, homosexuality or bisexuality among women (Johnson & Shrier, 1987; Krug, 1989; Rosencrans, 1996). Finally, Rosencrans (1996) found parenting to be problematic by all of nine men and most of the women who had been sexually abused in childhood by their mothers.

Stigmatisation

Sexual victimisation leaves victims feeling different from their peers and damaged, leading to feelings of shame and guilt, especially in relation to disclosure. Such feelings can lead to the individual withdrawing from others and experiencing isolation and alienation. This can also lead to self-destructive behaviours such as substance abuse, risk-taking, self-harm, suicidal gestures and acts, and behaviour designed to elicit punishment. To be sexually abused by a woman in a society which sees such abuse as 'extremely unusual' will increase the likelihood of stigmatisation and the associated feelings of shame and guilt. Lind (2004) describes having to form a separate group for women who had been sexually abused by females as they even felt stigmatised in survivor groups where the other participants had been sexually abused by males.

The stigmatisation, isolation and alienation of child victims make them far more vulnerable to internalising the beliefs about them held by the perpetrator. Briere (1995) stated that 'to understand the misconceptions and the assaulted identity of the victim/survivor, we must recognise the footprints on the soul that are the stamp of the misguided trespasser' (p. xvii). Women who sexually abuse children have a tendency to either denigrate or idealise those children. The sense of 'damaged goods' or 'defectiveness' that results from the internalisation of negative projections of the perpetrators is evident in comments made by the victims: 'I'm a nasty piece of work' (female aged 15); 'Mummy touched my tickle (vagina) because I was a bad sexy girl'; 'I can't see anything good about me, I never get anything right' (Saradjian, 1996a, p. 6); 'I became the unwanted, despicable rejected part of my mother. I believe that she projected onto me a view of herself as a bad child that she formed in response to her own abusive father and rejecting mother. . . I became the ugly death deserving one' (Rosencrans, 1996, p. 68).

Many male adolescents sexually abused by women are considered by some in society to be 'lucky', to be experiencing an initiation, a rite of passage. Influenced by these beliefs, some adolescent males initially perceive the abuse as benign or even in a positive light. Kelly and colleagues (2002) examined the relationship between positive initial perceptions of sexual abuse experiences on adult male psychosocial functioning. They found more adjustment problems among men (half of those had been abused by their mothers) who recalled an initial positive or mixed perception of the abuse than among men who recalled purely negative initial perceptions. The researchers concluded that sexually victimised males who experienced initial positive or mixed feelings about the abuse might be at increased risk for psychological impairment in adulthood, at least in clinical samples. These findings are supported by King, Coxell and Mezey (2002). They found that of nearly 2,500 men attending 18 medical practices, those with a history of sexual abuse ($n = 150$) were more likely than other men to report mental health, sexual or substance abuse problems. The highest risk of sexual problems, substance abuse and self-harm was found in those men who reported that the experience with the older person had been 'consensual', particularly among men who reported consensual sex with an older person before age 16. It is noted that men are more likely to construe sexual activity with *adult females* before the age of 16 as consensual while less likely to construe similar experience with adult males to be consensual (see Coxell, King, Mezey & Gordon, 1999).

Betrayal

The sexual abuse of a child is almost always the betrayal of a relationship of trust. This is especially significant when the perpetrator is a woman who is construed as being a protector and nurturer. A particularly significant betrayal is when the perpetrator is the child's mother. One adolescent victim of sexual abuse by a female perpetrator said 'You expect it of men don't you? You're aware. I'd have never got into a car with a man. But you trust women don't you, you'd never think a woman would do that, would you. I mean they just don't' (Saradjian, 1996a, p. 4) The impact of betrayal leaves the child with intense feelings of anger and mistrust that can border on paranoia and that can be expressed in various ways including physical and sexual violence. Some victims can also develop an over-dependence on specific others. The reaction to betrayal can also involve manipulating others, or maintaining the mistrust by engaging in further exploitive and damaging relationships.

In her study, Denov (2004b) found a number of similarities in how male and female victims responded to sexual abuse by a woman. All the participants reported feelings of rage as a result of the abuse, and all reported a strong mistrust of women. These findings replicate the findings in Rosencrans' (1996) study. In his study,

94 per cent of female victims and 66 per cent of male victims reported difficulties with trusting others, particularly women. In addition, 50 per cent of female victims and 66 per cent of male victims reported engaging in aggressive behaviours. Similarly, Lisak (1994) also found high levels of anger and difficulties trusting other people as significant factors in survivors of childhood sexual abuse by women.

Powerlessness

When a child experiences sexual victimisation by a woman in a society which does not accept the reality or extent of that form of abuse, the child has an increased sense of powerlessness, especially if the perpetrator is the child's mother. In such cases, the whole of the child's life is controlled by the offender. The impact of the powerlessness engendered by the abuse includes a terror of vulnerability and a perceived need to be in control. This can lead to identification with the perpetrator and an increased likelihood of aggression and exploitation towards others.

The possibility that males who are sexually abused by women may later sexually abuse others has been raised by several authors (Justice & Justice, 1979; Margolis, 1984; Rosencrans, 1997). Groth (1979) noted that rapists are sexually victimised more by females than by males and suggested that this partially explains their sexual attacks against women. High frequencies of sexual abuse in childhood by a female have been noted in the histories of sexual offenders (Allen, 1991; Briere & Smiljanich, 1993; Burgess, Hazelwood, Rokous, Hartman & Burgess, 1988; Groth, 1979; Petrovich & Templer, 1984). The finding of a high prevalence of sexual assault by female perpetrators in the lives of men who are sexually aggressive is evidence of the impact of this form of abuse (see Table 2.3). Victims also comment about their need to be in control: 'I have to be in control of sex. I can only get an erection if my partner is totally passive. If she makes any move on me at all, I just have to stop' (male victim sexually abused in adolescence by a friend of his mother; Saradjian, 1996a, p. 8).

Equally, the child may respond to the victimisation by becoming avoidant, repressing and dissociating emotions or by running away. Lind (2004) describes how the survivors of childhood sexual abuse by women had to briefly describe the abuse at the beginning of each therapy session as so many had coped by pretending that it had not happened. When unable to manage the negative emotions by avoidance strategies, the victim can experience anxiety which includes phobias, sleep problems and other related issues such as eating disorders and obsessive compulsive disorder (see Rosencrans, 1996). In extreme cases when infants are sexually abused by their mother over a sustained period, as the child cannot escape physically, the child 'escapes' psychologically by 'shutting down' their cognitive and social processes and consequently develops learning difficulties (Sinason, 1988).

Effect on Identity

Cole and Putnam (1992) propose that there is an interaction between the trauma of child sexual abuse and the stage(s) of development during which the sexual assaults occur. They suggest that sexual assault affects both the development of the self and social functioning of the child and influences the child's developing sense of identity. Thus, the younger the child is when the abuse begins and the more dependant the child is on the abuser, the more damaging the abuse is likely to be to the developing self. Victims of female sexual offenders tend to be younger on average (5.84 years) compared with victims of males (8.58 years). This age difference is often related to the fact that victims were more likely to be the son or daughter of the female abuser (Peter, 2009). Victims of females, especially when the offender is the mother of the child, struggle with high levels of enmeshment with the woman and experience difficulties in establishing a separate identity. One survivor summarised this difficulty: 'I still struggle with being as far away from my mother as possible identity-wise. I wanted to be as different as I could from my mother. I used to dress in men's clothes just so that I could be as different as I could from her' (Ogilvie & Daniluk, 1995, p. 600). Another said: 'Sometimes I can feel her on my skin. I can't explain ... I suppose it's like as if we are someway, we are melted into each other. I scrape and scrape at my skin but I cannot get deep enough into myself to get rid of her' (Saradjian, 1996a, p. 9). Others made statements such as 'I hate her but the worst thing of all is that I know that I am just like her, I look like her, I sound like her, I smell like her. I still feel her body is engulfing mine. I never feel free of her. It is as if . . .if I broke truly free, I would just fade away or drift into the air as if I never even existed except if I am attached to her' (Saradjian, 1996a). In her research, Denov (2004b) found similar findings. The majority of female participants abused by women reported difficulties in their sense of identity and self-concept, in many cases trying to deny a female identity from childhood through to adulthood (Denov, 2004b).

SUMMARY

The culture of resistance and denial has powerful implications for the victims of female sexual offenders. This is because the impact of sexual abuse depends less on the actual event and more upon how it is perceived and appraised by the victim (Woodward & Joseph, 2003). Whilst there is no intention of saying that for a child to be sexually victimised by a woman is worse than being sexually victimised by a male, society's construction of femaleness and the denial that women can and do sexually victimise children, can lead the child to perceive and appraise those experiences in a manner that exacerbates the impact of that abuse. The social construction of femaleness brings up specific issues for those survivors of sexual abuse by women that will need to be addressed in therapy. These issues are particularly evident when the perpetrator of that abuse is the victim's mother or a woman who is in a maternal role. Key issues for victims of female sexual offenders that need to be addressed include particular difficulties with trust/extreme dependency, problems with own sexuality/gender identity/sexualisation of all (or no) relationships, and intense anger and aggression, self-harm and violence towards others. When the offender is the child's mother, key additional impact will include significant difficulties in forming a sense of self separate from mother, an excessive need in the survivor to return to the mother, almost as if there is a need to validate his or her existence, and enmeshment that can be so extreme as to lead to psychosis. It is therefore imperative that professionals both accept that sexual abuse of children by women is less rare than once thought, and learn to identify the victims of such abuse. This is essential if the secret is to be exposed and the hidden victims receive appropriate therapy for their needs.

REFERENCES

Allen, C. M. (1991). *Women and men who sexually abuse children: A comparative analysis.* Orwell: The Safer Society Press.

Allen Consulting Group. (2003). *Protecting children: The child protection outcomes project.* Final report for the Victorian Department of Human Services. Melbourne, Australia.

Apfelberg, B., Sugar, C., & Pfeffer, A. Z. (1944). A psychiatric study of 250 sex offenders. *American Journal of Psychiatry, 100,* 762–770.

Aylward, A., Christopher, M., Newell, R. M., & Gordon, A. (2002, October). *What about women who commit sex offences?* Paper presented at the 22nd Annual Research and Treatment Conference of the Association for the Treatment of Sexual Abusers, St. Louis, Missouri, USA.

Banning, A. (1989). Mother–son incest: Confronting a prejudice. *Child Abuse & Neglect, 13,* 563–570.

Becker, J. V., Hall, S., & Stinson, J. D. (2001). Female sexual offenders: Clinical, legal, and policy issues. *Journal of Forensic Psychology Practice, 1,* 29–50.

Bender, L., & Blau, A. (1937). The reaction of children to sexual relations with adults. *American Journal of Orthopsychiatry, 7,* 500–518.

Bernard, P. (1886). *Des attentats à la pudeur sur les petites filles.* Paris: Octave Doin.

Briere, J. (1995). Preface. In A. Salter (Ed.), *Transforming trauma: A guide to understanding and treating adult survivors of child sexual abuse* (p. xvii). Newbury Park, CA: Sage Publications.

Briere, J., & Smiljanich, K. (1993, August). *Childhood sexual abuse and subsequent sexual aggression against adult women.* Paper presented at the 101st Annual Convention of the American Psychological Association, Toronto, Ontario.

Bumby, N. H., & Bumby, K. M. (2004). Bridging the gender gap: Addressing juvenile females who commit sexual offences. In G. O'Reilly, W. L. Marshall, A. Carr, & R. C. Beckett (Eds.), *The handbook of clinical intervention with young people who sexually abuse* (pp. 369–381). New York: Brunner-Routledge.

Bunting, L. (2005). *Females who sexually offend against children: Responses of the child protection and criminal justice systems.* NSPCC, NSPCC Policy Practice Research Series. NSCPP Publications.

Burgess, A. W., Hazelwood, R., Rokous, F., Hartman, C., & Burgess, A. G. (1988). Serial rapists and their victims: Reenactment and repetition. *Annals of the New York Academy of Sciences, 528,* 277–280.

Canadian Centre for Justice Statistics. (2001). Reported in Crime Statistics in Canada, 2001 Catalogue no. 85–002-XIE Vol. 22 no. by Josée Savoie Retrieved 25th March, 2009 from http://dsp-psd.communication.gc.ca/Collection-R/Statcan/85–002-XIE/0060285–002-XIE.pdf.

Chideckel, M. (1935). *Female sex perversions: The sexually aberrated woman as she is.* New York: Eugenics.

Cole, P. M., & Putnam, F. W. (1992). Effect of incest on self and social functioning: Developmental psychopathology perspective. *Journal of Consulting & Clinical Psychology, 60,* 174–184.

Condy, S. R., Templer, D. I., Brown, R., & Veaco, L. (1987). Parameters of sexual contact of boys with women. *Archives of Sexual Behavior, 16,* 379–394.

Cortoni, F., & Hanson, R. K. (2005). *A review of the recidivism rates of adult female sexual offenders* (Research Report No. R-169). Ottawa: Correctional Service of Canada. (Available from: www.csc-scc.gc.ca/text/rsrch/reports/r169/r169_e.pdf)

Cortoni, F., Hanson, R. K., & Coache, M. E. (2009). Les délinquantes sexuelles: Prévalence et récidive (female sexual offenders: Prevalence and recidivism). *Revue internationale de criminologie et de police technique et scientifique, LXII* (4), 319–336.

Coxell, A., King, M., Mezey, G., & Gordon, D. (1999). Lifetime prevalence, characteristics and associated problems of non-consensual sex in men: Cross sectional survey. *British Medical Journal, 318,* 846–850.

Coxell, A. W., King, M. B., Mezey, G. C., & Kell, P. (2000). Sexual molestation of men: Interviews with 224 men attending a genito-urinary medicine service. *International Journal of STD and AIDS, 11,* 574–578.

De Mause, L. (2008). Infanticide, child rape and war in early states. In L. De Mause (Ed.), *The origins of war in child abuse.* Available from http://www.psychohistory.com/originsofwar/08_infanticide.html.

Denov, M. S. (2001). A culture of denial: Exploring professional perspectives on female sex offending. *Canadian Journal of Criminology, 43,* 303–329.

Denov, M. S. (2003a). The myth of innocence: Sexual scripts and the recognition of child sexual abuse by female perpetrators. *The Journal of Sex Research, 40,* 303–314.

Denov, M. S. (2003b). To a safer place? Victims of sexual abuse by females and their disclosures to professionals. *Child Abuse & Neglect, 27,* 47–61.

Denov, M. S. (2004a). *Perspectives on female sex offending: A culture of denial.* Hampshire, England: Ashgate Publishing.

Denov, M. S. (2004b). The long-term effects of child sexual abuse by female perpetrators: A qualitative study of male and female victims. *Journal of Interpersonal Violence, 19,* 1137–1156.

Dimock, P. T. (1988). Adult males sexually abused as children. *Journal of Interpersonal Violence, 3,* 203–221.

Etherington, K. (1995). Findings of research on adult male survivors of childhood sexual abuse. *Counselling Psychology Quarterly, 8,* 233–241.

Etherington, K. (1997). Maternal sexual abuse of males. *Child Abuse Review, 6,* 107–117.

Finkelhor, D. (1984). *Child sexual abuse.* New York: The Free Press.

Finkelhor, D., & Browne, A. (1985). The traumatic impact of child sexual abuse: A conceptual model. *American Journal of Orthopsychiatry, 55,* 530–541.

Finkelhor, D. (1986). *Sourcebook on child sexual abuse.* Beverly Hills, CA: Sage.

Finkelhor, D., Hotaling, G., Lewis, I. A., & Smith, C. (1990). Sexual abuse in a national survey of adult men and women: Prevalence, characteristics and risk factors. *Child Abuse & Neglect, 14,* 19–28.

Finkelhor, D., Williams, L.M., & Burns, N. (1989). *Nursery crimes: Sexual abuse in daycares.* Newbury Park: Sage.

Ford, H. (2006). *Women who sexually abuse children.* Chichester, England: John Wiley & Sons.

Freud, S. (1896). The aetiology of hysteria and further remarks on the neuro-psychoses of defence. In *The standard edition of the complete psychological works of Sigmund Freud* (Vol. 3, pp. 191–221). Early Psycho-Analytic Publications. London: Hogarth Press.

Freund, K., Heasman, G., Racansky, I. G., & Glancy, G. (1984). Pedophilia and heterosexuality vs. homosexuality. *Journal of Sex and Marital Therapy, 10,* 193–200.

Gibb, T. W. (1894). Indecent assault upon children. In A. MacLane Hamilton & L. Godkin (Eds.), *A system of legal medicine* (Vol. 1, pp. 649–657). New York: E.B. Treat.

Giguere, R., & Bumby, K. (2007). *Female sex offenders.* Silver Spring, MD: Center for Sex Offender Management.

Groth, A. N. (1979). Sexual trauma in the life histories of rapists and child molesters. *Victimology, 4,* 10–16.

Hetherton, J. (1999). The idealisation of women: Its role in the minimisation of child sexual abuse by females. *Child Abuse & Neglect, 23,* 161–174.

Hetherton, J., & Beardsall, L. (1998). Decisions and attitudes concerning child sexual abuse: Does the gender of the perpetrator make a difference to child protection professionals? *Child Abuse & Neglect, 22,* 1265–1283.

Hislop, J. (2001). *Female sex offenders: What therapists, law enforcement and child protective services need to know.* Ravensdale, WA: Issues Press.

Home Office. (2002). *Statistics on women and the Criminal Justice System*. Accessed 24th August, 2009, http://www.homeoffice.gov.uk/rds/pdfs2/s95women02.pdf.

Johnson, R., & Shrier, D. (1987). Past sexual victimization by females of male patients in an adolescent medicine clinic population. *American Journal of Psychiatry, 144,* 650–662.

Johansson-Love, J., & Fremouw, W. (2006). Critique of the female sexual perpetrator research. *Aggression and Violent Behavior, 11,* 12–26.

Justice, B., & Justice, R. (1979). *The broken taboo: Sex in the family*. New York, London: Human Sciences Press.

Kaplan, M. S., & Green, A. (1995). Incarcerated female sexual offenders: A comparison of sexual histories with eleven female nonsexual offenders. *Sexual Abuse: A Journal of Research and Treatment, 7,* 287–300.

Kasl, C. D. (1990). Female perpetrators of sexual abuse: A feminist view. In M. Hunter (Ed.), *The sexually abused male: Vol. 1. Prevalence, impact and treatment* (pp. 259–274). Lexington: Lexington Books.

Kelly, R. J., Wood, J. J., Gonzalez, L. S., MacDonald, V., & Waterman, J. (2002). Effects of mother–son incest and positive perceptions of sexual abuse experiences on the psychosocial adjustment of clinic-referred men. *Child Abuse & Neglect, 26,* 425–441.

Kendall-Tackett, D. A., & Simon, A. (1987). Perpetrators and their acts: Data from 365 adults molested as children. *Child Abuse & Neglect, 11,* 237–245.

King, M., Coxell, A., & Mezey, G. (2002). Sexual molestation of males: Associations with psychological disturbance. *British Journal of Psychiatry, 181,* 53–157.

Kite, D., & Tyson, G. A. (2004). The impact of perpetrator gender on male and female police officers' perceptions of child sexual abuse. *Psychiatry, Psychology and Law, 11,* 308–318.

Krug, R. S. (1989). Adult male report of childhood sexual abuse by mothers: Case descriptions, motivations and long-term consequences. *Child Abuse & Neglect, 13,* 111–119.

Lawson, C. (1993). Mother–son sexual abuse: Rare or underreported? A critique of the research. *Child Abuse & Neglect, 17,* 261–269.

Lind, M. (2004, September). *When mother is the sexual abuser*. Paper presented at the 15th International Congress on Child Abuse and Neglect, Brisbane, Australia.

Lisak, D. (1994). The psychological impact of sexual abuse: Content analysis of interviews with male survivors. *Journal of Traumatic Stress, 7,* 525–548.

Margolis, M. (1984). A case of mother-adolescent son incest: A follow-up study. *Psychoanalytic Quarterly, 53,* 355–385.

Masson, J. M. (Ed.). (1985). *The complete letters of Sigmund Freud to Wilhelm Fliess, 1887–1904*. Cambridge: Harvard University Press.

Mathews, R., Matthews, J., & Speltz, K. (1989). *Female sexual offenders: An exploratory study*. Brandon, VT: The Safer Society Press.

NSPCC. (2004). *Calls to ChildLine about sexual abuse*. Retrieved 21st March, 2009, from http://www.nspcc.org.uk/Inform/factsandfigures/statistics/statistics_wda48748.html.

NSPCC. (2007). *Calls to ChildLine about sexual abuse*. Retrieved 21st March, 2009 from http://www.nspcc.org.uk/Inform/publications/casenotes/CLcasenotessexualabuse_wdf48189.pdf.

O'Brien, M. J. (1989). *Characteristics of male adolescent sibling incest offenders*. Orwell, VT: Safer Society Press.

O'Connor, A. A. (1987). Female sex offenders. *British Journal of Psychiatry, 150,* 615–620.

Ogilvie, B., & Daniluk, J. (1995). Common themes in the experiences of mother–daughter incest survivors: Implications for counselling. *Journal of Counselling and Development, 73,* 598–602.

Pereda, N., Guilera, G., Forns, M., & Gómez-Benito, J. (2009). The prevalence of child sexual abuse in community and student samples: A meta-analysis. *Clinical Psychology Review, 4,* 328–338.

Peter, T. (2009). Exploring taboos: Comparing male and female perpetrated child sexual abuse. *Journal of Interpersonal Violence, 24,* 1111–1128.

Peterson, K. D., Colebank, K. D., & Motta, L. L. (2001, November). *Female sexual offender recidivism*. Paper presented at the 20th Annual Research and Treatment Conference of the Association for the Treatment of Sexual Abusers, San Antonio, TX, USA.

Petrovich, M., & Templer, D. (1984). Heterosexual molestation of children who later become rapists. *Psychological Reports, 54,* 810.

Rallings, M., Webster, S. D., & Rudolph, B. (2001). *Early sexual experiences of sex offenders against adults and children.* London: Sex Offender Treatment Programme Statistics, H.M. Prison Service.

Ramsey-Klawsnik, H. (1990, April). *Sexual abuse by female perpetrators: Impact on children.* Paper presented at the National Symposium on Child Victimisation, Atlanta, GA.

Risen, L. I., & Koss, M. P. (1987). The sexual abuse of boys: Prevalence and descriptive characteristics of childhood victimization. *Journal of Interpersonal Violence, 2,* 309–323.

Rosencrans, B. (1996). *The last secret: Daughters sexually abused by mothers.* Brandon, VT: Safer Society Press.

Rosencrans, B. (1997). *The last secret: Daughters sexually abused by mothers.* Brandon, VT: Safer Society Press.

Rudin, M.M., Zalewski, C., & Bodmer-Turner, J. (1995). Characteristics of child sexual abuse victims according to perpetrator gender. *Child Abuse & Neglect, 19,* 963–973.

Russell, D. (1983). The incidence and prevalence of intrafamilial and extrafamilial sexual abuse of female children. *Child Abuse & Neglect, 7,* 133–146.

Saradjian, J. (1996a, September). *The subjective experience of victims who have been sexually abused by women.* Keynote Presentation at the National Organisation for the Treatment of Abusers (NOTA) Conference, Chester, England.

Saradjian, J. (1996b). *Women who sexually abuse children: From research to clinical practice.* Chichester: John Wiley & Sons.

Sarrel, P. M., & Masters, W. H. (1982). Sexual molestation of men by women. *Archives of Sexual Behaviour, 11,* 117–131.

Sgroi, S. M., & Sargent, N. M. (1993). Impact and treatment issues for victims of childhood sexual abuse by female perpetrators. In M. Elliott (Ed.), *Female sexual abuse of children: The ultimate taboo* (pp. 15–38). Chichester: John Wiley & Sons.

Shakeshaft, C. (2003). Educator sexual abuse. *Hofstra Horizons,* Spring, 10–13.

Shoop, R. (2003). *Sexual exploitation in schools: How to spot it and stop it.* Thousand Oaks, CA: Corwin Press.

Sinason, V. (1988). Smiling, swallowing, sickening and stupefying: The effect of sexual abuse on the child. *Psychoanalytic Psychotherapy, 3,* 97–111.

Snyder, H. (2000, July). Sexual assault of young children as reported to law enforcement: Victim, incident, and offender characteristics. *American Bureau of Justice Statistics Clearinghouse, Review, 27*(2), 284–300.

Snyder, H., & Sickmund, M. (2006). *Juvenile offenders and victims: 2006 national report.* Washington, DC: US Department of Justice, Office of Justice Programs, Office of Juvenile Justice and Delinquency Prevention.

Tardieu, A. (1857). *Étude médico-légale sur les attentats aux moeurs* (1st Ed.). Paris: Librairie JB Baillière et Fils.

The Press (2000, January 31st). *Call to change law Minster wants female offender review.* Canterbury, New Zealand: The Press.

Trocmé, N., MacLaurin, B., Fallon, B., Daciuk, J., Billingsley, D., Tourigny, M., et al. (2001). *Canadian incidence study of reported child abuse and neglect: Final report.* Ottawa, Canada: Minister of Public Works and Government Services Canada.

Ursel, J., & Gorkoff, K. (2001). Court processing of child sexual abuse cases: The Winnipeg Family Violence Court experience. In D. Hiebert-Murphy & L. Burnside (Eds.), *Pieces of a puzzle: Perspectives on child sexual abuse* (pp. 79–94). Halifax, Canada: Fernwood.

Vandiver, D., & Kercher, G. (2004). Offender and victim characteristics of registered female sexual offenders in Texas: A proposed typology of female sexual offenders. *Sexual Abuse: A Journal of Research and Treatment, 16,* 121–137.

Vizard, E. (2000, September). *Characteristics of a British sample of sexually abusive children.* Keynote presentation to the BASPCAN National Congress, University of York, UK.

Wolfe, F. (1985). *Women who commit sex crimes.* Unpublished manuscript.

Woodward, C., & Joseph, S. (2003). Positive change processes and post-traumatic growth in people who have experienced childhood abuse: Understanding vehicles of change. *Psychology & Psychotherapy: Theory, Research and Practice, 76,* 267–283.

Wulffen, E. (1934). *Women as sexual criminals.* New York: American Ethnological Press.

Yorukoglu, A., & Kemp, J. P. (1966). Children not severely damaged by incest with a parent. *Journal of American Academy of Child Psychiatry, 5,* 111–124.

Chapter 3

THEORIES OF FEMALE SEXUAL OFFENDING

DANIELLE A. HARRIS

Department of Justice Studies, San Jose State University, San Jose, CA, USA

If the development of theory on sexual offending by men remains in its adolescence (Marshall & Laws, 2003), then the development of theory that explains sexual offending by women is in its infancy. Our theoretical understanding of female sexual offending is hampered by significant obstacles. Criminology and psychology have long been ignorant to the possibility of women committing sexual offences. This has lead to the earnest construction of typological explanations that have not progressed beyond the original classificatory systems generated on samples of men. Meanwhile, criminology's neglect of the criminality of women altogether (Lilly, Cullen & Ball, 1995) has led to the application of male explanations to the apparently similar behaviours of women. In addition, feminist perspectives have concentrated exclusively on the role of women as victims. One of the greatest contributions of feminism has been the recognition of the effects of sexual abuse on female victims, especially by their male assailants (Naffine, 1996). The occurrence of sexual offending by women inverts this enduring assumption and poses a considerable threat to the credibility of the feminist paradigm (Young, 1993). The persistent belief that this phenomenon neither exists nor warrants our attention has made it difficult to move forward.

Most theories explain a phenomenon by trying to account for the broadest possible amount of variance in a particular dimension. Most theories in the social sciences also tend to acknowledge that there are exceptions to every rule. If female-perpetrated sexual abuse continues to be portrayed as isolated, atypical and inconsequential, it could be argued then, that no explanation (theoretical or otherwise) is actually necessary (Allen, 1997). In this way, it can be dismissed as an aberrant and uncharacteristic peculiarity (Schwartz & Cellini, 1995).

This chapter provides an overview of the theories that are available to explain sexual offending by women. It begins with a discussion of the application of criminological theories of male offending to female offending. Next, typological approaches as applied to female sexual offenders are presented. This includes

Female Sexual Offenders: Theory, Assessment, and Treatment   Edited by Theresa A. Gannon and Franca Cortoni
© 2010 John Wiley & Sons, Ltd

descriptions of what might be considered 'typical' examples of each classification. Finally, the chapter provides an examination of the types of theories that have been developed more recently in the field of female sexual offending and considers three separate offerings as level I, level II and level III theories, respectively.

APPLYING MALE THEORIES TO FEMALE OFFENDERS

Crime is an overwhelmingly male phenomenon that is frequently linked to masculine traits (Akers & Sellers, 2004; White & Haines, 1996). In fact, the y chromosome is often regarded as the single most compelling correlate of crime (Naffine, 1996; Vold, Bernard & Snipes, 2002). Sexual crime is likely the phenomenon where this gender ratio is demonstrated most convincingly. However, general sexual offending research has largely taken place outside the purview of conventional criminology (Simon, 2000). Criminology's reluctance to discuss sexual offenders as a distinct population has been attributed to its inability to reconcile such crimes within its sociological framework of offending (Simon, 2000). Evidently, the quest for a criminological explanation of female sexual offending requires an even bigger paradigm shift. Nonetheless, given the inherent criminality of this behaviour, conventional criminology is an appropriate place to search for an understanding of female sexual offending.

The typical approach to explain female offending so far has been to apply male theories to their behaviour. For example, Messerschmidt's 'Doing Masculinity' describes male and female criminality similarly (Cullen & Agnew, 2003). He argues that crime is a way of men 'doing gender', especially when they are not able to achieve masculinity through legitimate means (Akers & Sellers, 2004). Thus, when women commit a crime, it is conceivable that they too are behaving like men and embracing a masculine identity (Akers & Sellers, 2004; Miller, 2002).

Previous studies within the research on sexual offending have suggested that sexually aggressive men exhibit hypermasculine characteristics such as strength, power, forcefulness, domination and toughness (Allgeier & Lamping, 1998; Anderson, 1998). It would seem plausible then, that sexually aggressive women possess the same characteristics. Some components of sexual offending that have been found to be relevant for men (like the desire to gain control over a sexual partner) are also thought to be relevant, to some extent, for women (Anderson, 1998).

In a recent study that actually compared the sexually coercive behaviours of men and women on the same variables, Schatzel-Murphy, Harris, Knight and Milburn (2009) found that although men and women engaged in sexual coercion to a similar extent, the models developed for men did *not* effectively predict the same behaviours in women. Therefore, even though certain experiences might later manifest as similar behaviours, the experiences themselves are processed in extremely different ways. Specifically, this study concluded that where sexual coercion in men was predicted by sexual dominance and sociosexuality, it was predicted by sexual compulsivity in women (Schatzel-Murphy et al., 2009). These authors proposed that while male sexual coercion could be attributed to obtaining or maintaining a sense of power or control within relationships, the same behaviours in women were likely due to a desire to achieve interpersonal connection when feeling powerless or out of control (Schatzel-Murphy et al., 2009).

To summarise, although men and women who commit similar offences might do so by engaging in comparable behaviours, the latest research indicates that they do so for very different reasons. Thus, it is inappropriate to describe a woman's behaviour in terms that are used to describe the same actions of a man. Put simply, men and women are different, and warrant unique explanations of seemingly similar behaviours (Cortoni & Gannon, in press).

FEMALE SEXUAL OFFENDER TYPOLOGIES

Sexual offenders are often regarded as a heterogeneous population (Parkinson, Shrimpton, Oates, Swanston & O'Toole, 2004) with research indicating wide diversity across a range of factors. Such variables include personal characteristics, life experiences, and sexual and criminal histories (Ward, Polaschek & Beech, 2006). Typologies are a common tool used to make sense of this heterogeneity. Typologies 'zoom in' on individual differences and generate numerous groups to which an individual can theoretically be allocated (Blackburn, 1993; Brown & Forth, 1997). It is thought that typologies can contribute to theory development by illuminating clusters of demographic or other characteristics that appear related to offending (Gannon & Rose, 2008; Matravers, 2008).

In contrast to the now theoretically informed and empirically derived typologies of male sexual offenders (e.g. Knight & Prentky, 1990; Knight, 2009), the typologies that have been constructed for women are essentially descriptive in nature. In spite of everything, typologies have provided some direction in understanding the heterogeneity of female sexual offenders and have assisted clinicians who deal directly with these women (Gannon & Rose, 2008).

Typologies are typically constructed by arranging individuals into subtypes based on offender characteristics (e.g. age, history of childhood abuse, substance abuse, presence of a co-offender), offence characteristics (e.g. location of offence, motivation, recidivism, general criminal history) and victim type (e.g. age, gender and relationship) (Gannon & Rose, 2008; Matravers, 2008). Numerous female sexual offender typologies have emerged over the past two decades. Eight such examples are reviewed for this chapter (Faller, 1987; Finkelhor & Williams, 1988; Mathews, Matthews & Speltz, 1989; Matravers, 2008; McCarty, 1986; Sandler & Freeman, 2007; Sarrel & Masters, 1982; Vandiver & Kercher, 2004). Although some of this work comes from small and convenient samples, there *are* themes that transcend many of the available offender categories and a number of recognisable areas of convergence that exist (Ford, 2006).

This section describes four specific areas of convergence that are borne out of extant typological approaches. This discussion borrows most heavily from the typology developed by Mathews et al. (1989) which appears to have the most currency with both researchers and clinicians. These categories include women who abuse adolescent boys, women who sexually abuse their own or other young children, and women who co-offend with a man (Hunter & Mathews, 1997). A final group of women who sexually assault or coerce adults will also be discussed.

Women Who Abuse Adolescent Boys

A large proportion of the available typologies identify a specific group of female sexual offenders who exclusively abuse unrelated male adolescents. They are referred to, most often, as 'teachers/lovers' (Mathews et al., 1989), but subsequent typologies have labelled similar groups as 'heterosexual nurturers' (Vandiver & Kercher, 2004), 'adolescent abusers' (Faller, 1987) or 'criminally-limited hebephiles' (Sandler & Freeman, 2007).

Teacher/lover female sexual offenders typically elevate an adolescent boy to adult status and tend not to see the abusive behaviour as criminal (Atkinson, 1996; Cortoni, 2009). Instead, they believe the victim is a willing participant in a consensual relationship (Hunter & Mathews, 1997). This type of offender will typically act from a position of power that is achieved either through her age or her role in the boy's life (e.g. as his teacher or babysitter; Atkinson, 1996; Cortoni, 2009; Sarrel & Masters, 1982). Although the initial sexual encounter is often not premeditated, it might later become the result of calculation and careful planning.

Clinical experience indicates that these women are less likely than other subtypes to have been victimised sexually as children (Saradjian, 1996). However, they do tend to have experienced verbal or emotional abuse in their childhood and may have had a distant (or absent) father (Atkinson, 1996; Cortoni, 2009; Mathews et al., 1989).

Women Who Abuse Young Children

A small but identifiable group of female sexual offenders target younger, pre-pubescent children. Some typological approaches have separated these offenders by victim's gender (Sandler & Freeman, 2007) or by offender's relationship to the victim (McCarty, 1986; Sarrel & Masters, 1982), but it appears to be most helpful to consider them together. Referred to, most often, as 'predisposed' offenders (Mathews et al., 1989), these women typically act alone and victimise their own children, although some may also select victims outside the home (Atkinson, 1996; Faller, 1987; Vandiver & Kercher, 2004). According to Mathews et al. (1989), these women are especially likely to have experienced severe childhood trauma or have long histories of sexual abuse. Their adult relationships are frequently unhealthy or abusive (Cortoni, 2009; Mathews et al., 1989) and they tend to suffer additional emotional and psychological difficulties such as low self-esteem, extreme anger, anguish or distorted thinking (Mathews et al., 1989). Of the four types of female sexual offenders described in this chapter, women who abuse young children are most likely to have deviant fantasies about their sexual offending, display other sexually deviant behaviours and use violence during their offence (Atkinson, 1996; Cortoni, 2009).

Women Who Have Co-Offenders

The presence of a co-offender is an important dimension to be considered for female sexual offenders. So important in fact that it is included as a level II (or 'single factor') theory in a later part of this chapter. Women who are accompanied (or coerced) by men tend to account for the largest proportion of female sexual offenders in most of the existing classificatory schemes (Atkinson, 1996). In some typologies, male-coerced offenders are described separately from male-accompanied offenders (McCarty, 1986; Syed & Williams, 1996). The male-coerced offender is believed to typically abuse *only* in the presence of her male coercer. In such situations, the woman is thought to act out of fear of physical punishment or sexual assault at the hands of her partner, or due to extreme emotional dependency on her partner (Atkinson, 1996; Cortoni, 2009; Gannon, Rose & Ward, 2008; Mathews et al., 1989). The accompanied offender, on the other hand, is believed to participate more actively in the abuse, and over time, may come to initiate the sexual abuse independent of her accomplice (Atkinson, 1996).

In terms of reported characteristics, most information appears to be available for male-coerced women. Such women appear to be extremely non-assertive and emotionally dependent upon their male coercers (Atkinson, 1996; Gannon & Rose, 2008). Male-coerced women will also often subscribe to traditional gender roles that promote a man's dominance over a woman in the relationship context, and in society in general (Atkinson, 1996; Cortoni, 2009; Gannon & Rose, 2008). These women might participate directly in the abuse, or simply serve as a facilitator to procure or coerce victims into sexual activity. The victims in these cases are typically reported as being the women's daughters (Atkinson, 1996). However, it is also not unusual to find male-coerced women offending against boys and unrelated children (Faller, 1987; Matravers, 2008; McCarty, 1986).

Three of the eight typologies reviewed for this chapter neglect to include the involvement of a co-offender as a categorising variable (Sandler & Freeman, 2007; Sarrel & Masters, 1982; Vandiver & Kercher, 2004). The emphasis placed on the presence of a male co-offender in so much of the available knowledge on female sexual offending suggests that this is a substantial shortcoming of those classification schemes. Evidently, the presence or absence of a co-offender has important implications not only in terms of understanding one's behaviour, but also in guiding intervention, treatment and management decisions. This is certainly an area in need of more research.

Women Who Abuse Adults

Women who target adult victims constitute a small minority of female sexual offenders (Sarrel & Masters, 1982; Vandiver & Kercher, 2004). For example, only 8.3 per cent of Vandiver and Kercher's (2004) the total sample of 471 women were found to offend against adults. 'Homosexual criminals' ($n = 22$) and 'aggressive homosexual offenders' ($n = 17$) were the oldest groups in their typology with almost all of them (88 per cent) having female victims exclusively. The 'homosexual criminals' were described as a more general group of offenders with sexual offences (such as forcing females into prostitution) only constituting a small part of their overall offending behaviour. In contrast, the 'aggressive homosexual offenders' were the most likely to be arrested for a contact sexual assault against an adult. Schwartz and Cellini (1995) have suggested that these women are much less likely than other subtypes to come to the attention of authorities, which might account for their small representation in extant typologies.

To summarise, typologies are intended to classify individuals into theoretically useful categories that will facilitate a deeper understanding of their behaviour. In terms of clinical utility, it is also thought that descriptions of offender subtypes will help guide therapeutic interventions, management techniques and treatment alternatives. Although existing typologies provide descriptions of female sexual offenders, they are limited by their use of clinical descriptions of small samples, or alternatively, the use of descriptive demographic information within large samples (Cortoni, 2009). Further, clear areas of overlap within and between subtypes have been identified. Evidently, each individual will present with unique characteristics that might not be fully represented by a clear-cut classification scheme and further elements are needed to understand female sexual offenders. This is the focus of this next section.

THEORIES IN SEXUAL OFFENDING RESEARCH

Ward and Hudson (1998) suggest differentiating the broad array of existing theoretical perspectives on male sexual offending by their level of abstraction. They argue that a satisfactory theory will incorporate each of the three levels of explanation as it accounts for the onset, the development and the maintenance of a specific phenomenon.

Level I or 'multifactorial' theories provide a comprehensive or integrated explanation of sexual offending. Marshall and Barbaree's (1990) Integrated theory of sexual offending (for male sexual offenders) is considered a multifactorial theory which explains this behaviour as the result of a range of interrelated and empirically supported factors. Marshall and Barbaree's explanation combines developmental elements (that predispose someone to learn to express their sexuality through aggression) with situational and environmental factors (like stress, intoxication, anger and the presence of a potential victim).

Level II theories explain single factor or specific variables that are considered particularly important in the generation of sexual offending. These theories focus on a specific construct linked to male sexual offending such as deviant sexual arousal or empathy deficits. In this way, Level II theories could be seen to explain the occurrence of specific variables that are identified by Level I theories.

Level III theories, or micro-theories, 'provide the touchstone for all theoretical work' (Ward & Hudson, 1998, p. 49). They are much less common and involve the construction of descriptive models of the offence process (i.e. of how an offence or series of offences come to occur). Such models are typically developed *inductively* from detailed offence narratives and outline the specific cognitive, affective and contextual variables associated with the commission of an actual offence (Gannon et al., 2008).

When Ward and Hudson (1998) suggested differentiating male sexual offender theories according to these different categories, they did not specifically examine female sexual offender theory. In the sections that follow, I use the theoretical classification system suggested by Ward and Hudson to organise the scant contemporary literature regarding female sexual offender theories.

Level I Multifactorial Theories

The first level of theoretical abstraction requires that an explanation be comprehensive, encompassing multiple perspectives. Here, a specific behaviour is described as the result of a range of interrelated factors typically predetermined by existing empirical research. Traditional criminology is an apt example of this approach, where crime is often viewed through a macro lens as an outcome of a complex set of interconnected empirical variables. A potential Level I perspective regarding female sexual offenders may be borrowed from feminist criminology and focuses on the experience of *powerlessness*.

Although not previously considered in these terms, it seems that feminist criminology offers a description of two potential pathways that might help explain sexual offending by women: powerlessness through a pathway of *patriarchy* and powerlessness through a pathway of *victimisation*. The individual elements within each pathway have traditionally been used to explain various offending by women but this is the first time they have been integrated to approximate a multifactorial explanation of female sexual offending. Of course, there are limits to the validity of each component and these will be discussed below.

Powerlessness through a pathway of patriarchy is explained as occurring within the broader context of structural powerlessness. The predominantly female responsibility of raising a family provides a good description of this experience (White & Haines, 1996). Depending on one's individual circumstances, this task can be all-consuming, isolating, and both physically and emotionally demanding (Wolfers, 1993). This stress is exacerbated when there is an absence of a supportive partner. Here, a mother's structural powerlessness in the public sphere has the potential to become completely inverted in the private sphere of one's family (Wolfers, 1993). Abuse, neglect or over-discipline of a child might be the only opportunity a woman has to feel in control. Thus, abuse can be seen as a way of acquiring (or simulating) power in an otherwise powerless existence (Anderson, 1998). For example, almost all of Saradjian's (1996) sample of women who had sexually abused children expressed that they felt a sense of power during the offence.

A female sexual offender's powerlessness might also stem directly from her experiences of childhood sexual abuse and consequent feelings of having little control over her sexuality. Anderson (1998) posited that a social learning perspective, encompassing the intergenerational transmission of abuse hypothesis, likely constitutes the strongest explanation of female-perpetrated sexual offending. Early victimisation is thought to set the scene for some women to experience a number of adverse circumstances (such as eating disorders, running away, homelessness or unemployment; Chesney-Lind, 1989; Daly, 1998). Women with these experiences are at a greater risk of drug and alcohol abuse, shoplifting, prostitution or other sex-related offences (Chesney-Lind, 1989). Importantly, it has been suggested that these 'offences' could more accurately be recognised as methods of escape or survival that are directly linked to their victimisation history (Chesney-Lind, 1989).

Wolfers (1993) speculated that a woman with a history of sexual abuse might employ coercion to regain the sexual control she was stripped of as a child. The presence of a cycle of violence, especially in cases of female sexual offending, is supported by a considerable body of empirical research (Carnes, 1997; Schatzel-Murphy et al., 2009) and Wolfers (1993) posited that incest victims 'become offenders in an effort to resolve unresolved sexual trauma' (p. 101). Tired of being victimised, this might be a way of moving from defence to offence where a woman has the opportunity to recapitulate an experience through a role reversal where she at last has the upper hand (Anderson, 1998).

Evidently, the value of these two pathway explanations are limited by the fact that everyone's experiences are unique and not all of these elements will be relevant for every individual who experiences them. So, it is important to highlight two paradoxes here. First, as Ford (2006) reminds us, not all women who are abused as children go on to offend against others and not all female sexual offenders are victims of childhood abuse. Thus, just like with male sexual offenders, this explanation is likely not sufficient to explain the full range of offending behaviours by women. Further, an overemphasis on victimisation has the potential to conceal other important variables that place women and girls at risk of offending (Daly, 1998). Such factors might include larger examples of structural powerlessness such as racial, economic and educational marginality.

Second, it is difficult to reconcile two extremely well-established findings: that girls are much more likely than boys to be victimised and that men are much more likely than women to commit sexual offences (Cortoni & Gannon, in press). Evidently, if the intergenerational abuse hypothesis is able to be supported, then it is logical to expect that more female children will grow up to offend against others (Wolfers, 1993) and that the majority of adult sexual offenders would be female and not male (Herman, 1990). At the very least, it seems that if this theory were correct, then women would account for many more sexual offences than first thought. However, available statistics on the prevalence of female sexual offenders simply do not support this position (Cortoni & Hanson, 2005).

In summary, in the absence of any overarching multifactorial theory of female sexual offending, I have woven together a selection of single factor explanations to create a multifactorial theory of female sexual offending. Powerlessness may be expressed through two distinct pathways: the general experience of patriarchy and the personal experience of victimisation. In the next section, the individual variables that appear in these pathways (as well as other relevant factors) are presented in more detail.

Level II Single Factor Theories

Level II theories focus on specific single-factor variables to explain sexual offending behaviour. A range of individual vulnerability factors have been identified as strong correlates of female sexual offending. A selection of these is discussed below including childhood victimisation, coercion by a co-offender and cognitive distortions.

Childhood Victimisation

Many female sexual offenders report chaotic family backgrounds and adverse developmental experiences which are often characterised by neglect or abuse. Indeed, half of Gannon et al.'s (2008) sample reported multiple victimisations in childhood including sexual, physical and emotional abuse. Research also indicates that female sexual offenders experience more severe abuse, more often, than their male counterparts, often at the hands of a caregiver (Allen, 1997; Gannon et al., 2008; Hislop, 2001). Evidently, abuse alone does not predispose someone to offend and the extent to which it influences later behaviour remains to be seen. Victimisation has certainly emerged as a strong and compelling correlate of female sexual offending anyway. This is found to be especially true for women with particularly young victims (McCarty, 1986).

Coercion by a Co-Offender

It is known that a large proportion of identified female sexual offenders commit their offences in the company of a male co-offender (whether coerced or accompanied; Gannon & Rose, 2008). Traditional criminological theories that speak to the phenomenon of co-offending tend to do so with respect to juvenile delinquency, gang membership and deviant peer relationships. Unfortunately, none of these specific perspectives seems able to illustrate the kinds of behaviours with which we are concerned in this discussion.

Instead, sexual co-offending typically involves women who are in intimate relationships with men (or women) who influence or force them to engage in an offence. As noted earlier, coerced female sexual offenders are commonly regarded as holding non-assertive and extremely dependent characteristics (Gannon & Rose, 2008). Nevertheless, the extent to which solo female offenders and female co-offenders (either coerced or accompanied) are unique is unknown, but it is argued that they might differ in meaningful ways (Matravers, 2008). For example, women who co-offend sexually with men (either coerced or accompanied) have been found to have a greater number of arrests for non-sexual crimes than those who exclusively engage in solo offending (Vandiver, 2006). This suggests that women who co-offend with men might be prone towards more general criminality (Vandiver, 2006). Perhaps for these women, sexually offending with a male co-offender is simply part of a broader pattern of generally criminal behaviour in which they already engage.

So far, it is unknown whether the non-sexual crimes committed by women who co-offend with men are also committed in the company of a male co-perpetrator. This is an interesting gap in the existing body of knowledge regarding female offending. Two possible explanations would account for these findings. First, perhaps these women engage in a versatile range of criminal acts. Second, an alternative possibility is a third pathway to 'powerlessness'. This might be conceptualised as powerlessness through a pathway of interpersonal relationship dependence. Here, any coercion by men that these women experience might manifest itself in the commission of a range of criminal acts that are not restricted to sexual abuse. This hypothesis, of course, requires future empirical verification.

Cognitive Distortions

Cognitive distortions are frequently reported in the literature on male sexual offenders (especially for child sexual offenders) but the comparable literature on females is decidedly thin (Gannon & Rose, 2008). Regardless, there are a number of defence mechanisms that have been reported by women and they appear fairly similar to those expressed by men (although see Gannon, Hoare, Rose & Parrett, in press for an exception). Beech, Parrett, Ward and Fisher (2009) recently interviewed 15 female child sexual offenders to assess the existence of various implicit schemas that had previously been detected in male child sexual offenders (see Ward & Keenan, 1999). Beech et al. reported the general presence of each of the following implicit schemas previously identified in male child sexual offenders: the perception that children are seductive or sexually excited (*children as sexual objects*) or simply not violated or injured by the abuse (*nature of harm*), the general view that the world is uncontrollable and that 'things just happen' (*uncontrollability*), and the view that the world is inherently dangerous or threatening and that it is therefore preferable to engage in relationships with children (*dangerous world*; Beech et al., 2009). A final cognition that some people are superior to others and deserve to have their needs met (*entitlement*) has been detected in men but was not identified in the women in Beech et al.'s sample. However, in a follow-up study that recruited some of the same women, Gannon et al. (in press) found some support for the entitlement implicit schema previously identified in males. Yet Gannon noted that the exact nature of this schema appeared crucially different. Here, rather than female sexual offenders believing that they themselves were entitled to sexually abuse children, they instead voiced beliefs that their male co-offenders were *entitled* to control them and engage in sexual relationships with children (see Chapter 6 for more details).

In theoretical terms, most of these mechanisms are encapsulated by Sykes and Matza's (1957) criminological description of the five techniques of neutralisation. These include denial of responsibility, denial of injury, denial of victim, appeal to a higher loyalty and condemnation of the condemners. Cognitive distortions function as tools that enable an individual to deny their specific role in the offence, minimise injury and justify or excuse their behaviour. This is perhaps most often achieved by externalising blame on to other people or circumstances (Beech et al., 2009).

Although researchers agree on the importance of addressing cognitive distortions (Beech et al., 2009), the temporal order of the offence and the cognition is yet to be fully articulated and understood. Evidently, these explanations can be employed either in preparation of the offence (providing permission for an offender to offend) or simply as a post-hoc rationalisation for their behaviour. Since studies so far draw upon the recollections of already identified offenders who are reflecting on their pasts with the benefit of hindsight, it is impossible to determine whether any identified cognitions truly precede specific behaviours. This limitation of existing empirical explorations creates a substantial obstacle in the construction of sound theory. So, while an understanding of cognitive distortions remains theoretically promising, this potentially fatal flaw must be recognised.

In conclusion, this discussion of single-factor theories provides a number of individual variables that have been empirically related to female sexual offending. Evidently, the explanatory power of each one is limited if used in isolation. However, it is likely that our understanding of female sexual offenders will be sharpened when these individual factors are combined, as is the case in multifactorial theories, and micro-level theories described below.

Level III Micro-Level Theories

Micro-level theories are developed from actual offence accounts and seek to explain the offence process and its constituent parts (i.e. the planning processes and any particular offending styles). Gannon et al.'s (2008) Descriptive Model of Female Sexual Offending is the only current micro-level theory outlining the offence process of female sexual offenders (for both adult and child sexual offenders).

The recent development of Gannon et al.'s (2008) model of the offence process for women represents a substantial departure from the 'add women and stir' traditions described above. Instead, the authors interviewed 22 women incarcerated for sexual offences (almost half of all women imprisoned for sexual offences in England and Wales; Gannon et al., 2008) and developed the first model of female sexual offending that draws directly upon the narrative experiences of the women themselves (Gannon et al., 2008). Using grounded theory methodology, this approach provides a descriptive version of the women's offence pattern, addressing the question of 'how' rather than 'why' a sexual offence occurs. The product is a temporal model that encompasses the contributions of relevant cognitive, behavioural, affective and contextual variables.

The model is divided into three phases (see Figures 3.1–3.3 for a simplified reproduction of the model). The first phase, Background Factors (Figure 3.1), examines the influences of background factors that might 'prepare' someone to offend. This section is akin to the descriptions in Marshall and Barbaree's (1990) Integrated Theory which incorporates early life experiences. The second phase, the Pre-Offence Period (Figure 3.2), focuses on the period 12 months prior to and immediately before the offence. This stage of the model incorporates personal risk factors and illustrates how goals are established. The third phase, the Offence Period (Figure 3.3), is concerned with the offence itself, and the period of time immediately following the offence (although Figure 3.3 has been simplified to reduce focus on post-offence factors in the interests of brevity). In the sections that follow, the Descriptive Model and each of its constituent parts will be described in detail. Note that labels at the centre of the model (e.g. *cognition, affect*) represent factors that Gannon et al. (2008) noted as potential mediating factors associated with each stage.

Background Factors

The first phase categorises the background factors experienced by an individual into five dimensions: early family environment, abusive experiences, lifestyle outcomes, vulnerability factors and major life stressors. Gannon et al. (2008) found that

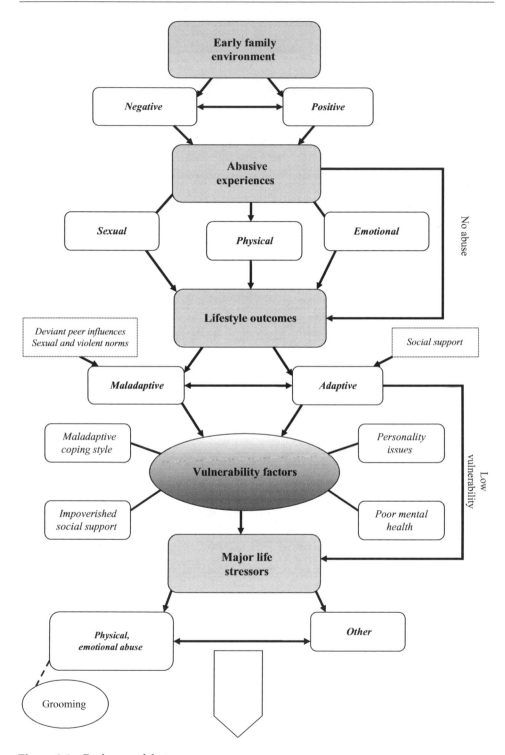

Figure 3.1 Background factors.

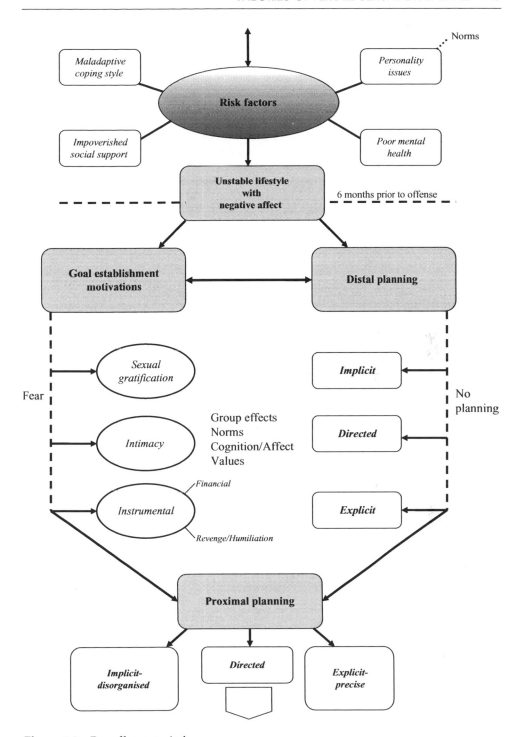

Figure 3.2   Pre-offence period.

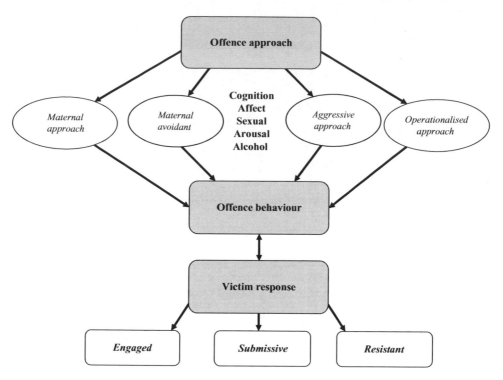

Figure 3.3 Offence period. © Sage Publications Ltd.*

early family environment could be either predominantly positive or predominantly negative. This variable measured a woman's childhood and adolescent family situations including caregiver relationships, parenting style and family cohesion. A negative family environment was characterised by parental neglect or rejection, prolonged periods of parental absence and ineffective or dysfunctional parenting style. A largely positive family environment was marked instead by family cohesion, parental stability and positive relationships with caregivers. Gannon et al. (2008) also found that an early family environment could be static but also might improve or deteriorate substantially.

Abusive experiences describe actual or vicarious abuse, be it sexual, physical or emotional. This is an intentionally broad variable that includes experiences such as witnessing domestic violence, physical punishment, sexual assault, school bullying and general criminal victimisation. It is important to note that this factor encompasses victimisation during childhood and adolescence as well as extending into early adulthood in some cases (Gannon, Rose & Ward, 2010).

Lifestyle outcomes are described as either adaptive or maladaptive and refer to a woman's responses and experiences through late adolescence and early adulthood. A maladaptive lifestyle is erratic or unstable and might involve crime, promiscuous sex and failure to resolve negative childhood experiences. In contrast, an adaptive

*The original, definitive version of this model was published in Sexual Abuse: A Journal of Research and Treatment, 20, 3, September, 2008.

lifestyle includes satisfactory employment, appropriate relationships and the development of adequate coping strategies. Gannon et al. (2008) found that deviant peer influences and sexual and violent norms appeared to function to increase the likelihood of a maladaptive lifestyle outcome, whereas strong social support appeared to increase the likelihood of an adaptive lifestyle outcome.

Many of the items encompassed in 'lifestyle outcomes' are also described by Gottfredson and Hirschi (1990) in their landmark General Theory of Crime. They consider a range of behaviours such as promiscuity, frequent short-term relationships, truancy and employment instability to be 'analogous to crime'. Their focus on situational variables and the attention they pay to measures of low self-control is reflected strongly in this stage of the Descriptive Model.

Vulnerability factors are divided into four clusters that illustrate individual traits and characteristics which can influence a woman's likelihood of offending. These include maladaptive coping styles, impoverished social support, personality issues and poor mental health (Gannon et al., 2008). *Coping style* refers to the way a woman might tolerate or rationalise instances of stress. Substance abuse would be an example of a maladaptive coping strategy to deal with stress. *Social support* reflects the extent to which family and friends are either practically or emotionally available to help a woman navigate these experiences. *Personality issues* refer specifically to traits or characteristics such as dependency or aggression that increase a woman's vulnerability. *Mental health* describes a woman's mental deficits, which might include depression, anxiety, disability or disorder.

The final background factor considered is *major life stressors*. These life experiences largely materialise during childhood, often within the context of a domestically violent personal relationship. Gannon et al. (2008) found that this often co-occurred with significant responsibilities including general caretaking of children or ailing family members and death or illness of a relative or loved one.

Gannon et al. (2010) recently re-examined the Descriptive Model to assess whether specific pathways could be identified. Approximately three quarters of the sample experienced a severely negative family environment, which included various kinds of abuse and vulnerability factors. With almost no variability in participants' experience of this first phase, it was impossible to identify any unique or specific pathways or to distinguish between women on the basis of their background factors. The frequency and severity of their experience of abuse and chaotic childhoods is certainly consistent with other theories detailed in this chapter. However, given the minimal variance detected in this component of the model, it might need to be restructured to increase its utility in future analyses.

Pre-Offence Period

Phase 2, the *pre-offence* period, explains how the vulnerability factors from Phase 1 become further entrenched into risk factors and place a woman at a higher likelihood of offending via the creation of an unstable lifestyle in the months prior to the offence. Again, this attention to such a multitude of variables that 'prepare' someone to offend is reminiscent of Marshall and Barbaree's (1990) Integrated Theory. Gannon et al. (2008) found that at this point in the woman's offence cycle, her lifestyle is usually marked by increased domestic disturbances, financial difficulties, significant responsibility (for children or ill family members) and general criminality. An appreciation of situational factors such as these is an important contribution of this model and reflects the increased emphasis that is now being placed on circumstantial variables in more general theories of crime and of male sexual offending.

At this point, Gannon et al. (2008) provide great detail on how offending goals are established and how offence planning occurs. Three main motivations are outlined: sexual gratification, intimacy and 'something else' (such as financial gain or vengeance). Sexual gratification and intimacy are sought with either the victim or co-offender. The final, more instrumental objective includes vengeance, humiliation or financial gain. The main motivation here is to seek retribution for a perceived wrong either committed by the victim or the group of people the victim represents (Gannon et al., 2008). Notably, this specific goal is not totally captured by the plethora of existing typological descriptions, and is another important contribution of this model. Gannon et al. (2008) also note that fear is likely to be one other reason why some women (typically those who are coerced into offending) are motivated to offend.

The types of offence planning described by Gannon et al. (2008) as occurring around the time offending goals are established (i.e. distal planning) are of three types: implicit, directed and explicit. Implicit planning refers to the unconscious manipulation of circumstances to make offending more likely, directed planning refers to the planning employed by a male co-offender, and explicit planning refers to explicit and conscious planning of the offence by the female sexual offender. This early or 'distal' planning of the offence appears to become crystallised as time passes such that nearer the time of the offence (i.e. proximal planning), women who implicitly planned become disinhibited and implement parts of their implicit plan impulsively (implicit-disorganised), women who were directed by a co-offending male continue to be directed by him (directed), and women who were explicit planners continue to implement their carefully formulated plan precisely (explicit-precise). Importantly, the model recognises that some women, who appear to act of their own volition, may not engage in any cognitive planning. The model also assumes that an individual's values, cognitions, affect, norms and the group conversations that they have will play a mediating influence in goal establishment and planning.

The identification of a pre-offence planning phase provides an excellent context for a description of the development of cognitive distortions. As outlined above, the extent to which cognitions truly precede an offence is unknown, but if research could be directed to this point in an offence cycle, it might shed some light on this important component and help to resolve the question of temporal ordering. This opportunity is theoretically exciting and extremely promising from a treatment provider's perspective.

Offence Period

Phase 3 describes the specific approaches that lead directly to an offence. These are arranged into four categories: maternal approach, maternal avoidant, aggressive approach and operationalised approach (Gannon et al., 2010). *Maternal approach* is especially characteristic of the 'teacher/lover' type. Here the woman takes a non-aggressive but coercive approach to their (usually male, adolescent) victim. Their decisions usually involve believing the victim is mature enough for the encounter, being sexually aroused, and sometimes the use of alcohol (Gannon et al., 2008). *Maternal avoidant* women are coercive and non-aggressive but actively want to avoid offending. *Aggressive approach* describes women who offend against adults or who offend in groups. They may have established an instrumental motivation to offend that focuses on humiliation or vengeance, and not sexual arousal. Finally, *Operationalised approach* also describes an instrumental motivation where the sexual nature of the specific offence is considered a necessary requirement for the achievement of a particular objective. Gannon et al. (2008) concluded that this was especially likely in instances of forced prostitution or human trafficking. Again, mediating factors of cognition, affect, sexual arousal and alcohol are all described as playing a role at this stage of the model.

The final phase of the Descriptive Model includes a description of the victim's response during the offence. This is another component of the model which is unique. Few if any theoretical perspectives pay specific attention to the victim (beyond simple demographic characteristics, as evidenced in the typologies described earlier in this chapter). Gannon et al. (2008) identified three types of victim responses: engaged, submissive and resistant. Engaged victims tend to be very young and appear to react positively to the abuse. Submissive victims interact minimally with the offender and tend not to react particularly strongly during the abusive event. Resistant victims express discomfort and ask the offender to stop. These victims are most likely to experience higher levels of force (Gannon et al., 2008).

Considering the victim in this way is certainly an interesting element to contemplate in our understanding of the execution of these behaviours. However, the extent to which it is theoretically relevant or simply descriptively interesting is unknown. Describing a victim's level of engagement or resistance appears to run the risk of suggesting the 'role' they played in their abuse. At the very least, this lays the foundation for the employment of the cognitive distortions (or techniques of neutralisation) discussed earlier. Blame can more easily be externalised if one can argue that their victim was aroused, engaged or simply did not resist. Although the observation of victim precipitation certainly has a place in more theoretical models of situational crime prevention (especially in cases of property crime), the extent to which it is appropriate in a discussion of the sexual abuse of children remains to be seen.

Pathways to Offending

A more recent study by the same authors (Gannon et al., 2010) examined the prevalence of specific patterns or pathways through the pre-offence and offence phases of the Descriptive Model. Here they were able to allocate 82 per cent of the total sample into one of three stable pathways: explicit approach, directed avoidant and implicit disorganised. In brief, the explicit approach group constituted just under half of Gannon et al.'s (2008) overall sample ($n = 9$). These women tended to demonstrate explicit planning of their offence behaviours and actively intended to offend. Note, that some of the women allocated into this category offended against adults, some offended against children and some offended alongside a co-offender male (i.e. they appeared to be male *accompanied* but not male *coerced*). Directed avoidant women, on the other hand, did not tend to plan the offence themselves, but instead were directed to offend by coercive male co-offenders. These women actively attempted to avoid offending and made up just less than one quarter of the interviewed women ($n = 5$). All of these women appeared to represent *male-coerced* offenders. The remaining four women (22 per cent) were identified as implicit disorganised and did not generally intend to offend. These women were instead characterised by their minimal planning, low self-control and impulsivity in the moments immediately before an offence. This category included offenders against both adults and children.

To review, the Descriptive Model provides a narrative version of a female sexual offender's offence pattern. In doing so, it is able to account for a broad range of specific offender characteristics and assign specific pathways through a series of phases, all without 'pigeon-holing' participants into simplistic and mutually exclusive categories (as is the case with some of the typologies noted previously). As a micro-level theory, the Descriptive Model focuses on the offence process *specifically* as opposed to a broader theoretical explanation of sexual offending by females. Nevertheless, it should be applauded for creating a step-by-step account of the interactions of such an extremely broad range of variables that borrow from both multifactorial and single factor theories.

Evidently, while promising, the utility of the model is limited at this time because of the small sample upon which it was constructed. Thus, it remains to be seen whether this approach can be replicated on larger or cross-cultural samples. But it certainly has the potential to guide future identification, treatment and management of these offenders and future research should be focused in this direction.

CONCLUSION

This chapter examined the current state of our theoretical understanding of female sexual offenders from both criminological and psychological traditions. It focused on previous attempts to apply male theories to (apparently similar) female behaviours. It described extant typological approaches and provided the dominant classifications currently available in this area. Finally, it provided a brief history of the development of theory in sexual offending research and detailed three separate levels of theory that attempt to explain why some women engage in sexually offending behaviour.

Research indicates that, superficially, women engage in similar acts to men. But how they arrive at that place (their pathway to offending) is uniquely female. Consequently, they warrant separate explanations than those constructed for their male counterparts. The Descriptive Model of Female Sexual Offending outlined above represents an important step in the direction of future theory development. Evidently, each perspective is limited in isolation and this underscores the need to integrate sociological, feminist and psychological viewpoints.

Future research would do well to attend to the further development of the theoretical perspectives outlined here and to other explanations that have not yet been articulated. A stronger theoretical explanation of sexual offending by women that can be validated empirically will certainly enhance future efforts to identify, treat, manage and understand this important population.

REFERENCES

Akers, R. L., & Sellers, C. S. (2004). *Criminological theories: Introduction, evaluation, and application* (4th ed.). California: Roxbury Publishing Company.

Allen, C. M. (1997). *Women and men who sexually abuse children: A comparative analysis*. Vermont: Safer Society Press.

Allgeier, E. R., & Lamping, J. C. (1998). Theories, politics, and sexual coercion. In P. B. Anderson & C. Struckman-Johnson (Eds.), *Sexually aggressive women: Current perspectives and controversies* (pp. 49–78). New York: The Guildford Press.

Anderson, P. B. (1998). Women's motives for sexual initiation and aggression. In P.B. Anderson & C. Struckman-Johnson (Eds.), *Sexually aggressive women: Current perspectives and controversies* (pp. 79–93). New York: The Guildford Press.

Atkinson, J. L. (1996). Female sex offenders: A literature review. *Forum on Corrections Research, 8*, 39–42.

Beech, A. R., Parrett, N., Ward, T., & Fisher, D. (2009). Assessing female sexual offenders' motivations and cognitions: An exploratory study. *Psychology, Crime & Law, 15*, 201–216.

Blackburn, R. (1993). *The psychology of criminal conduct: Theory, research and practice*. Chichester, UK: John Wiley & Sons.

Brown, S., & Forth, A. (1997). Psychopathy and sexual assault: Static risk factors, emotional precursors, and rapist subtypes. *Journal of Consulting and Clinical Psychology, 65*(5), 848–857.

Carnes, P. (1997). *Sexual anorexia: Overcoming sexual self-hatred*. Centre City, MN: Hazelden.

Chesney-Lind, M. (1989). Girls' crime and woman's place: Toward a feminist model of female delinquency. *Crime and Delinquency, 35*, 5–29.

Cortoni, F. (2009). Violence and women offenders. In J. Barker (Ed.), *Women and the criminal justice system: A Canadian perspective* (pp. 175–199). Toronto: Edmond Montgomery.

Cortoni, F., & Gannon, T. A. (in press). Female sexual offenders. In A. Phenix & H. Hoberman (Eds.), *Sexual offenders: Diagnosis, risk assessment and management*. New York: Springer.

Cortoni, F., & Hanson, K. (2005). *A review of the recidivism rates of adult female sexual offenders* (R-169). Ottawa: Research Branch, Correctional Service Canada.

Cullen, F., & Agnew, R. (2003). *Criminological theory: Past to present, essential readings* (2nd ed.). Los Angeles: Roxbury Publishing Company.

Daly, K. (1998). Gender, crime and criminology. In M. Tonry (Ed.), *The handbook of crime and justice* (pp. 85–108). Oxford: Oxford University Press.

Faller, K. (1987). Women who sexually abuse children. *Violence and Victims, 2* (4), 263–276.

Finkelhor, D., & Williams, L. M. (1988). Perpetrators. In D. Finkelhor, L. M. Williams, & N. Burns (Eds.), *Nursery crimes: Sexual abuse in day care* (pp. 27–69). Newbury Park, CA: Sage.

Ford, H. (2006). *Women who sexually abuse children*. London: John Wiley & Sons.

Gannon, T. A., Hoare, J., Rose, M. R., & Parrett, N. (in press). A re-examination of female child molesters' implicit theories: Evidence of female specificity? *Psychology Crime and Law*.

Gannon, T. A., & Rose, M. R. (2008). Female child sexual offenders: Towards integrating theory and practice. *Aggression and Violent Behaviour, 13*, 442–461.

Gannon, T. A., Rose, M. R., & Ward, T. (2010). Pathways to female sexual offending: Approach or avoidance? *Psychology, Crime & Law, 1–22* (iFirst).

Gannon, T. A., Rose, M. R., & Ward, T. (2008). A descriptive model of the offence process for female sexual offenders. *Sexual Abuse: A Journal of Research and Treatment, 20*, 352–374.

Gottfredson, M., & Hirschi, T. (1990). *A general theory of crime.* Stanford, CA: Stanford University Press.

Herman, J. L. (1990). Sex offenders: A feminist perspective. In W. Marshall, D. Laws & H. Barbaree (Eds.), *Handbook of sexual assault: Issues, theories and treatment of the offender* (pp. 177–193). New York: Plenum Press.

Hislop, J. (2001). *Female sex offenders: What therapists, law enforcement and child protective services need to know.* Ravensdale, WA: Idyll Arbor, Inc.

Hunter, J. A., & Mathews, R. (1997). Sexual deviance in females. In R. D. Laws & W. O'Donohue (Eds.), *Sexual deviance: Theory, assessment and treatment* (pp. 465–480). New York: Guilford Press.

Knight, R. A. (2009). Typologies for rapists: The generation of a new structural model. In A. Schlank (Ed.), *The sexual predator* (Vol. 4, pp. 17:1–17:28). New York: Civic Research Institute.

Knight, R. A., & Prentky, R. A. (1990). Classifying sexual offenders: The development and corroboration of taxonomic models. In W. Marshall, D. Laws, & H. Barbaree (Eds.), *Handbook of sexual assault: Issues, theories and treatment of the offender* (pp. 23–52). New York: Plenum.

Lilly, J. R., Cullen, F. T., & Ball, R. A. (1995). *Criminological theory: Context and consequences* (2nd ed.). Newbury Park, CA: Sage.

Marshall, W. L., & Barbaree, H. E. (1990). An integrated theory of sexual offending. In W. L. Marshall, D. R. Laws, & H. E. Barbaree (Eds.), *Handbook of sexual assault: Issues, theories and treatment of the offender* (pp. 257–275). New York: Plenum.

Marshall, W., & Laws, D. (2003). A brief history of behavioural and cognitive behavioural approaches to sexual offenders: Part 2. The Modern era. *Sexual Abuse: A Journal of Research and Treatment, 15*, 93–120.

Matravers, A. (2008). Understanding women who commit sex offences. In G. Letherby, K. Williams, P. Birch, & M. Cain (Eds.), *Sex as crime?* (pp. 299–320). Devon: Willan Publishing.

Mathews, R., Matthews, J. A., & Speltz, K. (1989). *Female sexual offenders: An exploratory study.* Orwell, VT: Safer Society Press.

McCarty, L. M. (1986). Mother–child incest: Characteristics of the offender. *Child Welfare, 65*, 447–458.

Miller, J. (2002). *One of the guys: Girls, gangs, and gender.* New York: Oxford University Press.

Naffine, N. (1996). *Feminism and criminology.* Philadelphia: Temple University Press.

Parkinson, P., Shrimpton, S., Oates, R., Swanston, H., & O'Toole, B. (2004). Nonsex offences committed by child molesters: Findings from a longitudinal study. *International Journal of Offender Therapy and Comparative Criminology, 48*, 28–39.

Sandler, J. C., & Freeman, N. J. (2007). Typology of female sex offenders: A test of Vandiver and Kercher. *Sexual Abuse: A Journal of Research and Treatment, 19*, 73–89.

Saradjian, J. (1996). *Women who sexually abuse children: From research to clinical practice.* Chichester, UK: Wiley.

Sarrel, P. M., & Masters, W. H. (1982). Sexual molestation of men by women. *Archives of Sexual Behaviour, 11*, 117–131.

Schatzel-Murphy, E. A., Harris, D. A., Knight, R. A., & Milburn, M. A. (2009). Sexual coercion in men and women: Similar behaviours, different predictors. *Archives of Sexual Behaviour,* DOI 10.1007/s10508–009-9481-y.

Schwartz, B. K., & Cellini, H. R. (1995). *The sex offender: Corrections, treatment and legal practice.* New Jersey: Civic Research Institute Inc.

Simon, L. M. J. (2000). An examination of the assumptions of specialization, mental disorder, and dangerousness in sex offenders. *Behavioral Sciences and the Law, 18*, 275–308.

Syed, F. & Williams, S. (1996). *Case studies of female sex offenders in the Correctional Service of Canada.* Ottawa: Correctional Service Canada.

Sykes, G. M., & Matza, D. (1957). Techniques of neutralization: A theory of delinquency. *American Sociological Review, 22*, 664–670.

Vandiver, D. M. (2006). Female sex offenders: A comparison of solo offenders and co offenders. *Violence and Victims*, *21*, 339–354.

Vandiver, D. M., & Kercher, G. (2004). Offender and victim characteristics of registered female sexual offenders in Texas: A proposed typology of female sexual offenders. *Sexual Abuse: A Journal of Research and Treatment*, *16*, 121–137.

Vold, G. B., Bernard, T. J., & Snipes, J. B. (2002). *Theoretical criminology* (5th Ed.). New York: Oxford University Press.

Ward, T., & Hudson, S. (1998). The construction and development of theory in the sexual offending area: A metatheoretical framework. *Sexual Abuse: A Journal of Research and Treatment*, *10*, 47–63.

Ward, T., & Keenan, T. (1999). Child molesters' implicit theories. *Journal of Interpersonal Violence*, *14*, 821–838.

Ward, T., Polaschek, D., & Beech, A. (2006). *Theories of sexual offending*. Chichester, UK: John Wiley & Sons.

White, R., & Haines, F. (1996). *Crime and criminology: An introduction*. Melbourne, Australia: Oxford University Press.

Wolfers, O. (1993). The paradox of women who sexually abuse children. In M. Elliott (Ed.), *Female sexual abuse of children: The ultimate taboo* (pp. 93–99). London: John Wiley & Sons.

Young, V. (1993). Women abusers – a feminist view. In M. Elliott (Ed.), *Female sexual abuse of children: The ultimate taboo* (pp. 100–112). London: John Wiley & Sons.

Chapter 4

THE JUVENILE FEMALE SEXUAL OFFENDER: CHARACTERISTICS, TREATMENT AND RESEARCH

LISA L. FREY

University of Oklahoma, OK, USA

The response of mental health professionals when the issue of female adolescent sexual offenders is discussed is illustrative of the challenges facing those who work with this population. Responses range from 'I know that boys do that, but girls? It's just not something a girl would do' to 'Any girl that does that should be locked up forever'. Whether such responses are evidence of the invisibility of female adolescents who sexually abuse or the rarity of female adolescent sexual offending are issues worth exploring.

Given the overlap among terms such as *sexual offender, sexual offence, sexual abuse* and so forth in the literature related to juveniles, these terms will be used interchangeably in the chapter. The use of the terms *offence* or *offender* in the juvenile literature does not necessarily imply that the behaviour has been labelled by the legal system unless characteristics of the sample (e.g. participants drawn from a sex offender registry) make this issue clear.

The Federal Bureau of Investigation (FBI) Uniform Crime Report (2007) documented that 1,174 young women under the age of 18 were arrested for forcible rape or other sexual offences (excluding prostitution) in 2007. In contrast, 13,034 young men under age 18 and 4,555 adult women (i.e. 18 years old or over) were arrested for these offences during the same time frame. Thus, arrests of young women under 18 years of age accounted for 8 per cent of juvenile arrests and 20 per cent of female arrests for all sexual offences. In addition, arrest trends for 1998–2007 indicated decreases of 52.5 per cent in forcible rape and 0.8 per cent in other sexual offence arrests (excluding prostitution) of females under 18 years old (FBI, 2007). These statistics compare to decreases of 31.2 per cent in forcible rape and 16 per cent in other sexual offence arrests of males under 18 years old and 35.4 per cent in forcible rape and 9.5 per cent in other sexual offence arrests of females of any age.

Female Sexual Offenders: Theory, Assessment, and Treatment   Edited by Theresa A. Gannon and Franca Cortoni
© 2010 John Wiley & Sons, Ltd

Of course, there are limitations to these statistics that obscure the true prevalence of female juvenile sexual offending including that arrest statistics are only reflective of offences that rise to the level of detection by the juvenile justice system. Also, they tell us nothing about the absolute numbers of victims. In presenting data on female adolescents' involvement in violent crimes, Chesney-Lind and Shelden (2004) pointed out that there has long been a discrepancy between self-report data and official statistics, with self-report data indicating increased involvement of girls. Irrespective of the numbers, however, there is general agreement that female juvenile sexual offenders represent a relatively small portion of the overall juvenile sexual offender population.

Several scholars have pointed out the impact of socioculturally influenced gender norms in masking the true prevalence of female sexual offending. For instance, ambivalence regarding women and sexuality, a focus on women as caretakers and the view of women as sexually passive (e.g. Denov, 2001; Schwartz & Cellini, 1995) may make it difficult for victims of female adolescents to disclose their abuse and for abusive female adolescents to seek help. However, once female adolescents' sexually abusive behaviour rises to the level that it is no longer possible to render it invisible, there may be a tendency to severely punish young women. For instance, MacDonald and Chesney-Lind (2001) found that adolescent girls engaging in delinquent behaviour tended to be more harshly sanctioned than male adolescents, even when charge seriousness was taken into account. In referring to the experiences of delinquent girls, Chesney-Lind and Shelden (2004) stated, 'It is simply not possible to discuss their problems, their delinquency, and their experiences with the juvenile justice system without considering gender in all its dimensions. Girls and boys do not inhabit the same worlds, and they do not have the same choices' (p. 4).

At the very least, it is clear that the paucity of research and theory relating to female juvenile sexual offenders serves no one. Likewise, demonising these young women is not an effective solution. Perhaps in view of the increased numbers of male versus female juvenile sexual offenders, directing the majority of resources towards treatment programmes for male adolescents is understandable. However, as Frey (2006) pointed out, '...the salient issue is not simply resource allocation but attention to gender disparities and the lack of gender-responsive services at many levels of system intervention. That is, it is an issue of quality not just quantity' (p. 250). It also must be kept in mind that the lack of attention to identification and treatment of female adolescents who sexually abuse marginalises the experiences of their victims.

In an effort to advance the body of knowledge regarding female adolescent sexual offenders, this chapter provides a critical analysis of the current empirical and theoretical literature regarding the characteristics and treatment of this population and offers recommendations about future directions for research. Of note is that the chapter focuses on adolescent females (i.e. age range 12–18) who sexually abuse and the terminology *juvenile* refers to this age range. Because the literature examining samples of juvenile females who sexually abuse sometimes tends to blur the line between childhood and adolescence, only studies with predominantly adolescent samples will be included in this review and, for clarity, the age range of sample participants will be reported whenever possible.

FEMALE JUVENILES WHO SEXUALLY OFFEND: COMMENTS ON THE CURRENT LITERATURE

A critical analysis of the scholarly literature regarding adolescent females who sexually offend results in more questions than answers. With a few exceptions, the clinical literature is composed of uncontrolled case studies or descriptions of a limited number of young women. Methodological and statistical problems, including small samples, questionable psychometric integrity of instruments, overly generous significance testing, over-interpretation of results and limited generalisability, are fairly commonplace in the empirical studies. The relatively small number of female adolescents who sexually offend and difficulties related to identification and recruitment help to explain some of the limitations in the literature. For instance, the tendency for many empirical studies to focus on young women who are incarcerated, are in residential treatment or are registered sexual offenders is understandable but results in serious threats to external validity. It is problematic when the results of these studies are generalised to all female adolescents who sexually offend, especially if applied to an individual client at the level of clinical practice. Therefore, in order to aid the reader in critically evaluating the reviewed literature and in making informed decisions regarding the generalisability of findings, characteristics of samples will be provided whenever possible.

CHARACTERISTICS OF FEMALE JUVENILES WHO SEXUALLY OFFEND

Race and/or Ethnicity

With some exceptions (e.g. Hunter, Lexier, Goodwin, Browne & Dennis, 1993; Matthews, Hunter & Vuz, 1997; Vandiver & Teske, 2006), the majority of studies investigating adolescent females who sexually offend do not report racial or ethnic demographic information. The literature on adolescent female delinquents points out differences between girls of colour and European American girls in regard to juvenile court processing, including rates of detention versus treatment facility placement (American Bar Association & National Bar Association [ABA/NBA], 2001; Chesney-Lind & Shelden, 2004). Therefore, the absence of racial and ethnic demographic information is a concerning omission.

Family History

Matthews et al. (1997) examined the characteristics of 67 juvenile females (age range 11–18), all who had documented histories of sexual perpetration. The majority of the young women ($n = 51$) were receiving community-based treatment for their sexual behaviour, with the remainder ($n = 16$) receiving intensive residential treatment. Matthews et al. reported moderate to severe family dysfunction and psychopathology, including neglect and incest, in the histories of the majority of these young women. Similarly, Tardif, Auclair, Jacob and Carpentier (2005) reported family dysfunction and instability in the majority of 15 juvenile female sexual abusers (age range 12–17) referred for assessment and/or treatment to a specialised outpatient sexual offender programme in Canada over a period of 10 years. In particular, Tardif et al. indicated that 50 per cent or more of the young women had experienced abandonment by a parent prior to the age of four and reported multiple and prolonged parental conflicts and/or conflictual mother–daughter relationships.

Some indirect corroboration of the previous findings can be found in Vick, McRoy and Matthews' (2002) description of 13 interviews with clinicians, each of whom reported treating at least 30 young female sexual offenders a year. Vick et al. indicated that all the clinicians reported evidence of family dysfunction, including substance abuse, attachment problems, mental illness, neglect and abuse, partner violence and poor boundaries, in the families of these young female offenders (defined as including both children and adolescents).

Fromuth and Conn (1997) studied 546 female college students and identified 22 (age range 17–21) who retrospectively reported sexually molesting one or more younger children. In contrast to the previous findings, no differences were found on Parental Support Scale (Fromuth, 1986) and Parental Bonding Instrument (Parker, Tupling & Brown, 1979) scores between the female students reporting perpetrating sexual molestation and those not reporting this behaviour; it is important to keep in mind the marked size difference in the comparison groups, however, which may have impacted the results. It is of note, also, that this data was exclusively self-report and none of the sexual incidents had been reported to the police or dealt with in counselling. In addition, the classification criteria for inclusion as sexual molestation were quite restrictive, with the required perpetrator–victim age differential ranging from 5–10 years (the 13–16 year old victim group required the participant to be at least 23–26 years old to be identified as an offender). Thus, it is possible that the 22 participants identified as sexual offenders may have been an underestimation.

Childhood Maltreatment History

One of the most robust findings in the literature related to female adolescents who sexually abuse is the high rate of childhood maltreatment. Histories of childhood sexual abuse were reported by (a) Bumby and Bumby (1997) in 100 per cent of two samples of young women (total $n = 30$, age range not specified) treated in a psychiatric inpatient facility; (b) Fehrenbach and Monastersky (1988) in 50 per cent of a sample of 28 young women (age range 10–18) treated in an outpatient evaluation and treatment programme; (c) Hendriks and Bijleveld (2006) in 90 per cent of a sample of 10 young women (age range 12–17) prosecuted for a sexual offence in the Netherlands over a 9-year period; (d) Hunter et al. (1993) in 100 per cent of a sample of 10 young women (age range 13–17) treated in a residential treatment programme; (e) Kubik, Hecker and Righthand (2002) in 64 per cent of a sample of 11 young women (age range 13–18) identified from State Department of Corrections records over a 1-year period as having sexually offended; (f) Matthews et al. (1997) in 78 per cent of the sample of juvenile female perpetrators described previously; and (g) Tardif et al. (2005) in 73 per cent of the Canadian sample of 15 juvenile female sexual abusers described previously. Fromuth and Conn (1997), in the previously described retrospective study, indicated that 77 per cent of the sample of 22 college women self-reporting sexual perpetration also reported childhood sexual abuse. Bumby and Bumby and Tardif et al. reported that the sexual abuse experienced by the young women in their studies was generally intrafamilial.

In addition to reported child sexual abuse experiences, other exposure to violence and/or neglect has been reported in the literature. Physical abuse frequencies ranging from 21 to 80 per cent have been found in samples of adolescent females who sexually offend (Bumby & Bumby, 1997; Fehrenbach & Monastersky, 1988; Hunter et al., 1993; Kubik et al., 2002; Matthews et al., 1997; Tardif et al., 2005). In addition, histories of neglect (Bumby & Bumby, 1997; Hendriks & Bijleveld, 2006; Kubik et al., 2002) and exposure to family violence (Bumby & Bumby, 1997; Tardif et al., 2005) have been reported.

Although the finding of child maltreatment history has been consistently supported in the literature on female adolescents who sexually abuse, the results must still be viewed tentatively in view of the methodological and sampling limitations previously discussed. Frey (2006) pointed out, however, that 'some support for the validity of this finding in adolescent female sexual abusers is provided by studies documenting the increased frequency of maltreatment in adolescent female non-sexual offenders as compared to adolescent male non-sexual offenders (e.g. Artz, 1998; McCormack, Janus & Burgess, 1986)' (p. 265). For instance, Chesney-Lind and Shelden indicated that physical and sexual abuse rates ranging from 40 to 73 per cent have been reported among delinquent girls.

Clinical History

A range of psychiatric diagnoses and learning problems have been reported in samples of female adolescents who sexually offend. Tardif et al. (2005) and Hunter et al. (1993) reported learning disabilities/disorders in 80 and 40 per cent, respectively, of the young women in their samples. Hendriks and Bijleveld (2006) found below average intellectual performance in more than 50 per cent of participants in their sample. Considering that school failure has been linked with delinquency in girls (Acoca, 2004), the incidence of learning problems and poor academic performance in adolescent females who sexually offend is a topic in need of further research.

A variety of psychiatric diagnoses have been reported in these young women, with the most consistently reported diagnoses being post-traumatic stress disorder (PTSD) and mood disturbances (Hunter et al., 1993; Kubik et al., 2002; Matthews et al., 1997; Tardif et al., 2005; Vick et al., 2002) and attention deficit hyperactive disorder (Kubik et al., 2002; Tardif et al., 2005). Also, Kubik et al. and Matthews et al. reported suicidal attempts and/or ideation in nearly half of participants in their samples (i.e. 46 and 44 per cent, respectively). Overall, however, the range of reported diagnoses makes it difficult to draw any firm conclusions, particularly considering that diagnoses were determined from treatment programme records, corrections records or clinician reports, thus reflecting only clinically-identified youth.

Other Problematic Sexual Behaviours

Few studies focused on assessing problematic sexual behaviours associated with sexually abusive behaviour. Exceptions include Hunter et al. (1993), Matthews et al. (1997) and Tardif et al. (2005), who found pornography use in 40, 51 and 47 per cent, respectively, of participants in their samples. Other sexual behaviours reported included exhibitionism (Hunter et al., 1993; Matthews et al., 1997; Tardif et al., 2005); frequent sexual encounters with no emotional involvement, voyeurism, compulsive masturbation and questions regarding sexual identity (Tardif et al., 2005); obscene phone calling (Hunter et al., 1993; Matthews et al., 1997); and frottage and bestiality (Hunter et al., 1993). The frequencies of these behaviours were relatively small (range 3–20 per cent), however, precluding any definitive conclusions. Likewise, Fromuth and Conn (1997) reported sexual masturbatory fantasies regarding children in 1–3 per cent of their sample of college women who had histories of sexually molesting, although the retrospective nature of the self-reports and the potential impact of socially desirable responding make it difficult to assess the validity of the results. Clearly this is a topic in need of further investigation.

Offence Characteristics

Available findings regarding offence characteristics present mixed results. Regarding the most frequently reported victim gender, Hunter et al. (1993), Matthews et al. (1997), Tardif et al. (2005) and Fromuth and Conn (1997) reported the targeting of predominantly male victims; Bumby and Bumby (1997), Fehrenbach and Monastersky (1988), Hendriks and Bijleveld (2006) and Vandiver and Teske (2006; $n = 61$ female adolescent registered sexual offenders, age 12–17 years) reported predominantly female victims; and Kubik et al. (2002) reported the targeting of (a) both genders or (b) male victims more than female victims. Some consensus exists regarding victim age, however, with the most frequently occurring age being 6 years or younger (Fehrenbach & Monastersky, 1988; Matthews et al., 1997; Tardif et al., 2005; Vandiver & Teske, 2006), although the victim age may simply be related to the similarly young age of participants (i.e. lower age range of study participants was 10–12 years).

Kubik and Hecker (2005), Kubik et al. (2002) and Tardif et al. (2005) found the most frequent age at first offence was 11–12 years, with Hunter et al. (1993) reporting a median age of 10 years. Although Hendriks and Bijleveld (2006) found that the majority of young women in their sample targeted only one victim, Hunter et al. (1993) and Matthews et al. (1997) reported a mean or median number of victims as greater than one. The majority of studies reporting the relationship of the victim to the offender indicated the victim was most frequently an acquaintance (Fehrenbach & Monastersky, 1988; Hendriks & Bijleveld, 2006; Kubik & Hecker, 2005; Kubik et al., 2002) or family member (Fromuth & Conn, 1997; Matthews et al., 1997; Tardif et al., 2005). One study (Hunter et al., 1993) reported primarily strangers as targeted victims.

Although it has been suggested that adult females frequently sexually abuse with a co-offender (e.g. Faller, 1995; Nathan & Ward, 2002), this pattern was found in only one study of juvenile female sexual offenders (i.e. Hendriks & Bijleveld, 2006). In contrast, Fehrenbach and Monastersky (1988), Hunter et al. (1993), Kubik and Hecker (2005) and Tardif et al. (2005) reported that the young women in their samples most often acted alone.

In regard to offence-related sexual behaviour, fondling was the most frequently reported behaviour (Hunter et al., 1993; Kubik & Hecker, 2005; Kubik et al., 2002; Matthews et al., 1997; Tardif et al., 2005). Aside from that particular result, there was little consensus regarding offence behaviour, with results suggesting vaginal intercourse frequencies, for example, of as much as 70 per cent (Hunter et al., 1993) and as little as 27 per cent (Kubik & Hecker, 2005; Kubik et al., 2002) and oral–genital contact frequencies ranging from 33 (Tardif et al., 2005) to 70 per cent (Hunter et al., 1993). Similarly, there was little consensus regarding the use of offence-related physical coercion or aggression, with Hunter et al. and Kubik et al. reporting frequency rates of 40 and 55 per cent, respectively, and Tardif et al. and Matthews et al. reporting rates of 13 and 19 per cent, respectively. It was possible that the variation in these reported frequencies were related to sample characteristics. For instance, the Tardif et al. and Matthews et al. participants were drawn from primarily outpatient populations whereas the Hunter et al. participants were drawn from a residential treatment programme. Thus, the level of risk of participants in the Hunter et al. sample was likely higher as compared with the other two samples.

COMPARISON OF JUVENILE FEMALE SEXUAL OFFENDERS WITH OTHER OFFENDER POPULATIONS

Juvenile and Adult Female Sexual Offenders

Studies comparing adult and adolescent females who sexually abuse are difficult to find. Although some studies have collapsed the two populations into one group (e.g. Freeman & Sandler, 2008; Miccio-Fonseca, 2000; Sandler & Freeman, 2007), there are potential pitfalls associated with this practice. For instance, Frey (2006) pointed out that adolescents and adults have developmental differences that present potentially significant statistical and interpretive confounds for studies that combine the age groups. Research has demonstrated that important differences exist between adolescent and adult male sexual offenders (e.g. Association for the Treatment of Sexual Abusers, 2000; Becker, Hunter, Stein & Kaplan, 1989; Chaffin & Bonner, 1998; Hunter, Goodwin & Becker, 1994), suggesting that findings regarding adult females should likewise not be generalised to adolescent females.

Tardif et al. (2005) provided descriptive details of female juvenile ($n = 15$) and adult ($n = 13$) sexual offenders. Of note was that a majority of participants in both groups (i.e. 62 per cent of adults, 60 per cent of juveniles) reported a history of sexual victimisation. Furthermore, a history of experiencing physical abuse was reported by 46 per cent of adults and 40 per cent of juveniles and exposure to family violence was reported by 53 per cent of juveniles in contrast to 31 per cent of adults. Diagnostic differences were also observed in the two samples, with adult females, perhaps predictably, being diagnosed with personality disorders at a much higher frequency as compared with adolescent females.

Offence characteristics varied to some extent in the two participant groups reported by Tardif et al. (2005). For instance, juveniles reported predominantly abusing male children (i.e. 60 per cent), whereas adults reported primarily abusing female children (i.e. 77 per cent). In terms of the number of incidents of sexual abuse perpetration, 39 per cent of adults and 33 per cent of juveniles chose the category designating 10–35 incidents. Regarding type of abuse, although a majority of adults and juveniles reported fondling victims (i.e. 62 and 93 per cent, respectively), adults also engaged in more intrusive sexually abusive behaviour (e.g. sexual intercourse, digital vaginal penetration) at a higher frequency. This finding may be understandable given differences in adult and adolescent sexual development and experiences. Overall, Tardif et al. concluded that both the adult and adolescent females showed evidence of developmental disturbances (e.g. parental abandonment, conflictual parent–child relationships) and impaired identification with the mother, resulting in a problematic 'feminine sexual identity' (p. 163) characterised by problems such as confusion regarding masculine and feminine roles, the expression of sexuality and the role of domination in relationships.

Juvenile Female and Male Sexual Offenders

The most frequently reported difference between adolescent female and male sexual abusers has been the increased incidence of sexual and physical victimisation in females (Bumby & Bumby, 1997; Kubik et al., 2002; Matthews et al., 1997). In addition, Kubik et al. and Matthews et al. found that female as compared with male participants were more likely to be abused by multiple perpetrators and reported an increased incidence of intrafamilial abuse. Furthermore, Matthews et al. found that the young women in their sample tended to be sexually abused at a younger age as compared with their male counterparts.

Vandiver and Teske (2006) compared 61 juvenile females with 122 juvenile males who were registered as sexual offenders. The two groups were matched on year of birth and race, and the age range for the time of the sexual offence arrest was similar for both groups. Chi-square analyses suggested significant differences on four characteristics: (a) age at arrest, with approximately half of the males in the 14–16-year-old category and half of the females in the 11–13-year-old category; (b) victim age, with females as compared with males more likely to victimise a child between infancy and 5 years of age and males more likely to victimise someone between 12 and 17 years of age; (c) victim sex, with males more likely to choose female victims and females choosing either gender equally; and (d) length of court-levied sentence. Of note is that, although females received shorter sentences as compared with males, potentially powerful mediators (e.g. seriousness of offence, aggravating circumstances) were not controlled.

Kubik et al. (2002) compared 11 adolescent female with 11 male sexual offenders on 'clinical/treatment factors' (p. 79; e.g. lack of remorse, inadequate guilt feelings, denial, actively rejecting help) and found that the two groups were similar. Data regarding the factors, however, were retrospectively collected from Department of Corrections records and coded by one person. Consequently, rater reliability could not be assessed.

In regard to diagnosis, Kubik et al. (2002) and Matthews et al. (1997) reported higher frequencies of PTSD diagnoses in females as compared with males, with Kubik et al. reporting 50 per cent of females as compared with 9 per cent of males being given this diagnosis. Kubik et al. also reported conduct disorder diagnoses in 9 per cent of females versus 46 per cent of males and adjustment disorder diagnoses in 0 per cent of females versus 36 per cent of males. No major between-group differences were observed in characteristics of the sexual offence (e.g. level and type of coercion, victim sex, age, relationship to victim, offence behaviours; Kubik et al., 2002; Matthews et al., 1997), in contrast to the Vandiver and Teske (2006) study, or in family characteristics, school behaviours and/or antisocial behaviours (Bumby & Bumby, 1997; Kubik et al., 2002; Matthews et al., 1997). Overall, further investigation of clinical and treatment factors seems crucial in order to provide guidance for treatment providers.

Juvenile Female Sexual Offenders, Non-Sexual Offenders and Non-Offenders

Kubik et al. (2002) compared adolescent female sexual offenders and non-sexual offenders (i.e. those who were identified as committing crimes that were not sex-related) and reported that the non-sexual offender group had significantly more problems with substance abuse, school problems and fighting. Maltreatment histories were reportedly similar in both samples. Of note was that the adolescent female sexual offenders reportedly tended to engage in their first sexual offence incident at a younger age as compared with the age of first criminal offence in the non-sexual offenders.

Kubik and Hecker (2005) compared adolescent female sexual offenders, non-sexual offenders and non-offenders on a variety of variables (e.g. cognitive distortions, beliefs about aggression, internalising and externalising behaviours). Of note, however, were the small study samples (i.e. 11 sexual offenders, 12 non-sexual offenders, 21 non-offenders), the number of statistical analyses that were performed, and the liberal alpha level (i.e. 0.10) used to determine significance despite the multiple analyses; thus, study results must be viewed tentatively. Using a vignette questionnaire designed for the study, a significant interaction (medium effect size) was found suggesting that, when victims responded to more serious levels of sexual contact by crying, female adolescent sexual offenders reported increased victim-related distortions as compared with the other two groups. In addition, there was some evidence that the female sexual offenders did not differ significantly from the other groups in terms of internalising and externalising behaviours.

ASSESSMENT OF FEMALE JUVENILES WHO SEXUALLY OFFEND

No empirically validated instruments or assessment protocols for the assessment of female adolescents who sexually abuse are currently available. Although there are some tools developed for the assessment of male adolescent sexual offenders, the application of these instruments to the assessment of young women has not been empirically examined and is not recommended (Hunter, Becker & Lexier, 2006; Worling & Langström, 2006). Clearly, the development of an empirically validated assessment tool is a pressing need. Nevertheless, tentative guidance can be provided to practitioners on the basis of the literature regarding characteristics of female juveniles who sexually offend. For instance, the thorough assessment of maltreatment experiences has emerged as a salient evaluation factor. As emphasised by Hunter et al. (2006), however, the identification of maltreatment is only helpful when balanced with an assessment of its impact on the development of sexual offending patterns (e.g. issues of identity development, cognition, mood, self-regulation, offence characteristics).

In addition to maltreatment experiences, it is recommended that the assessment of adolescent females who sexually abuse include a thorough evaluation of all areas suggested in the general juvenile sexual offender assessment literature (for instance, see Hunter et al., 2006; O'Reilly & Carr, 2006; Worling & Langström, 2006). However, the aetiology of offence-related behaviours, cognitions, emotions and psychological responses must be carefully assessed given that the underlying dynamics in female juveniles are not well-understood and are likely to differ from those of male juveniles (e.g. Frey, 2006; Kasl, 1990; Mayer, 1992). It is essential that the importance of assessing such aetiological differences not be minimised because the influence of sociocultural factors, including differences in gender socialisation, gender roles and gender inequities, differentially impact female and male identity development (e.g. Bloom, Owen & Covington, 2003; Chesney-Lind & Shelden, 2004). For instance, in youth that have experienced maltreatment, it has been hypothesised that the victim to victimiser cycle operates differently in females and males (Mayer, 1992).

TREATMENT OF FEMALE JUVENILES WHO SEXUALLY OFFEND

Burton, Smith-Darden and Frankel (2006) discussed results from the 2000 and 2002 Safer Society surveys, which collected data from community-based programmes, residentially-based programmes and private practitioners providing services to juvenile sexual offenders. Between 2000 and 2002, the number of community and residential programmes for female juveniles increased, although the male-to-female programme ratios remained relatively unchanged. In 2000, male programmes outnumbered female programmes by a 2 : 1 (community-based) and 9 : 1 (residentially based) male-to-female programme ratio; the 2002 survey indicated the male-to-female community-based and residentially based programme ratios were 2 : 1 and 6 : 1, respectively (Burton et al., 2006). A change was also noted in the theoretical orientation of programmes for young women; specifically, as compared with the 2000 survey results, the 2002 results suggested a decrease in the number of juvenile female sexual offender programmes relying on cognitive-behavioural, relapse prevention or social learning theories as their primary orientation. Instead, the 2002 survey found that a relatively greater number of programmes for young women reported using a sexual trauma or unspecified treatment orientation. Burton et al. suggested that these trends may be related to increased identification of juvenile female offenders overall. For instance, the awareness that programming for juvenile male offenders cannot automatically be applied to programmes for juvenile females and the need for a female continuum of services has recently been receiving increased attention (Community Research Associates, 1998).

The apparent increase in programmes addressing the treatment needs of juvenile female sexual offenders points to the importance of having reliable information regarding effective and evidence-based interventions. However, as is apparent from the previous literature review, female adolescents who sexually abuse are a poorly understood and understudied population. In fact, there are currently no evidence-based outcome studies to evaluate the effectiveness of treatment for these young women. Thus, treatment providers are confronted with a significant challenge. Two sources of information, the theoretical literature related to treatment needs of female juvenile sexual offenders and information that can be extrapolated from the literature regarding female juvenile and adult non-sexual offenders, can, however, provide some direction.

Theoretically Derived Treatment Implications

Matthews et al. (1997) outlined three provisional subtypes of sexually abusive female adolescents derived from their descriptive study comparing female and male adolescent sexual abusers. These subtypes cannot be uniformly applied, however, because they have not been examined empirically and were based on a small sample size. Although there are no empirically validated female juvenile sexual offender typologies available, clinical impressions underline the heterogeneity of this population and, thus, the importance of focusing treatment interventions on individual assessment.

Despite the heterogeneity of the population, some tentative recommendations can be offered. Certainly, the previous discussion regarding characteristics and aetiology point to the importance of intervening in individually identified dynamics including distorted or confused affective, cognitive and behavioural responses. Denov and Cortoni (2006), in discussing adult females who sexually abuse children, pointed out that the primary goals of treatment are to identify factors contributing to the sexually abusive behaviour, understand the needs met by the sexual behaviour and develop healthier and more effective ways to meet the needs. Specifically, Denov and Cortoni discussed the importance of addressing relationship needs, a treatment factor which has also been emphasised in the literature on female delinquents; emotional regulation; coping strategies, maladaptive cognitions, existing deviant fantasies and arousal patterns, and self-management strategies focused on eliminating the need for maladaptive and abusive behaviours.

As research suggests an increased incidence of maltreatment and PTSD diagnoses in female juvenile sexual offenders, interventions to address trauma experiences are undoubtedly an important aspect of treatment for female adolescents who sexually abuse (e.g. Hunter et al., 2006). This intervention must be balanced with facilitating responsibility for sexual offending behaviour, increasing understanding of the factors contributing to the offending behaviour and the development of strategies to manage the behaviour. For example, the presence of dissociative coping responses as a consequence of childhood maltreatment can have important implications for intervening in offending patterns. The central point is that balance is essential; a focus on victimisation experiences at the expense of offending behaviour has the potential to increase cognitive distortions and decrease responsibility (e.g. 'I couldn't help myself because I was abused') for the offending behaviour.

It is important to note that there is currently no evidence supporting the application of treatment models for adult or juvenile males to the treatment of female adolescents. Instead, the theoretical literature supports the importance of gender-specific treatment groups and placements, if necessary, in specialised settings for female juveniles who sexually offend (e.g. Bumby & Bumby, 2004; Hunter et al., 2006). The provision of specialised services targeting juvenile females who sexually abuse will help ensure that gender-specific needs (e.g. gender identity development, gender-related influences on offence development) are addressed.

Treatment Implications from the General Adult and Juvenile Female Offender Literature

The literature focused on females who sexually offend points to the gendered aspects of identification (e.g. Denov, 2001) and treatment (e.g. Bumby & Bumby, 2004; Tardif et al., 2005) of juvenile female sexual offenders. Similarly, the literature related to adult and juvenile female offenders in general (i.e. those committing sexual and/or non-sexual crimes) addresses this issue (e.g. ABA/NBA, 2001; Bloom et al., 2003; Chesney-Lind & Shelden, 2004; Office of Juvenile Justice and Delinquency Prevention [OJJDP], 1998). Thus, the gendered nature of offending cannot be ignored. Unfortunately, until recently, most theories of criminality were based on male characteristics and sociocultural experiences. Further, models of intervention have also traditionally been rooted in prototypes developed for male offenders (e.g. Chamberlain, 2003; Chesney-Lind & Shelden, 2004). As Chesney-Lind and Shelden (2004) aptly stated:

> A feminist approach to delinquency means construction of explanations of female behavior that are sensitive to its context in a male-dominated, or patriarchal, society. Clearly, the shape of female behavior and misbehavior is affected by gender stratification, as are the responses of a male-dominated system to female deviance. (p. 133)

The importance of gender-responsive services for female juvenile sexual offenders follows from the recognition that gender influences behaviour, identity development and social roles. Gender-responsive services recognise and incorporate women's experiences and relationships, including the unique developmental trajectory of abusive behaviour in adolescent females (e.g. Bloom et al., 2003; Frey, 2006). Although the empirical evidence supporting the effectiveness and necessity of gender-responsive services has not reached consensus, '. . .that girls deserve equitable (not equal) treatment and services is undeniable' (Chesney-Lind & Sheldon, 2004, p. 295).

Specific to female juveniles who sexually offend, Frey (2006) suggested several questions that emphasise the importance of gender-responsive treatment:

> How is the sexually abusive behaviour of these young women incorporated into their gender identity development? Is it possible that the desire to maintain some type of relational connection is an etiological factor in young women who experience alienation . . . from their family, social group, and the larger societal context? If it is true that a large number of young women who sexually victimize have also been victimized, what role does resistance [i.e., opposition to or rejection of sociocultural norms concerning gender, race, class, and other sociocultural differences; in this case, a maladaptive form of resistance] play in their sexually abusive behaviour? (p. 267)

An identified component of gender-responsive treatment services for adult and juvenile female offenders concerns the importance of relationships in women's lives (e.g. Bloom et al., 2003; Chesney-Lind & Shelden, 2004; OJJDP, 1998). The relational-cultural model (Jordan, Kaplan, Miller, Stiver & Surrey, 1991; Miller, 1984) provides a framework through which women's relational patterns can be better understood. The model suggests that women's development and maturity of the 'felt sense of self' (Jordan, 1997, p. 15) evolves through meaningful connections with others rather than through the process of separation-individuation (Miller & Stiver, 1997). According to the relational-cultural model, there are four core aspects of growth-enhancing relationships: (a) mutual engagement (i.e. mutual involvement, commitment and sensitivity to the relationship); (b) authenticity (i.e. the freedom to be genuine in the relationship); (c) empowerment (i.e. the capacity for action and sense of personal strength that emerges from the relationship); and (d) the ability to deal with conflict (i.e. the ability to express, receive and process diversity in the relationship) (Liang, Tracy, Taylor, Williams, Jordan & Miller, 2002). The consequence of a chronic absence of these qualities in relationships is a lack of interpersonal connection and a sense of isolation (Jordan & Dooley, 2001; Walker, 2004). Bloom et al. (2003) suggested that many incarcerated women have had multiple experiences of disconnection in relationships: 'As a result, they may lack empathy for both self and others, or they may be highly empathic toward others but lack empathy for themselves' (p. 55). Thus, it is imperative that female juvenile and adult offenders have the opportunity to experience authentic and mutual relationships.

In addition to relational needs, several additional factors have been identified as key to gender-responsive programming for young women. These include counselling services that are responsive to issues such as experiences of trauma and violence, skill-building in areas such as empowerment and assertiveness, and the need for access to medical and dental services, educational resources and stable living situations (Chesney-Lind & Shelden, 2004; OJJDP, 1998).

Conclusions Regarding Treatment Strategies

Muehlenhard (1998) emphasised the importance of moving beyond an exclusive focus on gender roles and socialisation to a multidimensional conceptualisation of female sexual aggression, including examining the intersection of gender and other social identities. Keeping this caution in mind, as well as the current dearth of empirically validated treatment interventions targeting female juveniles who sexually offend, the following guidelines are offered to practitioners and programme staff treating this poorly understood population:

1. Advocating for a safe and healthy living environment is vital. This includes protecting young women from further maltreatment but also advocating for the level of treatment necessary to protect young women from engaging in further sexual offending and to protect the community. Young women living in an unsafe environment cannot be expected to risk the level of interpersonal vulnerability and openness required for treatment.
2. As previously discussed, the aetiology of offence-related behaviours, cognitions, emotions and other psychological responses among female adolescents who abuse likely differ from those of male adolescents (e.g. Frey, 2006; Kasl, 1990; Mayer, 1992). Thus, distortions (cognitive or otherwise) underlying these responses must be carefully assessed. Understanding distortions unique to the individual lays the groundwork for the development of alternative methods for meeting needs.
3. The exploration of maltreatment experiences is important but must be balanced with facilitating responsibility for and increasing understanding of the development of sexual offending behaviour. This exploration should help inform the development of strategies for managing offending behaviour.
4. The influence of social identities and sociocultural factors, including gender socialisation, gender roles, gender inequities and cultural context, must be assessed and incorporated into treatment goals and interventions.
5. Training in skill development is imperative. For instance, skill building in the areas of interpersonal skills as well as the development of empowerment, emotional regulation and coping skills are essential (e.g. Bloom et al., 2003; Denov & Cortoni, 2006; OJJDP, 1998).
6. The need for substance abuse, psychiatric and counselling services should be carefully assessed. An awareness of the impact of differences in gender, race, ethnicity, religion or spiritual beliefs and sexual orientation must be incorporated into assessment, diagnosis and treatment.
7. The opportunity to experience a healthy relational context is a necessary part of intervention (Bloom et al., 2003; OJJDP, 1998). This can be partially accomplished through (a) offering group experiences that explore women's issues and the interrelationships between these issues and sexual offence behaviours; (b) ensuring the availability of healthy female role models and mentors; and

(c) fostering the building of healthy peer relationships. The monitoring of relationships to ensure that young women's patterns of victimising and victimisation experiences are not being re-enacted is also a key issue (Bloom et al., 2003).

8. Facilitating access to services to meet health and dental needs is essential (Bloom et al., 2003; OJJDP, 1998). Considering the traumatic and chaotic life experience of many of these young women, evaluation of HIV status, evaluation for sexually transmitted diseases and a thorough physical examination (including pelvic examination) should be routine. These medical interventions, of course, must be approached in a sensitive and supportive manner. A wellness focus can also be helpful in teaching young women respect for their bodies (OJJDP, 1998).

9. Attention to educational needs and career preparation are important interventions. Because academic performance and school failure are closely associated with delinquency in young women (Acoca, 2004), it is possible that a focus on education and career preparation could be key components in decreasing recidivism.

10. Practitioner training and experience focused on increasing cultural awareness, including but not limited to issues of gender, race, ethnicity, sexual orientation and religion, is recommended (Bloom et al., 2003; OJJDP, 1998). OJJDP emphasises the importance of including training topics such as adolescent female development, the impact of personal biases, cultural knowledge and risk and protective factors relevant to young women.

DIRECTIONS FOR FUTURE RESEARCH

There is still much to learn about female juveniles who sexually abuse. Arguably the two most pressing needs are for the development of psychometrically sound classification and assessment tools and the development of empirically validated and/or supported treatment interventions. One difficulty, however, in developing such tools and interventions is related to limitations imposed by the lack of consensus regarding characteristics of juvenile females who sexually offend. Thus, a logical first step might be to focus on designing rigorous studies exploring offence characteristics and personal traits and experiences. Keeping in mind the difficulties in identification and recruitment of this population, relatively small sample sizes may be unavoidable. However, attention to designs that include control groups, matching of participants on multiple factors and the use of psychometrically sound instruments would improve the validity of results. In addition, careful attention to setting up well-defined and developmentally appropriate participant groupings would be helpful; for instance, the importance of clearly defining populations of children versus adolescents versus adults is well-established in the developmental literature and would aid in clarifying similarities and differences in sexual behaviours among the three groups.

An additional issue relates to the fact that much of the current literature on female juvenile sexual offenders is heavily focused on young women who are receiving residential services or have been identified by the justice system as offenders.

This focus precludes examination of those young women who have not come to the attention of the juvenile justice system, including those who are receiving interventions for sexual aggressive behaviour without being labelled as having committed a sexual crime. In addition, the focus on female offenders identified by the criminal justice system introduces a potential racial and/or ethnic bias. As discussed previously, there is evidence that girls of colour and European American girls are processed differently in the juvenile justice system (e.g. ABA/NBA, 2001; Chesney-Lind & Shelden, 2004). Thus, in order to access a range of young women who sexually abuse, it would be advantageous in recruiting to target a broader group of professionals and programmes including private practitioners, Department of Human Services' caseworkers, foster parents and school counsellors. At a minimum, demographic information related to ethnicity and/or race should be included in studies. Overall, studies comparing characteristics of young women identified through sources other than registry or corrections records and programmes specifically targeting sexual offending behaviour would expand the literature base regarding characteristics of female adolescents who sexually abuse.

In responding to Wells' description of past programming for girls as 'throwaway services for throwaway girls' (as cited in Chesney-Lind & Shelden, 2004), Chesney-Lind and Shelden stated, 'We can and should do better for tomorrow's women' (p. 294). In the case of female adolescents who sexually offend, there is a dual benefit to 'doing better': doing better for these young women will also have important added benefits of decreasing the marginalisation and invisibility of their victims and improving community safety.

REFERENCES

Acoca, L. (2004). Outside/inside: The violation of American girls at home, on the streets, and in the juvenile justice system. In M. Chesney-Lind & L. Pasko (Eds.), *Girls, women, & crime: Selected readings* (pp. 77–96). Thousand Oaks, CA: Sage.

American Bar Association & National Bar Association. (2001). *Justice by gender: The lack of appropriate prevention, diversion and treatment alternatives for girls in the justice system.* Retrieved 18th April 2009, from http://www.abanet.org/crimjust/juvjus/justicebygenderweb.pdf.

Artz, S. (1998). *Sex, power, and the violent school girl.* Toronto: Trifolium Books.

Association for the Treatment of Sexual Abusers. (2000). *The effective legal management of juvenile sexual offenders.* Retrieved 7th July 2004, from http://www.atsa.com/ppjuvenile.html.

Becker, J. V., Hunter, J. A., Stein, R. M., & Kaplan, M. S. (1989). Factors associated with erection in adolescent sexual offenders. *Journal of Psychopathology and Behavioral Assessment, 11,* 353–363.

Bloom, B., Owen, B., & Covington, S. (2003). *Gender-responsive strategies: Research, practice, and guiding principles for women offenders.* Retrieved 18th April 2009, from the National Institute of Corrections: https://www.nttac.org/views/docs/jabg/grpcurriculum/research_practice_guiding_principles.pdf.

Bumby, N. H., & Bumby, K. M. (1997). Adolescent female sexual offenders. In B. K. Schwartz & H. R. Cellini (Eds.), *The sex offender: Corrections, treatment, and legal practice* (pp. 10.1–10.16). Kingston, NJ: Civic Research Institute, Inc.

Bumby, N. H., & Bumby, K. M. (2004). Bridging the gender gap: Addressing juvenile offenders who commit sexual offenses. In G. O'Reilly, W. L. Marshall, A. Carr, & R. C. Beckett

(Eds.), *Handbook of clinical intervention with juvenile sex offenders* (pp. 369–382). London: Routledge.

Burton, D. L., Smith-Darden, J., & Frankel, S. J. (2006). Research on adolescent sexual abuser treatment programs. In H. E. Barbaree & W. L. Marshall (Eds.), *The juvenile sex offender* (2nd ed., pp. 291–312). New York: Guilford.

Chaffin, M., & Bonner, B. (1998). "Don't shoot, we're your children": Have we gone too far in our response to adolescent sexual abusers and children with sexual behavior problems? *Child Maltreatment, 3*, 314–316.

Chamberlain, P. (2003). Antisocial behavior and delinquency in girls. In P. Chamberlain (Ed.), *Treating chronic juvenile offenders: Advances made through the Oregon multidimensional treatment foster care model* (pp. 109–127). Washington DC: American Psychological Association.

Chesney-Lind, M., & Shelden, R. G. (2004). *Girls, delinquency, and juvenile justice* (3rd ed.). Belmont, CA: Wadsworth/Thomson.

Community Research Associates. (1998). *Juvenile female offenders: A status of the states report*. Retrieved 12th April 2009, from the Office of Juvenile Justice and Delinquency Prevention: http://ojjdp.ncjrs.org/pubs/gender/.

Denov, M. S. (2001). A culture of denial: Exploring professional perspectives on female sex offending. *Canadian Journal of Criminology, 43*, 303–329.

Denov, M. S., & Cortoni, F. (2006). Women who sexually abuse children. In C. Hilarski & J. Wodarski (Eds.), *Comprehensive mental health practice with sex offenders and their families* (pp. 71–99). New York: Haworth.

Faller, K. C. (1995). A clinical sample of women who have sexually abused children. *Journal of Child Sexual Abuse, 4*(3), 13–30.

Federal Bureau of Investigation. (2007). *Crime in the United States, 2007.* Retrieved 28th March 2009, from http://www.fbi.gov/ucr/cius2007/index.html.

Fehrenbach, P. A., & Monastersky, C. (1988). Characteristics of female adolescent sexual offenders. *American Journal of Orthopsychiatry, 58*(1), 148–151.

Freeman, N. J., & Sandler, J. C. (2008). Female and male sex offenders: A comparison of recidivism patterns and risk factors. *Journal of Interpersonal Violence, 23*, 1394–1413.

Frey, L. L. (2006). Girls don't do that, do they? Adolescent females who sexually abuse. In R. E. Longo & D. S. Prescott (Eds.), *Current perspectives: Working with sexually aggressive youth & youth with sexual behavior problems* (pp. 255–272). Holyoke, MA: NEARI Press.

Fromuth, M. E. (1986). The relationship of childhood sexual abuse with later psychological and sexual adjustment in a sample of college women. *Child Abuse & Neglect, 10*, 5–15.

Fromuth, M. E., & Conn, V. E. (1997). Hidden perpetrators: Sexual molestation in a nonclinical sample of college women. *Journal of Interpersonal Violence, 12*, 456–465.

Hendriks, J., & Bijleveld, C. C. J. H. (2006). Female adolescent sex offenders—an exploratory study. *Journal of Sexual Aggression, 12*, 31–41.

Hunter, J. A., Becker, J. V., & Lexier, L. J. (2006). The female juvenile sex offender. In H. E. Barbaree & W. L. Marshall (Eds.), *The juvenile sex offender* (2nd ed., pp. 148–165). New York: Guilford.

Hunter, J. A., Goodwin, D. W., & Becker, J. A. (1994). The relationship between phallometrically measured deviant sexual arousal and clinical characteristics in juvenile sexual offenders. *Behavior Research and Therapy, 32*, 533–538.

Hunter, J. A., Lexier, L. J., Goodwin, D. W., Browne, P. A., & Dennis, C. (1993). Psychosexual, attitudinal, and developmental characteristics of juvenile female sexual perpetrators in a residential treatment setting. *Journal of Child and Family Studies, 2*, 317–326.

Jordan, J. V. (1997). A relational perspective for understanding women's development. In J. V. Jordan (Ed.), *Women's growth in diversity: More writings from the Stone Center* (pp. 9–24). New York: Guilford.

Jordan, J. V., & Dooley, C. (2001). *Relational practice in action: A group manual*. Wellesley, MA: Stone Center Publications.

Jordan, J. V., Kaplan, A. G., Miller, J. B., Stiver, I. P., & Surrey, J. L. (Eds.). (1991). *Women's growth in connection: Writings from the Stone Center.* New York: Guilford.

Kasl, C. D. (1990). Female perpetrators of sexual abuse: A feminist view. In M. Hunter (Ed.), *The sexually abused male: Vol. 1. Prevalence, impact, and treatment* (pp. 259–274). New York: Lexington Books.

Kubik, E. K., & Hecker, J. E. (2005). Cognitive distortions about sex and sexual offending: A comparison of sex offending girls, delinquent girls, and girls from the community. *Journal of Child Sexual Abuse, 14*(4), 43–69.

Kubik, E. K., Hecker, J. E., & Righthand, S. (2002). Adolescent females who have sexually offended: Comparisons with delinquent adolescent female offenders and adolescent males who sexually offend. *Journal of Child Sexual Abuse, 11*(3), 63–83.

Liang, B., Tracy, A., Taylor, C. A., Williams, L. M., Jordan, J. V., & Miller, J. B. (2002). The Relational Health Indices: A study of women's relationships. *Psychology of Women Quarterly, 26,* 25–35.

MacDonald, J. M., & Chesney-Lind, M. (2001). Gender bias and juvenile justice revisited: A multiyear analysis. *Crime & Delinquency, 47,* 173–195.

Matthews, R., Hunter, J. A., & Vuz, J. (1997). Juvenile female sexual offenders: Clinical characteristics and treatment issues. *Sexual Abuse: A Journal of Research and Treatment, 9*(3), 187–199.

Mayer, A. (1992). *Women sex offenders: Treatment and dynamics.* Holmes Beach, FL: Learning Publications.

McCormack, A., Janus, M. D., & Burgess, A. W. (1986). Runaway youths and sexual victimization: Gender differences in an adolescent runaway population. *Child Abuse & Neglect, 10,* 387–395.

Miccio-Fonseca, L. C. (2000). Adult and adolescent female sex offenders: Experiences compared to other female and male sex offenders. *Journal of Psychology and Human Sexuality, 11*(3), 75–88.

Miller, J. B. (1984). *The development of women's sense of self* (Work in Progress No. 12). MA: Wellesley College, Stone Center.

Miller, J. B., & Stiver, I. P. (1997). *The healing connection: How women form relationships in therapy and in life.* Boston: Beacon Press.

Muehlenhard, C. L. (1998). The importance and danger of studying sexually aggressive women. In P. B. Anderson & C. Struckman-Johnson (Eds.), *Sexually aggressive women: Current perspectives and controversies* (pp. 19–48). New York: Guilford.

Nathan, P., & Ward, T. (2002). Female sex offenders: Clinical and demographical features. *Journal of Sexual Aggression, 8*(1), 5–21.

Office of Juvenile Justice and Delinquency Prevention. (1998). *Guiding principles for promising female programming: An inventory of best practices.* Retrieved 18th April 2009, from http://www.ojjdp.ncjrs.org/pubs/principles/contents.html.

O'Reilly, G., & Carr, A. (2006). Assessment and treatment of criminogenic needs. In H. E. Barbaree & W. L. Marshall (Eds.), *The juvenile sex offender* (2nd ed., pp. 189–217). New York: Guilford.

Parker, G., Tupling, H., & Brown, L. B. (1979). A parental bonding instrument. *British Journal of Medical Psychology, 52,* 1–10.

Sandler, J. C., & Freeman, N. J. (2007). Typology of female sex offenders: A test of Vandiver and Kercher. *Sex Abuse: A Journal of Research and Treatment, 19,* 73–89.

Schwartz, B. K., & Cellini, H. R. (1995). Female sex offenders. In B. K. Schwartz & H. R. Cellini (Eds.), *The sex offender: Corrections, treatment, and legal practice* (pp. 5.1–5.22). Kingston, NJ: Civic Research Institute, Inc.

Tardif, M., Auclair, N., Jacob, M., & Carpentier, J. (2005). Sexual abuse perpetrated by adult and juvenile females: An ultimate attempt to resolve a conflict associated with maternal identity. *Child Abuse & Neglect, 29,* 153–167.

Vandiver, D. M., & Teske, R., Jr. (2006). Juvenile female and male sex offenders: A comparison of offender, victim, and judicial processing characteristics. *International Journal of Offender Therapy and Comparative Criminology, 50,* 148–165.

Vick, J., McRoy, R., & Matthews, B. M. (2002). Young female sex offenders: Assessment and treatment issues. *Journal of Child Sexual Abuse*, 11(2), 1–23.

Walker, M. (2004). How relationships heal. In M. Walker & W. B. Rosen (Eds.), *How connections heal: Stories from relational-cultural therapy* (pp. 3–21). New York: Guilford.

Worling, J. R., & Langström, N. (2006). Risk of sexual recidivism in adolescents who offend sexually: Correlates and assessment. In H. E. Barbaree & W. L. Marshall (Eds.), *The juvenile sex offender* (2nd ed., pp. 219–247). New York: Guilford.

Chapter 5

THE MENTAL HEALTH NEEDS OF FEMALE SEXUAL OFFENDERS

MYRIAM-MÉLANIE ROUSSEAU AND FRANCA CORTONI

School of Criminology, Université de Montréal, Quebec, Canada

Clinical and empirical studies relevant to our understanding of sexual abuse perpetrated by females have focused not only on documenting prevalence rates but also on examining distinctive characteristics of the female sexual offender population. Indeed, progress has been made in recent years towards a better understanding of female sexual offenders, although issues related to the mental health needs of these women are still poorly understood. A number of studies have consistently reported a high incidence of psychopathology and past sexual and physical victimisation among this group of sexual offenders (e.g. Faller, 1995; Fazel, Sjöstedt, Grann & Langström, 2008; Mathews, Hunter & Vuz, 1997; O'Connor, 1987; Rowan, Rowan & Langelier, 1990; Turner, Miller & Henderson, 2008), bringing attention to the importance of these issues. Mental health issues need to be considered in order to enhance the assessment and treatment of female sexual offenders and the prevention of further sexual offences for this small but distinct population. This chapter provides a review of the available research examining the prevalence, nature and diagnoses of mental health issues among female sexual offenders. In addition, implications for the assessment and treatment of female sexual offenders are outlined.

MENTAL HEALTH ISSUES IN FEMALE SEXUAL OFFENDERS

Prevalence

Mental illness, alcohol, drug abuse and victimisation histories have been found to be very important contributors to women's criminality (Laque, 2002). The American Correctional Association (1990) and the Bureau of Justice Statistics (1994)

Female Sexual Offenders: Theory, Assessment, and Treatment   Edited by Theresa A. Gannon and Franca Cortoni
© 2010 John Wiley & Sons, Ltd

estimate that more than 1 in 10 women in US state prisons received inpatient psychiatric care before being sent to prison, and 1 in 8 women received mood-altering medication for emotional or mental health problems while in prison (Laque, 2002). Among federally sentenced women in Canada (i.e. women who received sentences of 2 years and more), 21 per cent were identified at admission to custody as presenting mental health problems (Correctional Service of Canada, 2006). A mental disorder is defined as 'a clinically significant behavioural or psychological syndrome or pattern that occurs in an individual and that is associated with either present distress (a painful symptom) or disability (impairment in one or more areas of functioning) or a significant risk of suffering death, pain, disability or loss of significant freedom' (American Psychiatric Association, 1987, p. xxii).

Among female sexual offenders, research also documents high levels of mental health issues, with the vast majority experiencing at least one psychological disorder (Johansson-Love & Fremouw, 2006). Specifically, rates of serious emotional and mood disorders, personality disorders, psychotic disorders, substance use problems and trauma-related events, including histories of physical and/or sexual abuse, have all been found to be over-represented among female sexual offenders (e.g. Allen, 1991; Christopher, Lutz-Zois & Reinhardt, 2007; Faller, 1995; Fazel et al., 2008; Green & Kaplan, 1994; Hunter & Mathews, 1997; Matthews, 1993; Mathews, Matthews & Speltz, 1989; Miccio-Fonseca, 2000; O'Connor, 1987; Strickland, 2008; Travin, Cullen & Protter, 1990). For instance, in a sample of 40 women who had sexually abused 63 children, Faller (1987) found that 47.5 per cent of these offenders had mental difficulties. Lewis and Stanley (2000) conducted a chart review of 15 female sexual offenders referred to their psychiatric facility (William S. Hall Psychiatric Institute in Colombia, US) for a competency to stand trial/criminal responsibility evaluation. These authors found that two thirds of these women (67 per cent) had previously been seen in outpatient psychiatric clinics. Very similar findings have been reported by Fazel et al. (2008). In their study, the largest clinical investigation study of mental illness among female sexual offenders to date ($n = 93$), the prevalence of prior psychiatric hospitalisation among these women was 36.6 per cent ($n = 34$) (Fazel et al., 2008).

Although research has documented high prevalence rates of mental health issues among female sexual offenders, most studies suffer from methodological problems that limit the validity of their findings. The prevalence of mental disorders among female sexual offenders might be particularly overestimated in the literature due to a higher likelihood of reporting of cases where mental disorders are present (Fazel et al., 2008). Female sexual offenders with mental health disorders, compared with those without such issues, are more likely to be detected and sanctioned given society's views that only 'insane' or 'unnatural' women commit sexual offences (Ford, 2006). The reported prevalence of mental illness among female sexual offenders may also be artificially inflated because the subjects are often recruited from forensic and/or mental health institutions. Samples from forensic mental health settings would clearly include higher proportions of mentally disordered offenders than would, for example, samples drawn from prisons (Johansson-Love & Fremouw, 2006). Finally, given society's tendency to dismiss sexual offending by women (Denov, 2001), known female sexual offenders could be primarily those who have committed more serious offences. Women who commit less severe sexual offences may perhaps be less likely to be charged with a criminal offence, or more likely to be diverted from the criminal justice system, leading to an overestimation of the prevalence of mental health disorders among sexually offending women.

Another limitation involves the use of self-reports of psychopathology taken directly from the women. Miller, Turner and Henderson (2009) suggested that female sexual offenders who self-report extensive psychopathology may be exaggerating their symptoms as a possible 'cry for help'. Alternatively, an over-exaggeration of self-reported mental health disorders may also be an attempt on the part of female perpetrators to explain or excuse their abusive behaviour and elicit sympathy. Such excuses or attempts to externalise blame for the sexually offending behaviour is not uncommon among both male and female sexual offenders (Eldridge & Saradjian, 2000; Gannon & Rose, 2009). While, comparatively to males, female offenders do demonstrate a higher prevalence of mental health problems (Hammett, Roberts & Kennedy, 2001), a willingness of female sexual offenders to over-report psychopathology may partially explain why these women appear to have a particularly high prevalence of mental health issues (Miller et al., 2009).

In sum, research that examined the prevalence of mental health problems among female sexual offenders provides varying findings. Various methodological problems, including a lack of standardised assessments and an inconsistency of definitions across studies, complicate the interpretation of results regarding the true prevalence of psychopathology among female sexual offenders (Johansson-Love & Fremouw, 2006). Consequently, this body of research remains inconclusive and uncertain.

PSYCHOPATHOLOGICAL ISSUES AMONG FEMALE SEXUAL OFFENDERS

Despite limitations in the literature, a better understanding of psychopathological issues in female sexual offenders can be of value to health professionals and researchers. Specifically, it can enhance the understanding of aetiology of sexual offending by women and improve their assessment and treatment. These issues are reviewed below.

Paraphilias

The *Diagnostic and Statistical Manual of Mental Disorders [DSM-IV]* (American Psychiatric Association, 1987; revised in 2000) define paraphilias as sexual disorders characterised by recurrent, intense sexual urges, fantasies or behaviours that involve unusual objects, activities or situations and that occur over a period of at least 6 months. In addition, to meet the diagnosis criteria for a paraphilia 'The individual either has acted on these fantasies or is markedly distressed by them and the fantasies and behaviours cause significant impairments in social, occupational or other important areas of functioning' (Sheerin, 2004, p. 129). Paraphilias, not including sexual masochism, are almost never diagnosed in females (Becker, Hall &

Stinson, 2001). Consequently, research on paraphilias among female sexual offenders is nearly inexistent, perhaps due to its perceived irrelevance to females (Davin, Hislop & Dunbar, 1999). This could also be explained by the fact that the diagnostic criteria in the *DSM-IV* use the masculine pronoun to denote the symptoms of paraphilias, suggesting that they are not applicable to women (Fedoroff, Fishell & Fedoroff, 1999). These problems continued in the 2000 revised version regarding the diagnosis of paedophilia: the *DSM-IV-R* states that paedophiles 'develop complicated techniques for obtaining access to children, which may include..., marrying a woman with an attractive child' (APA, 2000, p. 571). As a result, clinicians who might observe paraphilias in females may be discouraged to make this diagnosis and/or explore the issue further (Mandelblatt, 2007).

The word *paedophilia* is derived from the Greek words for love (*philia*) of young children (*pedeiktos*). A diagnosis of paedophilia can be applied to two distinct types of persons: individuals who are only sexually attracted to children (exclusive type) and individuals who are also attracted to adults (non-exclusive type) (*DSM-IV*, 1994). Although female sexual offenders tend not to be diagnosed with paedophilia (Wakefield & Underwager, 1991), clinical observations suggest that women may better fit the diagnosis of the non-exclusive type rather than the exclusive type (Matthews, 1993; Nathan & Ward, 2001).

Although females, compared with males, are less likely to be diagnosed as paedophiles, deviant sexual fantasies and sexual arousal have been observed in some female sexual offenders. Chow and Choy (2002) described the clinical characteristics of a woman who had received a diagnosis of paedophilia. The authors highlighted that the woman had a lifelong sexual interests in female children, masturbated to fantasies involving children and had a specific erotic preference age range of 3–4 years old. In their study of 16 female sexual offenders, Mathews et al. (1989) found that 11 of these women experienced some sexual arousal and/or victim-related fantasies during their acts of abuse. Interestingly, these women also frequently indicated that this arousal stemmed from feelings of power or fantasies that their victims were actually adult men. In Hunter, Lexier, Goodwin, Browne and Dennis' (1993) study of 10 juvenile female sexual offenders in a residential treatment programme, six of the girls reported they had deviant sexual fantasies prior to their first offence and two admitted to masturbating to fantasies of significantly younger children. Similarly, in Fromuth and Conn's (1997) study of female college students, women who admitted having sexually abused a significantly younger child were significantly more likely than non-perpetrators to have expressed a sexual interest in children. Moreover, in Nathan and Ward's (2002) study of 12 convicted adult female sexual offenders in Australia, 41.7 per cent were found to have been motivated, in part, by deviant sexual arousal. These findings indicate that the presence of paedophilic sexual arousal and fantasies might provide an important motivating factor for the sexual offending behaviour and, just like with male offenders, increase the risk of becoming a sexual offender (Hanson & Morton-Bourgon, 2005).

Although females do report deviant sexual arousal and fantasies, it is unclear whether the nature of paraphilic preferences among females is the same as that of males or whether sexual deviancy in females reflects a differing condition (Nathan & Ward, 2001). Traditionally, the tendency in criminological psychology has been to indiscriminately apply to female offenders theories developed and validated for male offenders (Blanchette & Brown, 2006), including female sexual offenders (Cortoni & Gannon, in press; Chapter 3). Attempting to understand females' arousal patterns by applying current knowledge developed on males could lead to invalid theoretical postulations as research indicates that women's sexual arousal patterns are different than those of males. Specifically, Chivers and her colleagues have demonstrated that while men's physiological sexual arousal actually reflects their sexual preferences, women's arousal patterns are much more fluid and tend not to demonstrate such specificity (e.g. Chivers, Rieger, Latty & Bailey, 2004; Suschinsky, Lalumière & Chivers, 2009). These results suggest that sexual arousal patterns, like many factors related to offending among female sexual offenders, are gender-specific rather than gender-neutral (Cortoni & Gannon, in press) and that much more research is required before we can firmly establish the full nature of the patterns of deviant arousal among females.

As indicated in the literature, although some female sexual offenders do report deviant sexual fantasies and arousal, in general, these women are less likely to be diagnosed with paedophilia and other paraphilias than men (Chow & Choy, 2002). Despite this lower prevalence of paraphilias among women, clinicians and researchers should give more attention to the assessment of these issues among female sexual offenders in order to better understand the role sexual arousal and fantasies may have played in the offending behaviour and provide adequate treatment as necessary.

Psychiatric and Personality Disorders

A number of studies on female sexual offenders emphasise that although these women are heterogeneous in many ways, as a group, they do show signs of serious psychiatric disorders (e.g. Green & Kaplan, 1994; Faller, 1995; Fazel et al., 2008; Hislop, 2001; Lewis & Stanley, 2000; Nathan & Ward, 2001; Tardif, Auclair, Jacob, & Carpentier, 2005). In a comparison of incarcerated female sexual and non-sexual offenders, Green and Kaplan (1994) found that Axis I diagnoses of post-traumatic stress disorder, major depressive disorder and impulse control disorder were particularly prominent among female sexual offenders, with 64 per cent of their sample having experienced a past or current episode of major depression, while 73 per cent exhibited post-traumatic disorder (PTSD). Further, in comparison to the female non-sexual offenders, the sexual offenders were more frequently diagnosed with avoidant and dependent personality disorders while the comparison subjects were more often diagnosed with antisocial personality disorder. Overall, their results indicated that the female sexual offenders were more psychiatrically impaired than the women in the comparison group (Green & Kaplan, 1994).

The results from Green and Kaplan (1994) are not unusual. Tardif et al. (2005) collected clinical and evaluative data since 1992 from a sample of 13 adult females who sexually abused children. They found that these women had been diagnosed (according to the *DSM-IV*) with one or a combination of the following disorders: borderline (30.8 per cent), concurrent borderline and dysthymic disorders (15.4 per cent), dependent personality (15.4 per cent) and depression with dependent personality (30.8 per cent). Of course, these data should be treated with caution, given that both studies discussed here involved so few subjects (Green & Kaplan, 1994: $n = 11$; Tardif et al., 2005: $n = 13$). In spite of everything, similar findings were also obtained in other studies with rather larger samples of female sexual offenders. Specifically, in their study of 39 women, Travin et al. (1990) noted that a prominent presence of borderline, bipolar, paranoid schizophrenia and schizoaffective personality disorders. In her study of 81 female sexual offenders, O'Connor (1987) noted that as many as half of these offenders had some type of mental illness.

Other research, however, does not indicate a differential prevalence of psychiatric disorders among female sexual offenders. Strickland (2008) used the Personality Disorder Indicator subscale on the MSI-II (female version) to assess the personality characteristics of 130 incarcerated females: 60 sexual offenders and 70 non-sexual offenders. She found that both groups had similar rates of personality disorder indicators, although their nature slightly differed. The female sexual offenders had somewhat more schizoid, borderline and dependent indicators, while the non-sexual offenders had slightly more antisocial and significantly more histrionic personality disorder indicators (Strickland, 2008). In their study of 93 female sexual offenders, Fazel et al. (2008) did find that the rate of psychosis in their sample (8 per cent) was 16 times higher than that found in the general female population. In contrast, there were no differences in rates of psychotic or substance abuse disorders when these women were compared to violent (non-sexual) female offenders. These results suggest that while female sexual offenders do demonstrate more mental health problems when compared to non-offending women, their mental health problems are actually not that different from those of female offenders in general.

Intellectual Disabilities

There is some evidence that individuals with intellectual impairments are over-represented among sexual offenders (Lund, 1990). Not surprisingly, this issue has not been well investigated among female sexual offenders. Faller (1987, 1995) found that a substantial number of the female perpetrators in her study (47.5 per cent) had mental difficulties of some kind, with 32.5 per cent of the offenders suffering from brain damage or mental disabilities, as well as various impairments in judgement and impulse control. Consistent with Faller's findings, Lewis and Stanley (2000) also found that intellectual limitations were common among the women in their sample. One in five had borderline intellectual functioning and four (26.7 per cent) were mildly mentally retarded. Of course, like other research in this field, there are inherent problems with the Faller, and Lewis and Stanley studies: small sample size; the researchers use chart review rather than structured diagnostic interviews; and finally, no comparison groups. Consequently, the reported rates of female sexual offenders with intellectual disabilities may in fact be due to a number of factors that include imprecise use of the term (intellectual disabilities/impairment) (Johansson-Love & Fremouw, 2006), difficulties in the assessment of learning problems (Hislop, 2001) and the presence of adverse life experiences, such as repeated trauma, that can impact on intellectual development (Saradjian, 1996). Finally, female sexual offenders who present more obvious intellectual impairments, just like men with intellectual disabilities (Lindsay & Taylor, 2009), may also be among those who are more likely to be identified and sanctioned by the criminal justice system, hence highlighting the importance of ensuring that an accurate identification of potential intellectual limitations be conducted prior to conducting offence-specific assessment and treatment (Lindsay & Taylor, 2009).

Substance Abuse Disorders

Despite an apparent association, the causal impact of alcohol and drugs on sexual offending is unsubstantiated. Some research suggests that alcohol and other drugs are used by sexual offenders in general to excuse their behaviour or make their victim appear somehow responsible for the sexual offence (Messer, Maughan, Quinton & Taylor, 2004). Others argue that the use of alcohol prior to the offence may serve to facilitate sexual abuse by removing inhibitions against such behaviour (Morrison, Erooga & Beckett, 1994). According to Pithers and Cumming (1995), sexual offenders actually often use drugs or alcohol to control the anxiety often associated with the decision to commit a sexual offence. The general consensus is that alcohol and substance abuse may play a companion or contributing role in sex offending, but not a causal one.

Although substance abuse does not cause sexual offending, the use of alcohol and other drugs appears common among female sexual offenders. Faller (1987, 1995) found that about half of the female sexual offenders in her studies (55 and 51 per cent, respectively) had experienced past or current problems with some form of substance abuse. Similar results were also reported by Green and Kaplan (1994), who found that 8 of the 11 incarcerated female sexual offenders in their study had alcohol and substance abuse difficulties. Aylward, Christopher, Newell and Gordon (2002) also reported that 53 per cent of the women in their sample had difficulties with substance abuse. However, as noted by Johansson-Love (2007), in many of these studies, it is ambiguous if the authors referred to a history of substance abuse or the presence of the use of substances during the offence. The distinction between women who used drugs or alcohol purely to facilitate their offending and those who use substances more generally in their lives is important as it will have a differential impact on their assessment and treatment (Ford, 2006).

It is also important to remember that substance abuse is a characteristic that is *not* exclusive to female sexual offenders. Substance abuse is a common criminogenic factor (i.e. a factor related to the offending behaviour; Andrews & Bonta, 2007) among all types of both male and female offenders. Given this situation, while the above-noted studies found high rates of substance abuse problems among female sexual offenders, it is not surprising that studies with comparison populations do not find differences between female sexual offenders and other groups in prevalence rates of substance abuse disorders. Saradjian (1996) reported that substance abuse rates in her study did not differ between the female offenders and the non-offending comparisons. Actually, there was a tendency for the comparison women to be heavier users. Similarly, Fazel et al. (2008) found no difference in substance use disorders between sexual and non-sexual violent female offenders. Lewis and

Stanley (2000) also reported that substance abuse was not implicated as a major factor in the offences of the female sexual offenders.

As with male sexual offenders, the use of substances may be used by females to reduce inhibitions in order to offend, particularly among women who engage in solo offending (i.e. no co-offender; McCarty, 1986; Wilkins, 1990). Alternatively, the substance abuse may represent a strategy to cope with problems such as dysfunctional relationships (Blanchette & Brown, 2006; Laque, 2002), emotional dysregulation (Eldridge & Saradjian, 2000) or serious mental disorders (Hislop, 2001). These issues exemplify the importance of understanding the role substance use plays not only in the offending behaviour, but also in the overall lives of female sexual offenders.

VICTIMISATION HISTORIES AND MENTAL HEALTH ISSUES

Female offenders in general demonstrate high rates of physical, sexual and emotional victimisation in both childhood and adulthood (Blanchette & Brown, 2006). For example, Harlow (1999) found that the proportion of women prisoners who reported having a history of childhood sexual victimisation is two to three times greater than women in the general public. High rates of victimisation have also been documented among female sexual offenders, typically ranging from 50 to 80 per cent (e.g. Lewis & Stanley, 2000; Saradjian, 1996; Tardif et al., 2005). However, the victimisation histories among female sexual offenders appear to have been particularly severe, even in comparison with other female offenders; they tend to suffer more extensive and intrusive abuse at the hand of many perpetrators during both childhood and adulthood (Grayston & De Luca, 1999; Johansson-Love & Fremouw, 2006).

Mental health difficulties are often the direct result of victimisation, particularly when it is sexual in nature. Childhood victimisation frequently leads to chronic trauma, with victims being more likely than others to suffer from a variety of long-term consequences in cognitive, affective and behavioural domains (Putnam & Trickett, 1993). For example, a large body of research with diverse samples has also established a strong relationship between experiences of childhood sexual abuse and later symptoms of post-traumatic stress disorder (e.g. Elliott & Briere, 1992; Goodwin, 1988; Lindbergh & Distad, 1985; Matsunaga et al., 1999; McCleer, Callaghan, Henry & Wallen, 1994; McLeer, Deblinger, Henry & Orvaschel, 1992; Roesler & McKenzie, 1994; Williams, 1993). In addition, associations between sexual victimisation and somatic complaints (e.g. eating and sleep disturbances), anxiety, interpersonal difficulties, feelings of isolation, suicidal behaviour, depression and self-destructive behaviour are unfortunately too common among victims (for more information on negative consequences of childhood victimisation, see additional reviews by Beitchman, Zucker, Hood, DaCosta & Akman, 1991; Beitchman, Zucker, Hood, DaCosta, Akman & Cassavia, 1992; Cahill, Llewelyn & Pearson, 1991; Kendall-Tackett, Williams & Finkelhor, 1993; Neumann, Houskamp, Pollock & Briere, 1996; Oddone Paolucci, Genius & Violato, 2001).

At least among women, victimisation is linked to later mental health problems as well as offending (Bagley, Wood & Young, 1994; Dutton & Hart, 1992; Ford &

Linney, 1995; Hamilton, Falshaw & Brown, 2002; Prendergast, 1991). Many studies have shown that mental illness and violence share many of the same risk factors, including histories of childhood sexual abuse (see Hislop, 1999; Silver, Felson & Vaneseltine, 2008). In turn, although most people with mental health problems do not engage in violence, the likelihood of committing violence is greater for people with mental health problems than for those without (Silver et al., 2008). Although, as discussed earlier, the prevalence of mental health issues among female sexual offenders is still uncertain, diverse studies indicate that female offenders, specifically those who commit violent offences, seem to need an 'extra push' to engage in violence (Gorsuch, 1998; Mohan, Scully, Collins & Smith, 1997, cited by Miller, Turner & Henderson, 2009). It is likely that high levels of psychopathology, some of which would be related to their victimisation histories, could provide the 'extra push' for women to commit sexual offences (Miller et al., 2009). This is not to say, however, that victimisation causes sexual offending: a large majority of victims never go on to offend. Rather, it is more likely that the types of victimisation experiences of female sexual offenders, along with the environment in which it occurred, contributed to psychological and societal maladjustment, subsequent substance abuse, ineffective coping and dysfunctional relationships, and it is those elements that actually contribute to the offending behaviour (Blanchette & Brown, 2006; Eldridge & Saradjian, 2000). Of course, as this area of work is still in its infancy, these conclusions are still uncertain, and further research is needed.

IMPLICATIONS FOR ASSESSMENT AND TREATMENT

Since research on the mental health needs of female sexual offenders is still in its infancy, further consideration must be given to how to assess and address their specific treatment needs. Fazel et al. (2008) suggested that routine psychiatric screening of these women at court or on reception to prison would be warranted. Likewise, Hislop (2001) recommended that the assessment of female sexual offenders entering correctional and forensic facilities should be as comprehensive as possible. Given the current indications that female sexual offenders suffer from a number of DSM-IV Axis I and Axis II disorders, clinicians should assess the presence and the nature of those disorders, as well as their relationship to the circumstances that surrounded the sexually offending behaviour.

Attention to co-morbidity issues among female sexual offenders is essential to improve responsivity to treatment. The presence of mental health problems frequently interferes with any attempt to address the sexual offending behaviour, sometimes even precluding such work (Ford & Cortoni, 2008). In these circumstances, the goal should be, at a minimum, to ensure a stabilisation of the mental health issues and provide the woman with appropriate social support.

As stated by Cortoni (2010), the overarching goal of the treatment of female sexual offenders is to address the factors related to their sexually offending behaviour. To better address these factors, it is essential to clearly differentiate the impact mental health issues have on the woman's life from the impact they may have on offending behaviour. Only rarely will psychiatric issues be directly related to the offending behaviour (Blanchette & Brown, 2006; Bonta, Law & Hanson, 1997).

Consequently, while addressing the mental health needs of female sexual offenders is important, it is not sufficient when the goal is to reduce the likelihood of future offending; treatment must additionally address the factors directly related to sexually offending behaviour such as cognitions that support the offending, problematic relationships and the role sexual arousal and fantasies have played in facilitating the sexual offence (Cortoni & Gannon, in press).

The same important caveat exists in relation to the victimisation histories of female sexual offenders. As noted by Denov and Cortoni (2006), victimisation histories should not take precedence over the sexually offending behaviour. Addressing such issues is, of course, an important part of a holistic approach to the treatment of female offenders (Blanchette & Brown, 2006). Too much focus on the victimisation histories, however, takes away from the work necessary to address offence-specific issues. Further, such a focus might only serve to reinforce in the woman that she simply has no control over her own life, and by extension, her offending behaviour (Ford & Cortoni, 2008). As a result, rather than helping the woman, it could actually impair her ability to establish a healthier offence-free life.

CONCLUSION

Although studies have found a high rate of psychopathology among female sexual offenders, their methodological problems preclude the establishment of firm conclusions regarding the contribution of mental health issues to the aetiology of sexual offending. To improve our ability to draw firm conclusions from the literature, future research would do well to adopt universal definitions and standardised measures of mental health issues that have been validated for women to permit valid comparisons among studies.

Despite its methodological limitations, the current literature on the mental health issues of female sexual offenders does indicate that they are of sufficient magnitude to warrant additional investigations. Further analyses of the interconnections between psychopathology, paraphilias, substance abuse and histories of victimisation among female sexual offenders are crucial to develop not only a better understanding of the aetiology of female sexual offending, but also better assessment and treatment services.

REFERENCES

Andrews, D. A., & Bonta J. (2007). *The psychology of criminal conduct* (4th ed.). Cincinnati, OH: Anderson.

Allen, C. M. (1991). *Women and men who sexually abuse children: A comparative analysis*. Brandon, VT: Safer Society Press.

American Correctional Association. (1990). *The female offender*. Washington, DC: St-Mary's Press.

American Psychiatric Association. (1987). *Diagnostic and statistical manual of mental disorders (DSM-III-R)*. Washington, DC: APA.

American Psychiatric Association. (1994). *Diagnostic and statistical manual of mental disorders (DSM-IV)*. Washington, DC: APA.

American Psychiatric Association. (2000). *Diagnostic and statistical manual of mental disorders (DSM-IV-R)*. Washington, DC: APA.

Aylward, A., Christopher, M., Newell, R. M., & Gordon, A. (2002). *What about women who commit sex offences?* Paper presented at the 22nd Research and Treatment Conference, Association for the Treatment of Sexual Abusers, St-Louis, MO.

Bagley, C., Wood, M., & Young, L. (1994). Victim to abuser: Mental health and behavioral sequels of child sexual abuse in a community survey of young adult males. *Child Abuse & Neglect, 18*, 683–697.

Becker, J. H., Hall, S. R., & Stinson, J. D. (2001). Female sexual offenders: Clinical, legal, and policy issues. *Journal of Forensic Psychology Practice, 1*, 29–50.

Beitchman, J. H., Zucker, K. J., Hood, J. E., DaCosta, G. A., & Akman, D. (1991). A review of the short-term effects of child sexual abuse. *Child Abuse & Neglect, 15*, 537–556.

Beitchman, J. H., Zucker, K. J., Hood, J. E., DaCosta, G. A., Akman, D., & Cassavia, E. (1992). A review of the long-term effects of child sexual abuse. *Child Abuse & Neglect, 16*, 101–118.

Blanchette, K., & Brown, S. L. (2006). *The assessment and treatment of women offenders*. Chichester, UK: John Wiley & Sons.

Bonta, J., Law, M., & Hanson, R. K. (1997). The prediction of criminal and violent recidivism among mentally disordered offenders: A meta-analysis. *Psychological Bulletin, 123*, 123–142.

Bureau of Justice Statistics. (1994). *Women in prison*. Washington, DC: US Department of Justice.

Cahill, C., Llewelyn, S. P., & Pearson, C. (1991). Long-term effects of sexual abuse which occurred in childhood: A review. *British Journal of Clinical Psychology, 30*, 117–130.

Chivers, M. L., Rieger, G., Latty, E., & Bailey, J. M. (2004). A sex difference in the specificity of sexual arousal. *Psychological Science, 15*, 736–744.

Chow, E. W. C., & Choy, A. L., 2002. Clinical characteristics and treatment response to SSRI in a female pedophile. *Archives of Sexual Behavior, 31*, 211–215.

Christopher, K., Lutz-Zois, C. J., & Reinhardt, A. R. (2007). Female sexual-offenders: Personality pathology as a mediator of the relationship between childhood sexual abuse history and sexual abuse perpetration against others. *Child Abuse & Neglect, 31*, 871–883.

Correctional Service of Canada. (2006). *The changing federal offender population: Profiles and forecasts, 2006*. Ottawa, Canada: Research Branch. (Available from http://www.csc-scc.gc.ca/text/rsrch/special_reports/highlights-2006-eng.shtml)

Cortoni, F. (2010). Female sexual offenders: A special sub-group. In K. Harrisson (Ed.), *Dealing with high-risk sex offenders in the community: Risk management, treatment and social responsibilities* (pp. 159–173). Devon, UK: Willan Publishing.

Cortoni, F., & Gannon, T. A. (in press). Female sexual offenders. In A. Phenix & H. M. Hoberman (Eds.), *Sexual offenders: Diagnosis, risk assessment and management*. New York: Springer.

Davin, P. A., Hislop, J., & Dunbar, T. (1999). *Female sexual abusers: Three views*. Brandon, VT: Safer Society Press.

Denov, M. S. (2001). A culture of denial: Exploring professional perspectives on female sex offending. *Canadian Journal of Criminology, 43*, 303–329.

Denov, M. S., & Cortoni, F. (2006). Adult female sexual offenders. In C. Hilarski & J. Wodarski (Eds.), *Comprehensive mental health practices with sex offenders and their families* (pp. 71–99). New York: Haworth Press.

Dutton, D. G., & Hart, S. D. (1992). Risk markers for family violence in a federally incarcerated population. *International Journal of Law and Psychiatry, 15*, 101–112.

Eldridge, H. J., & Saradjian, J. (2000). Replacing the function of abusive behaviors for the offender: Remaking relapse prevention in working with women who sexually abuse children. In D. R. Laws, S. M. Hudson, & T. Ward (Eds.), *Remaking relapse prevention with sex offenders: A sourcebook* (pp. 402–426). Thousand Oaks, CA: Sage.

Elliott, D. M., & Briere, J. (1992). Sexual abuse trauma among professional women: Validating the Trauma Symptom Checklist (TSC 40). Child Abuse & Neglect, *16*, 391–398.

Faller, K. C. (1987). Women who sexually abuse children. *Violence and Victims, 2*, 263–276.

Faller, K. C. (1995). A clinical sample of women who have sexually abused children. *Journal of Child Sexual Abuse, 4*, 13–30.

Fazel, S., Sjöstedt, G., Grann, M., & Langström, N. (2008). Sexual offending in women and psychiatric disorder: A national case-control study. *Archives of Sexual Behavior*, Online May 2008, DOI 10.1007/s10508–008-9375–4.

Fedoroff, J. P., Fishell, A., & Fedoroff, B. (1999). A case series of women evaluated for paraphilic sexual disorders. *The Canadian Journal of Human Sexuality, 8*, 127–140.

Ford, H. (2006). *Women who sexually abuse children.* London: John Wiley & Sons.

Ford, H. J., & Cortoni, F. (2008). Assessment and treatment of sexual deviance in females. In D. R. Laws, S. M. Hudson, & W. O'Donohue (Eds.), *Sexual deviance* (2nd ed., pp. 508–526). New York: The Guilford Press.

Ford, M., & Linney, J. (1995). Comparative analysis of juvenile sexual offenders, violent non-sexual offenders, and status offenders. *Journal of Interpersonal Violence, 10*, 56–70.

Fromuth, M., & Conn, V. (1997). Hidden perpetrators: Sexual molestation in a nonclinical sample of college women. *Journal of Interpersonal Violence, 12*, 456–465.

Gannon, T. A., & Rose, M. R. (2009). Offence-related interpretative bias in female child molesters: A preliminary study. *Sexual Abuse: A Journal of Research and Treatment, 21*, 194–207.

Goodwin, J. (1988). Post-traumatic symptoms in abused children. *Journal of Trauma & Stress, 1*, 475–488.

Gorsuch, N. (1998). Unmet need among disturbed female offenders. *Journal of Forensic Psychiatry, 9*, 556–570.

Grayston, A. D., & De Luca, R. V. (1999). Female perpetrators of child sexual abuse: A review of the clinical and empirical literature. *Aggression and Violent Behavior, 4*, 93–106.

Green, A. H., & Kaplan, M. S. (1994). Psychiatric impairment and childhood victimization experiences in female child molesters. *Journal of the American Academy of Child & Adolescent Psychiatry, 33*, 954–960.

Hamilton, C. E., Falshaw, L., & Browne, K. D. (2002). The link between recurrent maltreatment and offending behavior. *International Journal of Offender Therapy and Comparative Criminology, 46*, 75–94.

Hammett, T., Roberts, C., & Kennedy, S. (2001). Health-related issues in prisoner reentry. *Crime & Delinquency, 47*, 390–409.

Hanson, R. K., & Morton-Bourgon, K. E. (2005). The characteristics of persistent sexual offenders: A meta-analysis of recidivism studies. *Journal of Consulting and Clinical Psychology, 73*, 1154–1163.

Harlow, C. W. (1999). *Prior abuse reported by inmates and probationers.* Washington, DC: Bureau of Justice Statistics.

Hislop, J. (2001). *Female sex offenders.* Ravensdale, WA: Issues Press.

Hislop, J. C. R. (1999). Female child molesters. In P. A. Davin, J. C. R. Hislop, & T. Dunbar (Eds.), *The female sexual abuser: Three views* (pp. 135–310). Brandon, VT: Safer Society Press.

Hunter, J. A., Lexier, L. J., Goodwin, D. W., Browne, P. A., & Dennis, C. (1993). Psychosexual, attitudinal, and developmental characteristics of juvenile female perpetrators in a residential treatment setting. *Journal of Child and Family Studies, 2*, 317–326.

Hunter, J. A., & Mathews, R. (1997). Sexual deviance in females. In D. R. Laws & W. O'Donohue (Eds.), *Sexual deviance: Theory, assessment, and treatment* (pp. 465–480). New York: The Guilford Press.

Johansson-Love, J. (2007). A two by two comparison of offense and gender: What characteristics do female sex offenders have in common with other offender groups? Unpublished doctoral dissertation, Morgantown, WV.

Johansson-Love, J., & Fremouw, W. (2006). A critique of the female sexual perpetrator research. *Aggression and Violent Behavior, 11*, 12–26.

Kendall-Tackett, K., Williams, L. M., & Finkelhor, D. (1993). Impact of sexual abuse on children: A review and synthesis of recent empirical studies. *Psychological Bulletin, 113*, 164–180.

Laque, J. (2002). *Childhood traumas, substance abuse and sexual experiences: A comparison study between incarcerated female sex offenders and non-sex offenders.* Unpublished doctoral dissertation, Houston, TX.

Lewis, C. F., & Stanley, C. R. (2000). Women accused of sexual offenses. *Behavioral Sciences and the Law, 18,* 73–81.

Lindbergh, F. H., & Distad, L. J. (1985). Post traumatic stress disorders in women who experienced childhood incest. *Child Abuse & Neglect, 9,* 329–334.

Lindsay, W. R., & Taylor, J. L. (2009). The assessment of treatment related issues and risk in sexual offenders and abusers with ID. In A. R. Beech, L. A. Craig, & K. D. Browne (Eds.), *Assessment and treatment of sexual offenders: A handbook* (pp. 217–236). Chichester, UK: Wiley-Blackwell.

Lund, J. (1990). Mentally retarded criminal offenders in Denmark. *British Journal of Psychiatry, 156,* 726–731.

Mandelblatt, A. W. (2007). *The stories that are not told: Female sexual offenders.* Unpublished doctoral dissertation, Chester, Pennsylvania.

Mathews, R., Hunter, J. A., & Vuz, J. (1997). Juvenile female sexual offenders: Clinical characteristics and treatment issues. *Sexual Abuse: A Journal of Research and Treatment, 9,* 187–199.

Mathews, R., Matthews, J. K., & Speltz, K. (1989). *Female sexual offenders: An exploratory study.* Orwell, VT: Safer Society Press.

Matsunaga, H., Kaye, W., McConaha, C., Plotnicov, K., Pollice, C., Rao, R., et al. (1999). Psychopathological characteristics of recovered bulimics who have a history of physical or sexual abuse. *Journal of Nervous and Mental Diseases, 187,* 472–477.

Matthews J. K. (1993). Working with female sexual abusers. In M. Elliott (Ed.), *Female sexual abuse of children* (pp. 57–73). New York: Guilford Press.

McCarty, L. (1986). Mother–child incest: Characteristics of the offender. *Child Welfare, 65,* 447–458.

McCleer, S. V., Callaghan, M., Henry, D., & Wallen, J. (1994). Psychiatric disorders in sexually abused children. *Journal of the American Academy of Child and Adolescent Psychiatry, 33,* 313–319.

McLeer, S. V., Deblinger, E., Henry, D., & Orvaschel, H. (1992). Sexually abused children at high risk for PTSD. *Journal of the American Academy of Child and Adolescent Psychiatry, 31,* 875–879.

Messer, J., Maughan, B., Quinton, D., & Taylor, A. (2004). Precursors and correlates of criminal behavior in women. *Criminal Behavior and Mental Health, 14,* 82–107.

Miccio-Fonseca, L. C. (2000). Adult and adolescent female sex offenders: Experiences compared to other female and male sex offenders. *Journal of Psychology & Human Sexuality, 11,* 75–88.

Miller, H. A., Turner, K., & Henderson, C. (2009). Psychopathology of sex offenders: A comparison of males and females using latent profile analysis. *Criminal Justice and Behavior, 36,* 778–792.

Mohan, D., Scully, P., Collins, C., & Smith, C. (1997). Psychiatric disorder in an Irish female prison. *Criminal Behaviour and Mental Health, 7,* 229–235.

Morrison, T., Erooga, M., & Beckett, R. C. (1994). *Sexual offending against children: Assessment and treatment of male abusers.* New York: Routledge.

Nathan, P., & Ward, T. (2001). Females who sexually abuse children: Assessment and treatment issues. *Psychology and Law, 8,* 44–55.

Nathan, P., & Ward, T. (2002). Female sex offenders: Clinical and demographic features. *Journal of Sexual Aggression, 8,* 5–21.

Neumann, D. A., Houskamp, B. M., Pollock, V. E., & Briere, J. (1996). The long-term sequelae of childhood sexual abuse in women: A meta-analytic review. *Child Maltreatment, 1,* 6–16.

O'Connor, A. A. (1987). Female sex offenders. *British Journal of Psychiatry, 150,* 615–620.

Oddone Paolucci, E., Genius, M. L., & Violato, C. (2001). A meta-analysis of the published research on the effects of child sexual abuse. *Journal of Psychology, 135,* 17–36.

Prendergast, W. E. (1991). *Treating sex offenders in correctional institutions and outpatients clinics: A guide to clinical practice.* New York: The Haworth Press.

Pithers, W. D., & Cumming, G. F. (1995). Relapse prevention: A method for enhancing behavioral self-management and external supervision of the sexual aggressor. In B. K. Schwartz & H. R. Cellini (Eds.), *The sex offender: Corrections, treatment, and legal practice* (pp. 20.1–20.32). Kingston, NJ: Civic Research Institute.

Putnam, F. W., & Trickett, P. K. (1993). Child sex abuse: A model of chronic trauma. *Psychiatry, 56,* 82–95.

Roesler, T. A., & McKenzie, N. (1994). Effects of childhood trauma on psychological functioning in adults sexually abused as children. *Journal of Nervous and Mental Diseases, 182,* 145–150.

Rowan, E., Rowan, J., & Langelier, P. (1990). Women who molest children. *Bulletin of the American Academy of Psychiatry and the Law, 18,* 79–83.

Saradjian, J. (1996). *Women who sexually abuse children: From research to clinical practice.* New York: John Wiley & Sons.

Sheerin, D. (2004). Psychiatric disorder and adolescent sexual offending. In G. O'Reilly, W. L. Marshall, A. Carr, & R. C. Beckett (Eds.), *The handbook of clinical intervention with young people who sexually abuse* (pp. 129–159). New York: Brunner-Routledge.

Silver, E., Felson, R. B., & Vaneseltine, M. (2008). The relationship between mental health problems and violence among criminal offenders. *Criminal Justice and Behavior, 35,* 405–426.

Strickland, S. M. (2008). Female sex offenders: Exploring issues of personality, trauma, and cognitive distortions. *Journal of Interpersonal Violence, 23,* 474–489.

Suschinsky, K. D., Lalumière, M. L., & Chivers, M. L. (2009). Sex differences in patterns of genital sexual arousal: Measurement artifacts or true phenomena? *Archives of Sexual Behavior, 38,* 559–573.

Tardif, M., Auclair, N., Jacob, M., & Carpentier, J. (2005). Sexual abuse perpetrated by adult and juvenile females: An ultimate attempt to resolve a conflict associated with maternal identity. *Child Abuse & Neglect, 29,* 153–167.

Travin, S., Cullen, K., & Protter, B. (1990). Female sex offenders: Severe victims and victims and victimisers. *Journal of Forensic Sciences, 35,* 140–150.

Turner, K., Miller, H. A., & Henderson, C. E. (2008). Latent profile analysis of offense and personality characteristics in a sample of incarcerated female sexual offenders. *Criminal Justice and Behavior, 35,* 879–894.

Wakefield, H., & Underwager, R. (1991). Female child sexual abusers: A critical review of the literature. *American Journal of Forensic Psychology, 9,* 45–69.

Wilkins, R. (1990). Women who sexually abuse children. *British Medical Journal, 300,* 1153–1154.

Williams, M. B. (1993). Assessing the traumatic impact of child sexual abuse: What makes it more severe? *Journal of Child Sexual Abuse, 2,* 41–59.

Chapter 6

THE ASSESSMENT OF FEMALE
SEXUAL OFFENDERS

Franca Cortoni

School of Criminology, Université de Montréal, Quebec, Canada

Just like with male sexual offenders, the assessment of women who have committed sexual offences is predominantly driven by the need to establish the likelihood of future occurrences of sexual offending behaviour and to identify interventions that would reduce their risk of recidivism. Because women are subjected to the same sanctions as males in the criminal justice system (e.g. Sexually Violent Predator laws in the USA), it is crucial that their assessment of risk and treatment needs be based on empirically validated approaches. Although tremendous advances have been made in establishing empirically based assessment practices among males (e.g. Hanson & Morton-Bourgon, 2005; Hart, Laws & Kropp, 2003; Quinsey, Harris, Rice & Cormier, 2006), the assessment of risk and treatment needs of female sexual offenders remains a difficult endeavour as research in this area is approximately 20 years behind the research on male sexual offenders. Despite these difficulties, there is now an, albeit limited, empirical foundation from which evaluators can draw to improve the validity of their assessment of female sexual offenders. This chapter reviews this empirical foundation and provides guidelines for the evaluation of female sexual offenders' risk and treatment needs.

RECIDIVISM RATES AMONG FEMALE SEXUAL OFFENDERS

Although we now have a solid understanding of the recidivism rates of male sexual offenders (e.g. Hanson & Morton-Bourgon, 2005), similar knowledge is only starting to accumulate for female sexual offenders. Understanding the base rates of recidivism is fundamental to the evaluation of risk of future offending (Hanson & Bussière, 1998; Quinsey, Lalumière, Rice & Harris, 1995). Base rates

Female Sexual Offenders: Theory, Assessment, and Treatment   Edited by Theresa A. Gannon and Franca Cortoni
© 2010 John Wiley & Sons, Ltd

are the proportion of the population that exhibit the phenomenon of interest – in our case, recidivism base rates of female sexual offenders. Recidivism rates vary according to factors such as jurisdictions, types of crimes being measured and how they were measured. In addition, base rates vary according to the length of follow-up time.

In an initial review of the recidivism base rates of 380 female sexual offenders, Cortoni and Hanson (2005) found a sexual recidivism rate of 1 per cent with a 5-year follow-up period. As with male sexual offenders, female sexual offenders also demonstrated other types of non-sexual reoffending. This review, however, was based on what is considered a small number of offenders when the purpose is to examine recidivism rates. Since that time, a number of studies with larger samples have appeared. In addition, Cortoni and Hanson (2005) did not provide a meta-analytic summary of recidivism rates; a meta-analytical approach provides much more precise estimates of the stability of the results. Also, meta-analysis can identify statistical outliers and moderator variables. Consequently, evaluators and policy makers can have the most confidence in results obtained from an aggregated meta-analytical review as opposed to results from individual studies that may be influenced by sample or methodological characteristics.

Given these issues, Cortoni, Hanson and Coache (in press) conducted an updated meta-analytic review of the recidivism rates of female sexual offenders. Their meta-analysis included the results from a total of 10 recidivism studies with an aggregated total number of 2,490 female sexual offenders. These recidivism studies were conducted in Canada, Australia, the USA, the UK and the Netherlands. The average follow-up time was 6.5 years. In efforts to standardise research methodology so that meaningful comparisons in recidivism rates between male and female offenders could be made, the same definition for recidivism as used in studies of males was utilised (e.g. Hanson & Morton-Bourgon, 2005). Specifically, recidivism was defined as being charged, convicted or incarcerated for a new offence. Sexual recidivism included a new charge, conviction or reincarceration for a sexual offence. Violent recidivism was defined as a new violent charge, conviction or incarceration for a new violent offence (including sexual offences). Any recidivism was defined as any new charge, conviction or incarceration, all categories confounded. Consequently, and consistent with research on the recidivism rates of male sexual offenders, the categories of recidivism were cumulative rather than mutually exclusive.

The meta-analysis revealed that there was more variability across studies than expected by chance, with one study consistently identified as the outlier (Vandiver, 2007). This finding was not surprising as in her study, Vandiver counted sexual recidivism as any offence that led to the registration of the woman as a sexual offender, as defined by the State of Texas (D. Vandiver, personal communication, 14 October, 2008). It appears therefore that Vandiver's study included behaviours that are not typically counted as sexual offences in the male sexual offender recidivism studies (e.g. compelling prostitution, kidnapping, Court or Board ordered registration), thereby likely artificially inflating the rate of sexual recidivism among the female sexual offenders. Specifically, while the female sexual offenders had sexual recidivism rates virtually identical to the male sexual offenders (10.8 per cent vs 11.4 per cent), only the female offenders had offences related to prostitution.

Given the variability among studies created by the Vandiver (2007) study, Cortoni et al. (in press) analysed the recidivism rates of female sexual offenders with and without the results from Vandiver. When the analyses included the Vandiver study, the weighted observed sexual recidivism rate for all studies was 3.2 per cent. Fixed and random effects from the meta-analysis showed that the aggregated estimates of sexual recidivism ranged from 1.2 to 2.4 per cent with an average 6.5 years follow-up. For violent recidivism, the fixed and random effects analyses showed aggregated estimates that ranged from 4.4 to 7.6 per cent. Finally, the fixed and random effects estimates for the presence of any recidivism (including violent and sexual recidivism) ranged from 22 to 24 per cent. However, when the data were re-analysed without the results from the Vandiver study, the variability across studies disappeared and the aggregated estimates of recidivism dropped significantly. Specifically, meta-analytical fixed and random effects showed sexual recidivism rates between 1.0 and 1.3 per cent. Violent recidivism ranged from 3.7 to 5.6 per cent, while the rate of any recidivism was at 21 per cent regardless of whether fixed or random effects were examined.

In contrast, meta-analyses of large samples of male sexual offenders show that the 5-year recidivism rates for male sexual offenders are 13–14 per cent for sexual crimes, 25 per cent for any violent crime (including sexual offending) and 36–37 per cent for any new crime (Hanson & Bussière, 1998; Hanson & Morton-Bourgon, 2005). Not surprisingly, Cortoni and Hanson (2005) noted in their earlier review that the differences between the recidivism rates for the male and female sexual offenders were statistically significant for all types of recidivism, confirming that female sexual offenders have much lower rates of all types of recidivism than male sexual offenders. The results from their 2009 meta-analysis confirmed that the rates of all types of recidivism among female sexual offenders are indeed significantly lower than those of males. Equally important, though, is the finding that female sexual offenders, just like males, are much more likely to recidivate with non-sexual crimes. This finding indicates the necessity of attending to issues related to criminal behaviour that go beyond risk of sexual recidivism.

In a recent separate study, Sandler and Freeman (2009) conducted a large-scale study of recidivism among female sexual offenders in the State of New York (included in the Cortoni et al. meta-analysis). Their study included a total of 1,466 women convicted of a registerable sexual offence in New York State between 1 January, 1986 and 31 December, 2006. In their study, recidivism was defined as a rearrest for a new offence and they found a rate of sexual recidivism of 1.8 per cent with a 5-year follow-up period. The rate of rearrest for a violent felony was 5.2 per cent while the rate for a rearrest for any new offence was 26.6 per cent. An important caveat in this study, however, must be noted. In New York State, like many other jurisdictions in the USA, offences related to prostitution that involve minors are considered 'sexual offences'. Consequently, this latest study on female sexual offenders included 79 women (5.4 per cent of the sample) who were not convicted for sexual offences per se; rather they received convictions for promoting prostitution of a minor, profiting from the prostitution of a child less than 16 years old, or promoting a sexual act by a child. Interestingly, out of the 32 (1.8 per cent) sexual recidivists, only 22 were women actually convicted of sexual offences, the other 10 'sexual' recidivists were actually part of the 79 women convicted of prostitution-related offences. When these women were removed from the main group, the sexual recidivism rate dropped to 1.2 per cent.

This finding raises an important issue related to the definition of sexual offending by women. As discussed earlier in this chapter, while jurisdictions may adopt various definitions to fit their legal requirements, the lack of standardised professional definitions of what constitutes sexual offending by women can lead to unwarranted conclusions. Specifically, results from Sandler and Freeman (2009) indicate that there are actually 2 distinct subgroups of women that are considered 'sexual offenders': those with actual hands-on or other sexually-related offences such as child pornography (this group could be called 'traditional sexual offenders' group), and those with prostitution types of offences (this group could be described as 'criminalised sex' group). Based on the finding of 22 recidivists in the first 'traditional' subgroup and 10 recidivists in the second 'criminalised sex' group, it appears that very different recidivism rates actually exist. The 'traditional' sexual offender group had very low rates of rearrest for new sexual offences (22 out of 1,387 or 1.2 per cent). In contrast, the 'criminalised sex' group had much higher rates of rearrest for new sexual offences: 10 out of the 79 or 12.66 per cent recidivism rate. Further, and consistent with their prior criminal history, these latter women were actually reconvicted for new prostitution-related offences as opposed to 'traditional' sexual offences (Sandler & Freeman, 2009).

The above certainly strongly suggests that there are actually two different types of women with different types of offending patterns and recidivism rates, yet all considered under the same generic label of 'sexual offenders'. By melding these two groups, some important distinctions between different types of female offenders appear to be hidden: not all women considered in various jurisdictions to be 'sexual offenders' are actually committing sexual crimes. Consequently, while this evidence is, of course, preliminary, it indicates that evaluators need to pay close attention to the offending and recidivism patterns of women considered 'sexual offenders' in their jurisdiction; those with only prostitution types of offences are likely to present different offending and recidivism patterns, and by extension, different treatment needs than those without such offences.

ASSESSING RISK OF RECIDIVISM

In order to make a determination of risk of recidivism, evaluators must consider the individual characteristics of the offender that increase or decrease the probability of recidivism (Hanson & Morton-Bourgon, 2004, 2005; Quinsey et al., 2006; Roberts, Doren & Thornton, 2002). These characteristics, referred to as *risk factors*, can be subsumed under two main dimensions: static and dynamic factors. *Static* factors are aspects in the offender's history that have a demonstrated empirically established link to recidivism – but that cannot be modified through an intervention. *Dynamic* factors are those characteristics of the offender that also have an empirically validated relationship to recidivism – but that are amenable to change. Consequently, dynamic risk factors are those elements that are addressed in treatment and in the management of offenders in order to manage and reduce risk of recidivism (Hanson, 2006).

While the static and dynamic risk factors of male sexual offenders are well-established (e.g. Hanson & Morton-Bourgon, 2005; Hanson, Harris, Scott & Helmus, 2007), similar knowledge does not yet exist for females. Essentially, the low base rates of recidivism, coupled with the low prevalence of sexual offending by women (Cortoni, Hanson & Coache, 2009) and the lack of general acknowledgment by professionals that women do engage in sexually offending behaviour (Denov, 2003; see also Chapter 2), have rendered, until recently, the empirical examination of risk factors related to sexual offending among women virtually impossible. Despite these limitations, recent research efforts have begun to provide some direction in the establishment of risk factors among women. The next section considers current findings in this area.

Before we turn to these studies, however, an explanation of the term 'higher risk' within the context of female offenders' risk for future recidivism must be provided. Across the ages and cultures, compared with men, women have universally shown not only a lower involvement in criminal activity, but also lower recidivism rates (Blanchette & Brown, 2006). Consequently, while, as discussed below, some factors may indicate a *higher* risk of recidivism among some women, the comparison is in relation with other female sexual offenders – not to some objective [actually non-existent] standard applied to both male and female offenders. If such an objective standard existed, since women consistently show lower rates of recidivism in contrast to males, they would virtually never be considered at *high risk* for recidivism. For example, in offenders released from the Correctional Service of Canada (CSC) during the 1990s, the 2-year rate of reconviction for any offence in male offenders ranged between 41 and 44 per cent, while the rates in female offenders ranged from 23 to 30 per cent (Bonta, Rugge & Dauvergne, 2003). In addition, still within CSC, the reconviction rate for new violent offences in the women was half that observed in the men (6.7 per cent vs. 13.2 per cent). Similarly, in the USA, in a 3-year follow-up of 272,111 offenders (including 23,674 women), 39.9 per cent of the women had been reconvicted for a new offence as compared with 47.6 per cent of the men (Langan & Levin, 2002). These findings indicate the importance of understanding the difference between relative and absolute rates of recidivism (see Babchishin & Hanson, 2009 for a discussion of this issue).

Static Risk Factors

Among male offenders, static risk factors for *general and violent (non-sexual)* recidivism include being at a younger age, being single and having a history of lifestyle instability, rule violations and prior criminal history (Andrews & Bonta, 2007; Hanson & Morton-Bourgon, 2005). Static factors specifically related to *sexual* recidivism include prior sexual offences and having male, stranger and/or unrelated victims (Hanson & Thornton, 2000).

An examination of the research on female sexual offenders shows that, just like with males, a prior criminal history is indicative of a *higher* risk of recidivism among women. In her follow-up of 471 women, Vandiver (2007) found that the number of prior convictions for any type of offence predicted rearrest for new *general* and *violent* offences. Vandiver could not, however, establish any factor that specifically predicted new sexual offences among the women in her sample.

Freeman and Sandler (2008a), in their study of 390 female sexual offenders registered in the State of New York, also noted that a prior criminal history was related to recidivism. Specifically, the number of prior drug offence arrests, the number of prior violent offence arrests, the number of prior incarceration terms and being younger at arrest for the index sexual offence were related to a rearrest for new general (i.e. non-sexual and non-violent) offences. In addition though, Freeman and Sandler (2008b) found that a high risk (as assessed by the New York State risk assessment system), the number of prior arrests for sexual offences, and interestingly, the number of prior child abuse offences (of any type) were specifically related to sexual recidivism among the women in their sample. In their updated study, Sandler and Freeman (2009), however, found different patterns of factors related to recidivism. Specifically, prior misdemeanours, prior drug offences and prior violent offences were *only* related to non-sexual recidivism, while prior child abuse offences of any type were *only* related to sexual recidivism (whether all females or only the 'traditional sexual offender' females were considered). In addition, Sandler and Freeman found that a younger age (less than 30) was only related to non-sexual recidivism. In contrast, and contrary to the well-established finding among male sexual offenders in which a younger age is related to higher sexual recidivism, being older was actually linearly related to sexual recidivism among females, but *only* for the prostitution-related offenders; age was not related to recidivism for the 'traditional' group of female sexual offenders.

The finding that prior criminal history is related to future non-sexual recidivism among female sexual offenders is not surprising. It is indicative of an antisocial orientation and is common to all types of offenders, whether males or females (Andrews & Bonta, 2007; Blanchette & Brown, 2006). As female sexual offenders also engage in other type of offending, they would be expected to demonstrate some of the antisocial characteristics common to all offenders.

Interestingly, the finding by Sandler and Freeman (2009) that prior child abuse (non-sexual) offences were related only to sexual recidivism appears, however, unique to women. Perhaps because women tend to be the primary caregivers, they are more likely than men to come to the attention of the criminal justice system for non-sexual abuse of children. Alternatively, it could be that the sexual abuse of children, for these women, is part of a broader pattern of abuse against children. This issue appears unique to females and certainly warrants further empirical investigation to clarify its role in their sexually offending behaviour.

Finally, a potentially useful, albeit extremely limited, finding comes from Williams and Nicholaichuk's (2001) follow-up of 61 female sexual offenders incarcerated in Canada between 1972 and 1998. It is now well-established that a number of female sexual offenders commit their offences in company of a co-offender, typically their male romantic partner (e.g. Vandiver, 2006). In their detailed analysis, Williams and Nicholaichuk (2001) found that the two sexual recidivists in their study were the only ones who had exclusively engaged in solo offending. This particular finding is noteworthy and may serve as an important risk marker for sexual recidivism among women, but it requires additional validation. Unfortunately the presence of a co-offender was not explicitly examined by Vandiver (2007) or by Sandler and Freeman (2009; Freeman & Sandler, 2008a, b), rendering any direct comparison of this factor among different samples impossible. As discussed later in this chapter, the frequent presence of a co-offender is a unique feature of female sexual offenders and future research will need to attend to its impact on recidivism patterns among women.

Dynamic Risk Factors

Among male sexual offenders, the main changeable characteristics associated with sexual offending are *deviant sexual interests, cognitions supportive of sexual offending, problematic socioaffective functioning* and *poor self-regulation* (Beech, Fisher & Thornton, 2003; Craig, Browne, Beech & Stringer, 2006; Hanson & Harris, 2001; Hanson & Morton-Bourgon, 2005; Thornton, 2002, 2005). Although dynamic risk factors are well established for male sexual offenders, the dynamic risk factors of women are unknown. Consequently, the assessment of potential dynamic risk factors, and by extension, their treatment needs, can only be based on the elements that appear common among female sexual offenders and that are suggestive of a relationship with the offending behaviour.

Generally, clinical research suggests that while female sexual offenders possess some unique features, they do share some of the same characteristics as males. However, the accumulating evidence indicates that these characteristics manifest themselves in different ways for women (e.g. Gannon, Rose & Ward, 2008). Evaluators need to be aware that a simple transfer of knowledge from the male sexual offender literature to females is simply not appropriate. An understanding of the literature on female sexual offenders and indeed of women offenders in general (e.g., Barker, 2009; Blanchette & Brown, 2006) is necessary to conduct the evaluation.

On the basis of available evidence, common to both male and female sexual offenders are denial or minimisation of the offending behaviour, distorted cognitions about the sexual offending and sexual abuse in general, problematic relationship and intimacy deficits and the use of sex to regulate emotional states or fulfil intimacy needs (Gannon et al., 2008; Grayston & De Luca, 1999; Nathan & Ward, 2002). Sexual gratification, a desire for intimacy (with either a victim or a co-defendant), or instrumental goals such as revenge or humiliation are also associated with female sexual offending (Gannon et al., 2008). Finally, as female sexual offenders, just like their male counterparts, also engage in other criminal behaviour, factors such as the presence and extent of antisocial attitudes, antisocial associates and substance abuse as a precursor to the offending behaviour should also be considered in the assessment (Ford & Cortoni, 2008; see also Chapter 5, Chapter 7 for detailed discussions of these issues).

CONDUCTING THE ASSESSMENT

The assessment of a female sexual offender should follow the accepted practices in the general offender literature. Areas to be examined include dispositional factors such as antisocial personality characteristics, historical factors including factors such as adverse developmental experiences and prior criminal history, contextual elements including details and circumstances of the offences, social network and support, and personal life circumstances (e.g. marital and parental status, educational, work and social functioning), and clinical factors such as presence of mental health issues or substance abuse issues (Craig, Browne & Beech, 2008). An exploration of these areas helps establish not only the woman's personal circumstances, but also the likely pathway taken by the woman towards her offending (Gannon et al., 2008; Gannon, Rose & Ward, in press).

An examination of the developmental and family history of the offender is often a good starting point in the assessment. It helps the woman open up and become more comfortable during the evaluation before the focus turns to the offending behaviour itself. The woman's history also helps set the stage for examining and understanding her current functioning. This information provides clues to the elements that have likely contributed to the offending behaviour, including whether a co-offender played a role. The background information also helps establish how a past history of physical, emotional or sexual victimisation may be linked to her offending via her pattern of relating to others as well as her pattern of coping. Finally, it helps determine the role of sexual relationships in the woman's life, the cognitions related to the offending, the type and extent of problematic relationships, and the presence and extent of general antisocial characteristics, all elements that appear important in the offending process of female sexual offenders (Gannon et al., 2008).

Women Who Co-Offend

A factor unique to female sexual offenders is the frequent presence of a co-offender (Grayston & De Luca, 1999; Vandiver, 2006). While early research posited that women were predominantly coerced into the offending by a male (e.g. Mathews, Matthews & Speltz, 1989), we now know this is not the case. More recent findings indicate that while a subgroup is clearly identified as having been coerced into the offending, another subgroup co-offends willingly, including initiating the abuse (Gannon et al., 2008; see also Chapter 9). It is noted as well that some female offenders engage in both solo and co-offending. As part of the assessment, the full extent of the woman's willingness to participate in the abuse needs to be examined. Different treatment needs are likely to emerge if the woman was coerced into the abuse, as opposed to being a willing participant or an initiator. For example, a coerced offender may demonstrate significant deficits in assertiveness and an exaggerated dependence on her co-offender (Eldridge & Saradjian, 2000; Gannon et al., in press). Deviant arousal and fantasising, and attitudes that condone sexual abuse may appear more frequently in initiators or willing participants (Gannon et al., in press).

Sexuality

The assessment of female sexual offenders must include an examination of the potential presence of sexually deviant thoughts and behaviours to ascertain the role they may have played in the offending behaviour. As with a segment of male sexual offenders, deviant arousal and fantasies are part of the dynamics of the offending behaviour in some female sexual offenders (Eldridge & Saradjian, 2000; Grayston & De Luca, 1999; Mathews et al., 1989; Nathan & Ward, 2002). Eldridge and Saradjian (2000) theorised that in females, deviant sexual fantasies are simply a stage between negative emotions and offending rather than an indication of a true sexual preference for deviant sex. They further posited that for some women, deviant fantasies may also be related to her history of victimisation. Beside these postulations, little is actually known about the role these fantasies and arousal may play in the aetiology of sexual offending among females and caution should be taken not to indiscriminately apply male knowledge to females (see Chapter 5 for a more in-depth discussion on paraphilias and deviant arousal among women).

In addition to the assessment of sexual deviance, evaluators need to examine the sexual developmental history and the role sex generally plays in the woman's life. The woman's beliefs about sexual activity, including sexual abuse, may be linked to her beliefs about sex in general, gender roles, a sense of entitlement (her own or her co-offender) and/or a refusal to acknowledge the harm caused by the abuse (Beech, Parrett, Ward & Fisher, 2009; Gannon, Hoare, Rose & Parrett, in press). Consequently, the meaning assigned to sex in general by the woman may have a motivational role in her offending. Within this context, a careful examination of the coping patterns of women is required to determine whether she uses sex to alleviate negative emotional states (Ford & Cortoni, 2008).

Cognitions

The link between pro-offending attitudes and criminal behaviour for all types of offenders of both genders is firmly established (Andrews & Bonta, 2007; Blanchette & Brown, 2006). In male sexual offenders, pro-abuse cognitions and grievance thinking type of cognitions are major dynamic risk factors (Hanson & Harris, 2001). Female sexual offenders also have distorted beliefs about themselves and about children as well as deny or minimise their involvement in the abuse (Grayston & De Luca, 1999; Saradjian, 1996). Core beliefs about relationships, children and gender roles also require examination as they are likely intertwined with pro-offending attitudes (Beech et al., 2009; Eldridge & Saradjian, 2000; Gannon et al., in press). Recent research also suggests that women may hold different types of cognitions depending on whether she offended alone or with a co-offender (see Chapter 7 for a detailed review of the research on the cognitions of female sexual offenders). The assessment would therefore need to elucidate the presence of denial and minimisation, pro-offending cognitions and other distorted beliefs and determine their likely contribution to the offending behaviour.

Problematic Relationships

The nature of problematic relationships and intimacy deficits appear quite different for female sexual offenders in contrast to males. Among male sexual offenders, intimacy deficits tend to manifest themselves through some form of emotional identification with children, instability in his current intimate relationship, hostility towards women, general social rejection/loneliness and a general lack of concern for others (Hanson et al., 2007). In contrast, female sexual offenders appear to exhibit a pattern of relationships characterised by abuse. For example, in their examination of the offence process among female sexual offenders, Gannon et al. (2008) found that female sexual offenders were frequent victims of domestic violence. Similarly, in their study of 132 female sexual offenders, Wijkman and Bijleveld (2008) established that the presence of a prior violent partner, a history of having been physically abused and having been bullied while at school were related to the number of sexual offences committed by these women. Eldridge and Saradjian (2000) noted that an excessive dependence or an over-reliance on the men in their lives is an element that characterises female sexual offenders. Finally, Gannon et al. (2008) found that practical and emotional support from family and friends were lacking in all of their female sexual offender cases. Women tend to be in more need of extensive appropriate supportive social networks as these are an important part of their ability to deal with stress (Rumgay, 2004). Therefore, the assessment needs to focus not only on the dynamics of the woman's romantic relationships, but also the general quality of their social and familial support.

Victimisation

Although past victimisation is not related to future recidivism among female offenders in general, it is a common enough factor among these women to warrant special attention (Blanchette & Brown, 2006). Among female sexual offenders, a past history of physical, emotional or sexual victimisation may be linked to the woman's sexually offending behaviour. It is important, however, to not assume it as the cause of her sexual offences. For example, not all female sexual offenders have a history of sexual victimisation (Wiegel, Abel & Jordon, 2003). It is highly unlikely that victimisation alone is the main reason why the woman chose to sexually abuse. Rather, a history of past victimisation (physical, psychological or sexual) is more likely to be related to the offending behaviour via dysfunctional patterns of relating to others, as well as patterns of coping, that the woman developed as a result of the victimisation (Blanchette & Brown, 2006; Ford & Cortoni, 2008).

General Antisociality Characteristics

An often-neglected aspect of female sexual offenders is the extent to which they may also demonstrate general antisocial characteristics. These characteristics include antisocial attitudes and associates, substance abuse as precursor to offending and emotional dyscontrol (see Blanchette & Brown, 2006 for a review of these issues among female offenders in general). Some women who engage in sexually deviant behaviour do present with egocentric or antisocial features (Grayston & De Luca, 1999; Nathan & Ward, 2002) indicating that for at least a portion of female sexual offenders, the antisociality factor commonly found among male sexual offenders is also present. Unknown at this time, however, is the extent to which antisociality plays a role in sexual offending among women. Individual offending processes as well as general lifestyle issues should be carefully evaluated for the potential presence of antisocial characteristics to determine additional treatment requirements.

CONCLUSION

Many jurisdictions have adopted risk tools for male sexual offenders (e.g. *STATIC-99*; Hanson & Thornton, 1999) to assess female sexual offenders. Because tools for male sexual offenders have not been validated for women, using these tools to assess risk of recidivism among female sexual offenders is inappropriate. There are two reasons for this. First, these tools provide estimates of risk of recidivism that are predicated on the base rate of recidivism among adult male sexual offenders. Consequently, given the significantly lower rates of sexual recidivism of female sexual offenders, these tools would grossly overestimate risk among these women.

Second, the items in these risk assessment tools were selected based on their established empirical relationship with recidivism. For example, factors such as prior sexual offences, and having male, stranger and/or unrelated victims have a well-established relationship to sexual recidivism among male offenders (Hanson & Thornton, 2000). However, the state of our current knowledge is weak and conclusions regarding likely risk factors among female sexual offenders continue to be tentative. Further, other than the finding that prior criminal history is related to non-sexual recidivism, the only indicator that appears related to the potential for sexual recidivism among women is the presence of prior child abuse offences – a factor that does not appear in any risk assessment tools for males. Finally, there is no empirical evidence to suggest that factors such as having a particular type of victim are related to sexual recidivism among women. Hence, risk assessment tools for males not only overestimate risk in women, but they provide such overestimates on the basis of items that have no demonstrated links to sexual recidivism among women.

Since general (i.e. non-sexual) recidivism is much more common than sexual recidivism among female sexual offenders, evaluators tasked with the assessment of female sexual offenders should instead select a risk assessment tool that has been validated to assess general risk of recidivism among female offenders (e.g. *LSI-R*; Andrews & Bonta, 1995; Smith, Cullen & Latessa, 2009). The use of general risk assessment tools, however, still require an understanding of the research on risk factors and recidivism among female offenders in general as these issues differ according to the gender of the offender (e.g. Blanchette & Brown, 2006; Folsom & Atkinson, 2007; Holtfreter & Cupp, 2007; Manchak, Skeem, Douglas & Siranosian, 2009).

To specifically assess potential risk for sexual recidivism, an empirically guided clinical judgment of risk should be used. This approach to risk assessment normally entails that the prediction of risk for sexual recidivism is based on a clinical judgment of the extent and combination of *established* (i.e. empirically validated) risk factors in a given case. The complicating issue here is that risk factors for sexual recidivism among females have not been validated. However, they could plausibly include the dynamic elements, discussed earlier in this chapter, that have been found in clinical samples and that appear common to both male and female offenders. Again, the ways in which these factors manifest themselves in female sexual offenders, are likely to be different from the typical patterns found in male sexual offenders (e.g. Gannon et al., 2008). Finally, when conducting an assessment of female sexual offenders, it must be remembered that the base rate of sexual recidivism among women is extremely low. Consequently, conclusions on the likely risk of sexual recidivism in a given case must be framed within that context.

REFERENCES

Andrews, D. A., & Bonta, J. (1995). *Level of service inventory – revised*. Toronto: Multi-Health Systems.

Andrews, D. A., & Bonta J. (2007). *The psychology of criminal conduct* (4th ed.). Cincinnati, OH: Anderson.

Babchishin, K. M, & Hanson, R. K. (2009). Improving our talk: Moving beyond the "low", "moderate", and "high" typology of risk communication. *Crime Scene, 16,* 11–14. Available at www.cpa.ca/sections/criminaljustice/publications/.

Barker, J. (Ed.). (2009). *Women and the criminal justice system: A Canadian perspective*. Toronto: Emond Montgomery.

Beech, A. R., Fisher, D. D., & Thornton, D. (2003). Risk assessment of sex offenders. *Professional Psychology: Research and Practice, 34,* 339–352.

Beech, A. R., Parrett, N., Ward, T., & Fisher, D. (2009). Assessing female sexual offenders' motivations and cognitions: An exploratory study. *Psychology, Crime & Law, 15,* 201–216.

Blanchette, K., & Brown, S. L. (2006). *The assessment and treatment of women offenders: An integrated perspective*. Chichester, UK: John Wiley & Sons.

Bonta, J., Rugge, T., & Dauvergne, M. (2003). *The reconviction rate of federal offenders* (User Report No. 2003–03). Ottawa, ON: Public Safety Canada. Retrieved 9th August 2009, from http://www.publicsafety.gc.ca/res/cor/rep/_fl/2003-02-rec-rte-eng.pdf.

Cortoni, F., & Hanson, R. K. (2005). *A review of the recidivism rates of adult female sexual offenders* (Research Report R-169). Ottawa: Correctional Service Canada.

Cortoni, F., Hanson, R. K., & Coache, M. E. (2009). Les délinquantes sexuelles: Prévalence et récidive (Female sexual offenders: Prevalence and recidivism). *Revue internationale de criminologie et de police technique et scientifique, LXII,* 319–336.

Cortoni, F., Hanson, R. K., & Coache, M. E. (in press). *The recidivism rates of female sexual offenders are low: A meta-analysis*. Sexual Abuse: A Journal of Research and Treatment.

Craig, L. A., Browne, K. D., & Beech, A. (2008). *Assessing risk in sex offenders: A practitioner's guide*. Chichester: Wiley.

Craig, L. A., Browne, K. D., Beech, A., & Stringer, I. (2006). Psychosexual characteristics of sexual offenders and the relationship to reconviction. *Psychology, Crime & Law, 12*(3), 231–244.

Denov, M. S. (2003). The myth of innocence: Sexual scripts and the recognition of child sexual abuse by female perpetrators. *The Journal of Sex Research, 40,* 303–314.

Eldridge, H., & Saradjian, J. (2000). Replacing the function of abusive behaviors for the offender: Remaking relapse prevention in working with women who sexually abuse children. In D. R. Laws, S. M. Hudson, & T. Ward (Eds.), *Remaking relapse prevention with sex offenders: A sourcebook* (pp. 402–426). Thousand Oaks, CA: Sage.

Folsom, J., & Atkinson, J. L. (2007). The generalizability of the LSI-R and the CAT to the prediction of recidivism in female offenders. *Criminal Justice and Behavior, 34,* 1044–1056.

Ford, H., & Cortoni, F. (2008). Sexual deviance in females: Assessment and treatment. In D. R. Laws & W. O'Donohue (Eds.), *Sexual deviance* (2nd ed., pp. 508–526). New York: Guilford Press.

Freeman, N., & Sandler, J. (2008a). Female and male sex offenders: A comparison of recidivism patterns and risk factors. *Journal of Interpersonal Violence, 23,* 1394–1413.

Freeman, N. J., & Sandler, J. C. (2008b). *Correlates of female sex offender sexual re-arrest*. Unpublished Manuscript.

Gannon, T. A., Hoare, J., Rose, M., & Parrett, N. (in press). A re-examination of female child molesters' implicit theories: Evidence of female specificity? *Psychology Crime and Law.*

Gannon, T. A., Rose, M. R., & Ward, T. (in press). Pathways to female sexual offending: A preliminary study. *Psychology, Crime & Law.*

Gannon, T. A., Rose, M. R., & Ward, T. (2008). A descriptive model of the offense process for female sexual offenders. *Sexual Abuse: A Journal of Research and Treatment, 20,* 352–374.

Grayston, A. D., & De Luca, R. V. (1999). Female perpetrators of child sexual abuse: A review of the clinical and empirical literature. *Aggression and Violent Behavior, 4,* 93–106.

Hanson, R. K. (2006). Stability and changes: Dynamic risk factors for sexual offenders. In W. L. Marshall, Y. M. Fernandez, L. E. Marshall, & G. A. Serran (Eds.), *Sexual offender treatment: controversial issues* (pp. 17–31). Chichester, UK: John Wiley & Sons.

Hanson, R. K., & Bussière, M. T. (1998). Predicting relapse: A meta-analysis of sexual offender recidivism studies. *Journal of Consulting and Clinical Psychology, 66,* 348–362.

Hanson, R. K., & Harris, J. R. (2001). A structured approach to evaluating change among sexual offenders. *Sexual Abuse: A Journal of Research and Treatment, 13,* 105–122.

Hanson, R. K., Harris, A. J. R., Scott, T. L., & Helmus, T. (2007). *Assessing the risk of sexual offenders on community supervision: The Dynamic Supervision Project* (User Report No. 2007–05). Ottawa: Corrections Research, Public Safety Canada. (Available from: www.publicsafety.gc.ca/res/cor/rep/_fl/crp2007-05-en.pdf)

Hanson, R. K., & Morton-Bourgon, K. E. (2004). *Predictors of sexual recidivism: An updated meta-analysis* (User Report No. 2004–02). Retrieved 12th August 2009, from www.publicsafety.gc.ca/res/cor/rep/2004-02-pred-se-eng.aspx.

Hanson, R. K., & Morton-Bourgon, K. E. (2005). The characteristics of persistent sexual offenders: A meta-analysis of recidivism studies. *Journal of Consulting and Clinical Psychology, 73,* 1154–1163.

Hanson, R. K., & Thornton, D. (1999). *Static 99: Improving actuarial risk assessment for sex offenders* (User Report No. 99–02). Ottawa: Corrections Research, Public Safety Canada. (Available from www.ps-sp.gc.ca)

Hanson, R. K., & Thornton, D. (2000). Improving risk assessments for sex offenders: A comparison of three actuarial scales. *Law and Human Behavior, 24,* 119–136.

Hart, S., Laws, D. R., & Kropp, P. R. (2003). The promise and the peril of sex offender risk assessment. In T. Ward, D. R. Laws, & S. M. Hudson (Eds.), *Sexual deviance: Issues and controversies* (pp. 207–243). Thousand Oaks, CA: Sage.

Holtfreter, K., & Cupp, R. (2007). Gender and risk assessment: The empirical status of the LSI-R for women. *Journal of Contemporary Criminal Justice, 23,* 363–382.

Langan, P. A., & Levin, D. J. (2002). *Recidivism of prisoners released in 1994 [Special report].* Washington, DC: Bureau of Justice Statistics, US Department of Justice. Retrieved 12th August 2009, from www.ojp.usdoj.gov/bjs/pub/pdf/rpr94.pdf.

Manchak, M. A., Skeem, J. L., Douglas, K. S., & Siranosian, M. (2009). Does gender moderate the predictive utility of the level of service inventory—revised (LSI-R) for serious violent offenders? *Criminal Justice and Behavior, 36,* 425–442.

Mathews, R., Matthews, J. K., & Speltz, K. (1989). *Female sexual offenders: An exploratory study.* Orwell, VT: Safer Society Press.

Nathan, P., & Ward, T. (2002). Female sex offenders: Clinical and demographic features. *The Journal of Sexual Aggression, 8*(1), 5–21.

Quinsey, V. L., Harris, G. T., Rice, M. E., & Cormier, V. L. (2006). *Violent offenders: Appraising and managing risk, second edition.* Washington, DC: American Psychological Association.

Quinsey, V. L., Lalumière, M. L., Rice, M. E., & Harris, G. T. (1995). Predicting sexual offenses. In J. C. Campbell (Ed.), *Assessing dangerousness: Violence by sexual offenders, batterers, and child abusers* (pp. 114–137). Thousand Oaks, CA: Sage.

Roberts, C. F., Doren, D. M., & Thornton, D. (2002). Dimensions associated with assessments of sex offender recidivism risk. *Criminal Justice and Behavior, 29,* 569–589.

Rumgay, J. (2004). Living with paradox: Community supervision of women offenders. In G. McIvor (Ed.), *Women who offend* (pp. 99–125). London: Jessica Kingsley Publishers.

Sandler, J. C., & Freeman, N. J. (2009). Female sex offender recidivism: A large-scale empirical analysis. *Sexual Abuse: A Journal of Research and Treatment, 21,* 455–473.

Saradjian, J. (1996). *Women who sexually abuse children: From research to clinical practice.* Chichester, UK: John Wiley & Sons.

Smith, P., Cullen, F. T., & Latessa, E. J. (2009). Can 14,737 women be wrong? A meta-analysis of the LSI-R and recidivism for female offenders. *Criminology & Public Policy, 8,* 183–208.

Thornton, D. (2002). Constructing and testing a framework for dynamic risk assessment. *Sexual Abuse: A Journal of Research and Treatment, 14,* 137–151.

Thornton, D. (2005, November). *Evaluating risk factor domain and clusters.* Paper presented at the 24th Research and Treatment Conference of the Association for the Treatment of Sexual Abusers, Salt Lake City, UT.

Vandiver, D. M. (2006). Female sex offenders: A comparison of solo offenders and co-offenders. *Violence and Victims, 21,* 339–354.

Vandiver, D. (2007, March). *An examination of re-arrest rates of 942 male and 471 female registered sex offenders.* Seattle, WA: Academy of the Criminal Justice Sciences, Feature Panel on Sex Offenders.

Wiegel, M., Abel, G. G., & Jordan, A. (2003, October). *The self-reported behaviors of adult female child abusers.* Paper presented at the 22nd Annual Research and Treatment Conference, Association for the Treatment of Sexual Abusers, St. Louis, MO.

Wijkman, M., & Bijleveld, C. (2008, September). *Female sex offenders: Recidivism and criminal careers.* Paper presented at the 8th Annual Conference of the European Society of Criminology, Edinburgh, Scotland.

Williams, S. M., & Nicholaichuk, T. (2001, November). *Assessing static risk factors in adult female sex offenders under federal jurisdiction.* Paper presented at the 20th Research and Treatment Conference, Association for the Treatment of Sexual Abusers, San Antonio, TX.

Chapter 7

THE TREATMENT NEEDS OF FEMALE SEXUAL OFFENDERS

HANNAH FORD

Dudley and Walsall Mental Health Partnership NHS Trust, West Midlands, UK

Until comparatively recently, sexual offences were typically construed as acts committed by males, which women were neither motivated nor physically equipped to commit. Although this male-centric conceptualisation is being challenged and attention is increasingly being paid to sexual offending by women, our understanding of female sexual offenders remains patchy and scant in comparison to the knowledge accrued for males. Eldridge and Saradjian (2000) suggested that as sexual offences by women so strongly transgress expectations of female behaviour, there may have been greater scrutiny of these women's life histories, relationships and the demographics of their offences, perhaps in an effort to understand how *women* could act in this way. As a consequence, however, the treatment needs of these women and associated theoretical developments have not received the full research focus they require.

This poses challenges for those responsible for treating female sexual offenders. Perhaps it is the lack of a female-specific theoretical underpinning to inform assessment and treatment that has led to reliance on male sexual offender treatment models and methods. Gannon and Rose (2008) feel that theoretical developments have barely ventured beyond the construction of descriptive female sexual offender typologies. While typological classifications may hold *some* clinical utility in outlining the differential development of female sexual offending and subsequent treatment needs, such typologies continue to be primarily based upon demographic and offence characteristics (Turner, Miller & Henderson, 2008), thereby perpetuating the narrow focus of female sexual offender research. Nor can typologies encompass the true heterogeneity of female sexual offenders, leading Gannon and Rose (2008) to question the utility of these for clinicians working with individual female sexual offenders.

Female Sexual Offenders: Theory, Assessment, and Treatment   Edited by Theresa A. Gannon and Franca Cortoni
© 2010 John Wiley & Sons, Ltd

At the commencement of this chapter, it is important to acknowledge that the treatment needs of females are not fully understood. Therefore, the aim is to discuss a number of potential treatment needs drawn from the limited literature currently available, to highlight gaps in our knowledge and suggest areas for further consideration. Treatment needs that may overlap with those exhibited by male sexual offenders will be noted and potential gender differences within these raised. As most studies presented in this chapter use samples comprising primarily, or exclusively, women who have sexually offended against children, the needs highlighted are suggested to be most applicable to this offender group. There is currently insufficient literature to be able to comment on potential differences in treatment needs for women who have sexually offended against other victims. While the chapter discusses treatment needs for female sexual offenders in general terms, treatment planning should, of course, be guided by detailed individual assessment and case formulation.

POTENTIAL AREAS OF TREATMENT NEED

Offence-Supportive Cognitions

Compared with male sexual offenders, little is known about offence-supportive cognitions in women. While there is clear anecdotal evidence of distorted beliefs held by sexually abusive women (see Saradjian, 1996, for numerous examples), until very recently, there was little empirical investigation of these. Preliminary efforts have been made to assess these attitudes and beliefs in small numbers of women (e.g. Beckett, 2005; Ring, 2005), but these have been limited to some degree by reliance on measures developed for a male population, which may be less applicable to women, or miss important female-specific aspects.

Researchers are beginning to redress this gender imbalance. Recently, Beech, Parrett, Ward and Fisher (2009) interviewed a small sample of UK female sexual offenders ($n = 15$) to investigate whether the five core implicit theories previously identified in male sexual offenders (see Marziano, Ward, Beech & Pattison, 2006; Ward & Keenan, 1999) were identifiable in females. Beech et al. found evidence of four implicit theories: (1) the uncontrollability of the world and events within it [Uncontrollability]; (2) the world as a dangerous and threatening place [Dangerous World]; (3) beliefs around children as sexual objects [Children as Sexual Beings]; and (4) beliefs about the nature and degree of harm caused by some sexual acts [Nature of Harm]. Beech et al. suggest that their findings indicate that many attitudes, beliefs and goals originally identified in male sexual offenders are shared by females. Interestingly, however, some subtle, female-specific slants were noted within these broadly shared categories. Within the Dangerous World category, for example, much of the female data focussed primarily on the negative environment often created by their male co-perpetrator. Actions on the part of a male co-perpetrator also appeared to contribute to situations/events feeling uncontrollable to the women. Therefore, while four of the five male categories were identifiable in women, there were subtle differences. In addition, one male category (i.e. beliefs about one's *entitlement* to sexually abuse children) was absent from this female sample.

Gannon, Hoare, Rose and Parrett (in press) replicated Beech et al.'s (2009) study and identified all five male implicit theories in their female sexual offender sample. On the basis of their findings, however, they argued for more gender-specific interpretations of these theories. For example, neither this study, nor that of Beech et al., found evidence that female child molesters viewed themselves as being entitled to abuse others. However, Gannon et al. noted that some women expressed beliefs that men are entitled to *control* others sexually. Gannon et al. therefore contend that female child molesters' cognitions may not stem from the same theories as from those of males, hypothesising that they arise instead from implicit theories about gender, which develop through women offenders' prior experiences and sociocultural norms. Thus, whilst they are very preliminary, these findings raise queries about the extent to which we should draw upon the male research literature when considering cognitive distortions in women.

However, both Beech et al.'s (2009) and Gannon et al.'s (in press) findings could have been influenced by the self-report nature of their data. To reduce such difficulties, Gannon, Rose and Williams (2009) used a computerised Implicit Association Test to examine whether the implicit association between children and sexual concepts observed in male child molester research was also present in females. Gannon et al. found no evidence for this, stating that their findings support 'clinical contentions that female molesters generally hold little sexual interest in children' (p. 59). Interestingly, however, Beech et al. (2009) found that in almost half the women they interviewed, there was evidence of them sexualising the children they had abused and Gannon et al. (in press) stated that 63 per cent ($n = 10$) of their sample appeared to view their victim sexually. In Saradjian's (1996) work, many women who abused young children rated the children as having a high sex drive and interpreted the child's behaviour as indications that they wanted sex. Eldridge and Saradjian (2000) similarly noted that many women who abused their own children sexualised those children's behaviours. Gannon et al. (2009) acknowledge this discrepancy and suggest that while women may sexualise their own child victims, they may not hold associations between children and sex more generally.

A further study by Gannon and Rose (2009) also found no evidence for a general sexualised schema about children among female child molesters. However, their findings did suggest that women who sexually abused children were more likely to interpret ambiguous information about males in a threatening way, whether or not they had co-offended with men. This appears to accord with the dangerousness ascribed to men in both Beech et al.'s (2009) and Gannon et al.'s (in press) implicit theory studies. As Gannon and Rose (2009) note, however, it is not yet clear how this interpretive bias contributes to female sexual offending.

Gannon and Rose (2008) suggest that female sexual offenders' cognitions may differ according to context and the length of time she has been offending. Ring (2005) reported that women abusing alone held significantly higher levels of cognitive distortions (as measured by the Children and Sex Questionnaire, Beckett, 1987) than women who were brought into offending by males, although the appropriateness of this measure is questionable, as it was originally developed for males. There may also be qualitative differences in the cognitions of these offender types. Gannon, Rose and Ward (2008) found that women who abused alone valued the experience of intimacy with their victim and their cognitions were evidenced through statements such as 'he is old for his age'. Examples of the cognitions of male-coerced women, meanwhile, included, 'the victim is young and so won't remember this', or beliefs that perpetrating abusive acts themselves would result in less harm (e.g. 'if I do this, it will be less harmful than if he messes with her'). Additionally, some coerced women expressed beliefs that the coercive male must know more than she did; for example, one female sexual offender stated, 'I suppose I thought well I've been left to bring her up on my own, he knows more about kids than I do' (p. 364).

Recently, Strickland (2008) compared female sexual and non-sexual offenders using the *Multiphasic Sex Inventory II* (*MSI-II*, female version). Both groups of women had scores indicating a strong lack of accountability for their actions, a tendency towards blaming others for their situations and the taking of a victim's stance. Furthermore, there was little difference in their mean scores. While this study gave insufficient information about the presence of male co-perpetrators in the sexual offender group, the findings accord with the high frequency of uncontrollability themes found in Beech et al.'s (2009) interviews with women. The findings are also in keeping with Allen's (1991) finding that women offenders are more reluctant to admit abusing children, and feel that they have been wrongly accused, even in the face of supporting evidence. However, Matthews (1993) suggested that women are less likely to deny abusive acts and more willing to accept responsibility. There must be further investigation of the extent to which these issues constitute a treatment need for women given that the current research appears contradictory in nature.

Further understanding of female sexual offenders' cognitions is essential. While recent research has highlighted areas of overlap between males and females, it has also pointed to areas of difference. Gannon, Rose et al. (2009) neatly summarise the conundrum this lack of clarity presents to treatment providers who 'feel that females may generally depart from males in terms of children and sexual cognitions...[but who] persist with work on these issues "just in case"' (p. 59). In addition, Denov and Cortoni (2006) feel that treatment must extend beyond simply targeting offence-related cognitions to also address broader maladaptive cognitive patterns that influence other aspects of the woman's life, such as relationships and emotion regulation. These difficulties are discussed later.

Deviant Sexual Interests

There is an interesting contrast in the extent to which deviant sexual interests have been explored in male and female sexual offenders. While deviant sexual interests have been described as 'one of the most distinctive and important problems for [male] child molesters' (Laws, Hanson, Osborn & Greenbaum, 2000, p. 1297) and have received a corresponding degree of research attention, similarly detailed examinations of deviant sexual interests in females have not occurred. This creates difficulties in assessing the extent to which deviant interests form an important treatment target, particularly as methods of assessment have been developed primarily for a male population. Furthermore, even when female-specific assessments are available, there is little published research to guide clinicians (Ford & Cortoni, 2008).

There are some small-scale studies documenting the importance of deviant sexual interests in some women. Nathan and Ward (2002), for example, reported that nearly half of their female sexual offender sample (41.6 per cent, $n = 5$) admitted being motivated to offend partly by deviant sexual arousal. In their descriptive model of the offence process for female sexual offenders, Gannon et al. (2008) reported that one of the three main motivators for female sexual offenders was that of sexual gratification, in which women offended to gain sexual pleasure. Beech et al.'s (2009) study – described earlier – identified two sex-related cognitive clusters. In the first, offenders appeared to be sexually motivated, but also fearful of violence (often from a male co-perpetrator). In the second, women appeared to have no fear of violence and sexual gratification was the sole motivation for their offence. Women with a sexual motivation for their offence were defined by Beech et al. as those women who admitted sexual attraction or arousal to the victim. There are some reports of female sexual offenders having sexual fantasies about children, either while offending or between offences (see Grayston & De Luca, 1999; Saradjian, 1996). Saradjian (1996) found that women who initially abused young children admitted to repeated images and thoughts of sexual activity with children and many felt aroused by these thoughts. However, only 35 per cent ($n = 5$) said they masturbated to sexual fantasies when not engaging in sex with children. Women who abused adolescents reported sexual thoughts about their victims, although of a romantic and idealised nature. A much larger proportion (80 per cent, $n = 8$) of these women admitted masturbating to fantasies involving their victims. Eldridge and Saradjian (2000) note that even if women do not masturbate to fantasies about abusing children, these fantasies form part of the overall thinking that appears to support and maintain their sexual offending.

While sexual arousal or gratification is unlikely to play a role in *all* female sexual offending, it is important to ascertain whether deviant sexual interests motivate or maintain offending behaviour in some women. Deviant sexual arousal could be more important for females acting alone, or for women abusing adolescents, as they may be more likely to select victims according to their own sexual orientation or view them as surrogate partners. Gannon et al. (2008) provide some support for this, since they found that sexual arousal was primarily linked to a *maternal* style of sexual offending (i.e. a coercive, yet non-aggressive modus operandi). Women who took this approach to sexual offending were primarily solo female sexual offenders, especially those who abused teenage boys, but sometimes also male-accompanied offenders.

Gannon and Rose (2008) caution against assuming that deviant interests are not relevant to male-coerced sexual offenders. In support of this, many of the male-coerced women in Saradjian's (1996) sample admitted sexual thoughts about children although, in all but one case, these thoughts only began *after* the women had been coerced into abusing. However, many of these male-coerced women also stated that their arousal gradually became conditioned to sexual acts with children so that they eventually felt more arousal in the abuse situation than in adult sexual activity. Therefore, a thorough assessment of the sexual interests of female sexual offenders is important. However, this is currently only likely to be achieved through clinical interview, with its associated limitations. Although vaginal photo-plethysmography offers a possible method of physiological assessment, a number of concerns have been raised in relation to this (see Ford & Cortoni, 2008). There-fore, we also need to develop female-specific methods of assessing deviant sexual interests and require further guidance on how to modify those identified in the programmes we provide.

Empathy

Although victim empathy work forms a key part of treatment programmes for male sexual offenders, there has been little formal investigation of victim empathy in female sexual offenders. There are indications that victim empathy may be lacking in some female sexual offenders, as it is in some males. Fromuth and Conn (1997), for example, found that among college women who self-reported sexually molesting children, two thirds believed the effects would have been neutral and only one third felt they would have been negative. Saradjian (1996) reported that among her sample, 'the lack of ability of the women perpetrators to genuinely empathise with the children whom they sexually abuse is ubiquitous' (p. 114). Ring (2005) reported that women abusing alone had poorer victim empathy scores than high deviance male sexual offenders, although she also notes that as many of these women abused adolescents, they may have been particularly likely to report that the victim enjoyed or encouraged the abuse. It should also be noted that this victim empathy measure (the Victim Empathy Distortion Scale – Beckett & Fisher, 1994) was adapted from one originally developed for male sexual offenders.

In constructing their descriptive model of female sexual offending, Gannon et al. (2008; see also Chapter 3) noted differences in post-offence affect and cognition. In women who had previously viewed their victim as sexual, or for whom the offence had been motivated by revenge, there was little consideration of harm caused to the victim and consequent positive affect regarding the offence. However, some of the women coerced by males described not thinking anything, or pushing away negative thoughts about the offence, an action possibly suggestive of greater variation in their levels of empathy for their victims.

However, these comments are largely speculations drawn from the very limited literature available. This is clearly an area requiring further study to deepen clin-icians' understanding of the relevance of victim empathy for their female clients. In particular, further thought should be given to the possible relationship between a female sexual offender's empathy for her own victim and any victimisation she experienced. While this is also true for male sexual offenders, the high rates of childhood abuse reported by female sexual offenders (discussed later in this chapter) may make this a particularly pertinent consideration for women.

Social and Sexual Relationships

The literature frequently refers to female sexual offenders' difficulties in their re-lationships with others. Early relationships with parents are often reported to be very poor. For example, Saradjian (1996) found that women sexual offenders chose words such as 'cold', 'rejecting' or 'unloving' to describe their mothers, while Allen (1991) noted that female sexual offenders reported high levels of negative interaction with their mothers. Green and Kaplan (1994) similarly found that female sexual offenders viewed their relationships with primary caregivers as overwhelmingly negative and predominantly abusive. Negative relationship experiences appear to continue for many women as they grow up, with descriptions of poor relationships both with peers and adult partners (e.g. Gannon et al., 2008; Lewis & Stanley, 2000; Saradjian, 1996). For many women, then, negative beliefs about themselves and others formed through poor early relationship experiences appear not to have been challenged by more positive experiences later in life, resulting in poor social skills and difficulties in both forming relationships and experiencing appropriate intimacy. Many sexual offenders have very limited social networks and social support; Saradjian (1996) noted that at the time they were abusing children, no woman in her sample could name a friend. Strickland (2008) compared female sexual and non-sexual offenders, using the female version of the *MSI-II*. Sexual offenders scored significantly higher on the Social and Sexual Inadequacies subscale suggesting that they are more inhibited and feel more insecure and inferior in social and sexual contacts than women who commit other types of offences.

Given these poor relationship experiences and the high reported rates of childhood sexual abuse, it is perhaps not surprising that many female sexual offenders report difficult feelings about their sexual relationships. When Saradjian (1996) asked her sample what sex meant to them, all reported at least one negative feeling about sexual experiences with adult partners and negative feelings were particularly marked among women who had initially abused young children or been coerced into sexual offending. In comparison, non-offending women reported fewer negative feelings and more positive aspects such as warmth and bonding with their adult partners. However, this difference may simply be a product of comparing offenders with non-offenders. It may be more informative to compare sexually offending women with women who have committed other, non-sexual offences, but who may also have had poorer relationship and early life experiences.

Allen and Pothast (1994) reported that female sexual offenders had higher levels of sexual needs in their relationships than male sexual offenders and that offenders generally felt less fulfilled in their sexual relationships. If women's needs are not being met in their adult relationships, this raises the question of whether abuse of children could be an attempt to fulfil missing needs, or an inappropriate attempt at seeking closeness. Gannon et al. (2008) identified a subgroup of women for whom the major goal of sexual offending appeared to be experiencing intimacy and warmth with either the victim or co-perpetrator. It is interesting to note the similarity this bears to the positive feelings ascribed to adult sexual experiences by non-offending women in Saradjian's (1996) work. Although there was variation, Saradjian also found that women who had sexually offended endorsed more positive statements about sex with children than they did about sex with adults.

In contrast to this possible intimacy goal, Russell and Oswald (2001) found that women who sexually coerced others were more likely to show a 'Ludic lovestyle' – a pattern of being emotionally uninvolved and manipulative in relationships, and preferring to be in control. When Saradjian (1996) asked women about their feelings during sexual activity with children, feelings of power and control were most frequently endorsed. Given their life experiences, however, some women may only have experienced physical closeness in situations in which there were abusive power inequalities, or intimacy may feel threatening if they do not hold control.

Female sexual offenders may therefore have a number of interpersonal difficulties for consideration in treatment. Gannon et al. (2008) suggest that female sexual offenders' responses to their relationship experiences play a key role in their offence process, via their contribution to risk factors such as social isolation, poor coping strategies and mental health difficulties. In addition, women's poor experiences and expectations of relationships may facilitate them being targeted by men who wish to coerce them into sexually abusive behaviour. Tewksbury (2004) found that almost 40 per cent of women on the Sexual Offender Registries in Indiana and Kentucky, USA, had lost a friend when their sexual offending became public knowledge. Vandiver, Cheeseman Dial and Worley (2008) similarly reported that sexual offender registry had the greatest effect on women's personal relationships. This may be a particularly hard consequence for women whose social support is often already very limited. Therefore, without help to develop skills to form appropriate relationships, as well as manage difficulties within them, women are likely to remain vulnerable.

Coping Skills

Given the high levels of adverse life experiences reported by women who sexually offend, it is important to understand how they have learned to cope, particularly as they may have had to do so against a backdrop of continued adversity, limited social support and negative beliefs about themselves and their own efficacy. Saradjian (1996) reported that women who sexually abuse children rate themselves as experiencing more stress than non-offenders, but as having fewer internal or external resources to manage this. Saradjian additionally observed that it was when women were not sexually abusing children that many reported indicators of psychological distress such as self-harm, depression or anxiety and researchers have postulated that women may use sex or sexual abuse in order to regulate negative emotions (Eldridge & Saradjian, 2000; Nathan & Ward, 2002). A similar sexual coping response has been proposed for non-offending women who were sexually abused as children; Merrill, Guimond, Thomsen and Milner (2003) suggested that some abused women use sex to escape from or lessen emotional distress. Growing up in abusive, violent and traumatic environments can impact on brain development, resulting in chaotic patterns of relating to others and difficulties in regulating emotions (Stien & Kendall, 2004). For some women, the act of sexually abusing could soothe heightened emotional states; Saradjian (1996) reported that among women who initially abused young children, the most commonly endorsed statement about their abusive activity was 'it gives me a release of tension and makes me feel calm' (p. 135).

A sexual coping style has also been identified in male sexual offenders. Cortoni and Marshall (2001) found that male sexual offenders reported using both deviant and non-deviant sexual activities to cope with stressful situations or negative emotional states. Higher levels of emotional loneliness and low ratings of intimate engagement with others were both associated with increased sexual activity to relieve the resulting negative feelings. The extent to which this may be true for female sexual offenders requires closer investigation; Feelgood, Cortoni and Thompson (2005) note that ineffective coping may lead to re-occurring cycles in which stressors are dealt with by ineffective coping strategies, resulting in increased negative emotion and further difficulties, but no effective method of managing these.

As women appear to have experienced a number of life stressors prior to sexually offending (Gannon et al., 2008), Denov and Cortoni (2006) suggest that treatment should focus on helping women develop coping patterns which will be beneficial across a variety of stressful situations. Clearly, life stressors do not disappear after treatment is completed. In Tewksbury's (2004) sample of registered female sexual offenders, 42 per cent of respondents ($n = 40$) lost their job and more than 30 per cent had lost or been denied somewhere to live or experienced harassment once their sexual offending was publicly known. The proportion of women reporting these consequences increased as time on the registry also increased, suggesting that these difficulties were longer-term ones. Although there was no comparison with the experiences of male sexual offenders, such experiences are clearly not beneficial, and highlight the importance of helping women develop coping methods effective for a broad range of stressors.

Enhancing women's belief in their self-efficacy must occur alongside this work. Saradjian (1996) noted that all the female sexual offenders in her sample believed themselves to have far less control over their own lives than other adults and even children. A similar theme appears in Beech et al.'s (2009) study, with the most frequent implicit theory in their sample of female sexual offenders concerning the uncontrollability of the world and events within it. This, the authors state, suggests that these women feel that their ability to control events or aspects of their lives is severely limited, although they query whether the findings reflect 'the way offenders actually interpreted their lives at the time of the offence. . .[or] a self-preservation mechanism in place as a result of the offence' (p. 210). Either way, to help women develop and feel able to adopt new ways of coping, they may also need to enhance their self-esteem and sense of personal agency in all aspects of their lives.

Mental Health Difficulties

Peter (2006) comments that the mental health of female sexual offenders has received frequent attention in the literature, while male sexual offenders 'have not been pathologised to the same extent' (p. 291). Perhaps this reflects attempts to understand how *women* could act in sexually deviant ways; as Allen (1991) notes, sexual abuse by women was once thought so rare that this behaviour in itself was taken to indicate psychiatric disturbance.

Research studies have yielded mixed results (see also Chapter 6). Some have reported high levels of mental health difficulties in female sexual offenders. For example, O'Connor (1987) reported that of women convicted of gross indecency with children and indecent assault on persons under 16, 48 per cent ($n = 12$) had a psychiatric diagnosis and history of psychiatric treatment. Green and Kaplan (1994) found that their female sexual offenders had a mean of 3.6 personality disorders each, compared with 2.4 for women imprisoned for non-sexual offences, with a diagnosis of *avoidant* or *dependent* personality disorder most likely. All the female sexual offenders showed post-traumatic stress disorder (PTSD) symptoms, which were attributed to past victimisation experiences. However, other researchers have not found high rates. In Saradjian's (1996) study, for example, only three women abused children while in a psychotic state and were described as 'atypical perpetrators'. The more 'typical' sexual offenders did not demonstrate psychotic symptoms. These discrepant findings are likely to be at least partly accounted for by wide methodological variation, including different diagnostic tools, different definitions of mental health difficulties and different samples.

Studies of female non-sexual offenders have also identified high rates of mental health concerns. Although often focussed on imprisoned women, who may not represent female sexual offenders as a whole, studies have suggested substance dependency to be common, as well as high rates of depressive and neurotic disorders (Messer, Maughan, Quinton & Taylor, 2004). Christopher, Lutz-Zois and Reinhardt (2007) found that personality disorder tendencies did not distinguish female sexual offenders and non-sexual offenders, while Fazel, Sjöstedt, Grann and Långström (2008) reported no significant differences in the prevalence of psychotic and substance dependence disorders between female sexual offenders and women who had committed other violent offences. The extent to which female sexual offenders differ from female non-sexual offenders in this respect is therefore uncertain.

Clearly, such studies do not always distinguish current mental health concerns or clarify whether such difficulties contributed to sexual offending, directly or indirectly. Gannon et al. (2008) provide an interesting example of the indirect contribution of poor mental health to sexual offending. They describe a woman whose husband prevented her taking her antidepressant medication, thereby precipitating further deterioration in her mental health and ability to cope, an increasing sense of isolation and greater susceptibility to her husband's sexual grooming. Fazel et al. (2008) found that compared with general population women, there was significantly increased risk among female sexual offenders of psychiatric hospitalisation and diagnosis of a psychotic or substance use disorder. However, female sexual offenders did not appear to differ from non-sexual female offenders on such aspects. This study suggests that professionals working with female sexual offenders should undertake a thorough assessment of any mental health difficulties. If these are present, they may require management before a woman can undertake treatment, particularly if these difficulties are severe. Ford and Cortoni (2008) caution that failure to address mental health issues significantly limits the extent to which a woman may be able to participate in treatment or the benefits she may gain if she does. In the Correctional Service Canada, these authors note that some women have demonstrated such profound mental health difficulties that treatment for their sexual offending was not feasible. Instead, intervention for these women focussed on providing psychiatric care and intensive support to help them manage their mental health problems.

A related issue is that of substance misuse. Although their sample may not have been representative as it comprised women specifically selected to undertake their treatment programme, Turner et al. (2008) identified a subset of female sexual offenders with elevated scores on scales measuring substance abuse problems. Aylward, Christopher, Newell and Gordon (2002) reported that 53 per cent ($n = 18$) of the abusive women in their sample had substance abuse problems, while Saradjian (1996) found no differences in substance abuse rates between women sexual offenders and non-sexual offender comparisons. In fact, there was a tendency for the comparison women to be heavier users. Nevertheless it is important that there is full individual assessment of substance usage, the needs it meets for women and any role it played in the offence. If usage is current, this may also require management prior to commencing treatment to ensure that it does not impact on a woman's ability to engage in and benefit from intervention.

Male Coercion/Dependency

While the literature presents differing opinions regarding the similarity between male and female sexual offending, there is some consensus that a distinguishing feature of female sexual offending is the presence of co-perpetrators, primarily male, in a proportion of offences. The actual proportion of co-perpetrators is not clear. Grayston and De Luca (1999), for example, stated that research fairly consistently finds female sexual offenders to be most likely to abuse with another offender, while Johansson-Love and Fremouw (2006) note that in the 13 studies they reviewed, only three found the majority of female sexual offenders to have a co-offender. For those assessing female sexual offenders' needs and offering treatment to them, it is important to be clear about whether women abused *in conjunction* with men or were *coerced*. Nathan and Ward (2002), for example, reported that most of the abusive women in their sample co-offended with men, but less than half reported coercion from them. Research findings are likely to be confounded by variation in the ease of establishing coercion versus co-perpetration and may be further confused by women who were initially coerced into sexual offending, but who subsequently offended independently. However, as this distinction may have influenced the woman's motivations, offence patterns and beliefs and attitudes, it is an important clarification to make.

Women who have been coerced into sexual offending have a number of difficulties for consideration in treatment. Current knowledge regarding their offence-supportive cognitions has been outlined previously. Another difficulty highlighted in the literature is the woman's dependence on the relationship with the coercive male. Eldridge and Saradjian (2000) noted that many women were excessively dependent or overly reliant on the coercive men in their lives, with some even placing their relationships with these men above those with their own children (Saradjian, 1996). The intense importance placed on these relationships may be linked with the social and relationship difficulties described previously. With already impoverished social support networks, women coerced by male partners may find these limited networks further eroded by the male himself; Gannon et al. (2008) noted that a common pattern was the gradual process of isolation from friends and family, orchestrated by the coercive male partner.

This gradual loss of sources of support, combined with difficulties in forming new relationships and negative beliefs about oneself are strong potential contributors to the importance attached to the relationship with a coercive male partner. Matthews (1993) described male-coerced women as feeling unloved and unlovable, expecting rejection and remaining in abusive relationships as they thought no one else would want them. Saradjian (1996) noted a trend for male-coerced women to believe that they had even less control over their lives than other female sexual offenders, a belief they largely attributed to their relationship with the coercive male. These difficulties may be further exacerbated by experiences of domestic abuse, which Gannon et al. (2008) reported to be present in a very large proportion of their sample, prior to the onset of sexual offending. While this was not exclusive to women coerced into sexual offending by males, Gannon et al. noted that some men targeted women who had been victims of domestic abuse, 'providing them with a false sense of security that would ironically place them at higher risk of sexually offending' (p. 362). In addition, the authors note, some men began desensitising women to inappropriate sexual behaviour through this violence. The fear engendered by some coercive males was clear in the accounts of women interviewed by Beech et al. (2009) and these fears comprised many of the Dangerous World implicit theories identified.

There is a clear need for relationship-focussed work for these women, along-side work to address their poor self-esteem, underassertion and low self-efficacy. Gannon and Rose (2008) further suggest that some women may require education about early signs that men are targeting them and their children. However, such education should take place in conjunction with the aforementioned work. Without help to build and maintain supportive relationships and enhance self-belief, iden-tification of such targeting alone may be insufficient. Belief in one's self-efficacy to deal with high-risk situations is an important variable in whether attempts to behave differently will be successful (Casey, Day & Howells, 2005). Without this, women may continue to feel that their world is an uncontrollable and dangerous place, perhaps particularly as far as men are concerned (Gannon et al., in press; Gannon & Rose, 2009).

Previous Victimisation

A very high proportion of sexually offending women report histories of sexual, physical or psychological abuse (e.g. Lewis & Stanley, 2000; Saradjian, 1996; Tardif, Auclair, Jacob & Carpentier, 2005; Travin, Cullen & Protter, 1990). Not only are high levels of abuse reported, but some women also received little support or recogni-tion of these experiences when they happened. Travin et al. (1990) noted that in many cases, the women's abuse experiences had been ignored or minimised by caregivers and the women themselves blamed. Saradjian (1996) also reported that among female sexual offenders who had been physically abused, less than half received appropriate treatment for their injuries, unless these were very serious. Although high levels of victimisation are also reported by female non-sexual of-fenders (Blanchette & Brown, 2006), there are suggestions that these experiences are more severe in sexual offenders (Grayston & De Luca, 1999). Christopher et al. (2007) found that women imprisoned for sexual offences against children not only reported more frequent instances of child sexual abuse than women imprisoned for non-sexual offences, but had also suffered this abuse for significantly longer time periods.

Past abuse experiences are presented as a treatment need because of their potential to impact on many of the other needs discussed in this chapter. Abusive experiences may have impacted on the development of the woman's self-concept, mental health, ability to empathise with her own victims or relationship formation, potentially influencing not just the woman's functioning within the community, but also in the therapeutic relationship (Ford & Cortoni, 2008). Previous victimisation may also have shaped her coping patterns, whether or not these have a sexual aspect. Merrill et al. (2003) cite studies which have noted an association between the severity of sexual abuse and greater use of maladaptive coping strategies. As stated previously, sexual abuse experiences may have been particularly severe among female sexual offenders. Sexual abuse may also have impacted on the woman's developing sexuality and her experience and beliefs about sexual relationships and herself as a sexual being. Meston, Rellini and Heiman (2006) found that women with a history of childhood sexual abuse showed greater levels of negative sexual affect (such as anger, fear or disgust) than women with no abuse history, which accords with the negative feelings reported by sexual offending women in Saradjian's (1996) sample when they described their adult sexual experiences.

While understanding the impact of a female sexual offender's own abuse and helping her to address issues arising from it are legitimate treatment targets, Denov and Cortoni (2006) caution against this taking precedence over her abusive sexual behaviour. However, Ward and Moreton (2008) contend that treatment programmes should be able to address both. While not considering women specifically, they state that a goal of treatment should be to help offenders understand how life experiences have influenced their development and functioning and to identify changes required to help them lead better future lives. Focusing solely on offence issues, they state, potentially signifies to the offender that their own abuse experiences are not important, a response which may inadvertently mirror the disregard others showed to some women at the time of their own abuse. Instead, 'giving the offender an opportunity to talk about his or her own victimisation issues can help him or her to become more ethically attuned to those of his or her victim and pave the way for accepting responsibility' (p. 318).

CONCLUSIONS

This chapter has not intended to map out a comprehensive list of treatment targets, or give details of specific programmes, as this is available elsewhere (e.g. Chapter 8; Ford, 2006; Ford & Cortoni, 2008; Gannon & Rose, 2008). Instead, this chapter has highlighted a number of potential treatment targets for female sexual offenders. In some ways, the identified needs overlap broadly with the treatment needs of male sexual offenders, an unsurprising finding, given that the offences committed by females and the processes through which they are achieved do not necessarily diverge entirely from abusive acts committed by males (Kaufman, Wallace, Johnson & Reeder, 1995; Nathan & Ward, 2001). However, similar behaviours do not automatically constitute similar treatment needs. Within the broadly similar target areas we need to explore potential gender differences and consider how to address these in our interventions (see Chapter 10). For example, research has suggested both similarities, but also important areas of divergence, in male and female sexual offenders' offence-supportive beliefs. Despite some convergence in overall belief categories, important gender differences were observed in specific category contents (Beech et al., 2009). Furthermore, Gannon et al. (2008) noted that like their male counterparts, women hold either approach or avoidant goals towards sexual offending. However, both women's goals, and the steps taken to achieve them, were subtly different to those of males. Other broad areas of similarity such as deficits in coping skills need to be contextualised in previous life experiences, as these may differ between male and female sexual offenders. Therefore, similarity in areas of need should not necessarily be interpreted as identical needs, either in terms of specific treatment targets or methods used to address them. A key message from this chapter is that further research is needed, particularly to determine the *specific* treatment needs of women.

Gannon and Rose (2008) stress that each female sexual offender has individual circumstances, motivators and attitudes that contribute to her sexual offending, clearly pointing to the importance of an individual case formulation and treatment plan. However, we lack a strong theoretical perspective to guide us in this and there are few female-specific assessment measures to help us identify needs, or monitor treatment progress. This is not specific to female sexual offenders; Blanchette and Brown (2006) state that further work is needed to determine how to identify general women offender's needs. However, these limitations may be even truer of the sexual offender group, for whom the entire research endeavour is comparatively new and has tended to focus only on particular areas.

A female sexual offender discussing her treatment experiences commented that, 'treatment is not geared for women' (Vandiver et al., 2008, p. 190) and it is important to consider the extent to which she could be right. The difficulties described above potentially leave clinicians in a position of uncertainty, wondering exactly what the content of their programme should be and how to deliver it, to ensure that their intervention *is* geared for women. Levenson, Macgowan, Morin and Cotter (2009) caution that 'treatment programmes all too often provide similar services to diverse populations, perhaps diluting the effectiveness of the services' (p. 39). The absence of female-specific theoretical development perhaps places us at risk of this, as we have had little choice but to draw on models from other offender groups. However, Gannon and Rose (2008) argue that progress will continue to be hampered unless researchers desist from using measures and theories derived from male sexual offenders. Even Beech et al.'s recent (2009) study allocated female data to male-derived categories, rather than independently categorising the women's data and then comparing it with male studies. While their aim was to examine whether male sexual offender categories fitted female sexual offenders and record any gender differences, attempting to slot female data into a predetermined male framework could sideline important aspects of women's experiences. Furthermore, Gannon and Rose suggest that using male models and methods to inform treatment of women, without fully understanding the (in)appropriateness of this, risks damaging the therapeutic relationship and limiting the effectiveness of treatment.

We need to understand more about the process of delivering treatment to women. Saradjian (1996), for example, states that therapy raises many emotional difficulties for female sexual offenders, for which they may need support to manage, particularly given their potential difficulties with emotion regulation. As the social supports and networks of female sexual offenders are also often very limited and they may have to undertake treatment individually without support from other group members, it may be important to ensure that support is available for women prior to treatment (Saradjian, 1996). Therefore, not only do we need to better understand the specific treatment needs of women, but also the most effective processes of meeting those needs.

Currently, it is hard to know how well we are doing. Establishing outcome is hampered by small offender numbers, variation in programme content, methods or format, few female-specific measures on which to plot change and low female sexual recidivism (Cortoni, Hanson & Coache, 2009), which indicates that much larger sample sizes than those currently available are needed to evaluate this effectively. However, it is essential that we are able to effectively evaluate our interventions for women, particularly if we believe that they should not unquestioningly follow the format of the better-evidenced male sexual offender programmes.

In summary, then, our knowledge of the treatment needs of female sexual offenders remains basic and further research is required across the entire treatment process. We need to better understand the process through which women come to sexually offend, their specific treatment needs and to ascertain gender-appropriate means of identifying these. Alongside this, we need to further investigate treatment approaches for women and how identified needs can be most effectively addressed through intervention. However, this must be underpinned by the development of theory which should guide us in these other aspects of our work.

REFERENCES

Allen, C. M. (1991). *Women and men who sexually abuse children: A comparative analysis.* Brandon, VT: The Safer Society Press.

Allen, C. M., & Pothast, H. L. (1994). Distinguishing characteristics of male and female child sex abusers. *Journal of Offender Rehabilitation, 21*(1–2), 73–88.

Aylward, A., Christopher, M., Newell, R. M., & Gordon, A. (2002, October). What about women who commit sex offences? Paper presented at the 22nd Annual Research and Treatment Conference, Association for the Treatment of Sexual Abusers, Montréal, QC, Canada.

Beckett, R. (1987). *The children and sex questionnaire.* (Available from Richard Beckett, The Oxford Clinic, Littlemore Health Centre, Sandford Road, Littlemore, Oxford OX4 4XN, UK)

Beckett, R. C. (2005). What are the characteristics of female sex offenders? *NOTA News, 51,* 6–7.

Beckett, R. C., & Fisher, D. (1994, November). *Assessing victim empathy: A new measure.* Paper presented at the Conference of the Association for the Treatment of Sexual Abusers, San Francisco, USA.

Beech, A. R., Parrett, N., Ward, T., & Fisher, D. (2009). Assessing female sexual offenders' motivations and cognitions: An exploratory study. *Psychology, Crime & Law, 15,* 201–216.

Blanchette, K., & Brown, S. L. (2006). *The assessment and treatment of women offenders.* Chichester, UK: John Wiley & Sons.

Casey, S., Day, A., & Howells, K. (2005). The application of the transtheoretical model to offender populations: Some critical issues. *Legal and Criminological Psychology, 10,* 157–171.

Christopher, K., Lutz-Zois, C. J., & Reinhardt, A. R. (2007). Female sexual offenders: Personality pathology as a mediator of the relationship between childhood sexual abuse history and sexual perpetration against others. *Child Abuse & Neglect, 31,* 871–883.

Cortoni, F., Hanson, R. K., & Coache, M. E. (2009). *The recidivism rates of female sexual offenders are low: A meta-analysis.* Manuscript submitted for publication.

Cortoni, F., & Marshall, W. L. (2001). Sex as a coping strategy and its relationship to juvenile sexual history and intimacy in sexual offenders. *Sexual Abuse: A Journal of Research and Treatment, 13,* 27–43.

Denov, M. S., & Cortoni, F. (2006). Adult female sexual offenders. In C. Hilarski & J. Wodarski (Eds.), *Comprehensive mental health practices with sex offenders and their families* (pp. 71–99). New York: Haworth Press.

Eldridge, H. J., & Saradjian, J. (2000). Replacing the function of abusive behaviours for the offender: Remaking relapse prevention in working with women who sexually abuse children. In D. R. Laws, S. M. Hudson, & T. Ward (Eds.), *Remaking relapse prevention with sex offenders: A sourcebook* (pp. 402–426). Thousand Oaks, CA: Sage.

Fazel, S., Sjöstedt, G., Grann, M., & Långström, N. (2008). Sexual offending in women and psychiatric disorder: A national case-control study. *Archives of Sexual Behavior.* E-publication ahead of print.

Feelgood, S., Cortoni, F., & Thompson, A. (2005). Sexual coping, general coping and cognitive distortions in incarcerated rapists and child molesters. *Journal of Sexual Aggression, 11,* 157–170.

Ford, H. (2006). *Women who sexually abuse children.* Chichester, UK: John Wiley & Sons.

Ford, H. J., & Cortoni, F. (2008). Assessment and treatment of sexual deviance in females. In D. R. Laws, S. M. Hudson, & W. O'Donohue (Eds.), *Sexual deviance* (2nd ed., pp. 508–526). New York: The Guilford Press.

Fromuth, M. E., & Conn, V. E. (1997). Hidden perpetrators: Sexual molestation in a nonclinical sample of college women. *Journal of Interpersonal Violence, 12,* 456–465.

Gannon, T. A., & Rose, M. R. (2008). Female child sexual offenders: Towards integrating theory and practice. *Aggression and Violent Behavior, 13,* 442–461.

Gannon, T. A., & Rose, M. R. (2009). Offence-related interpretative bias in female child molesters: A preliminary study. *Sexual Abuse: A Journal of Research and Treatment, 21,* 194–207.

Gannon, T. A., Hoare, J., Rose, M. R., & Parrett, N. (in press). *A re-examination of female child molesters' implicit theories: Evidence of female specificity? Psychology Crime and Law.*

Gannon, T. A., Rose, M. R., & Ward, T. (2008). A descriptive model of the offence process for female sexual offenders. *Sexual Abuse: A Journal of Research and Treatment, 20,* 352–374.

Gannon, T. A., Rose, M. R., & Williams, S. E. (2009). Do female child molesters implicitly associate children and sex? A preliminary investigation. *Journal of Sexual Aggression, 15,* 55–61.

Grayston, A. D., & De Luca, R. V. (1999). Female perpetrators of child sexual abuse: A review of the clinical and empirical literature. *Aggression and Violent Behavior, 4,* 93–106.

Green, A. H., & Kaplan, M. S. (1994). Psychiatric impairment and childhood victimization experiences in female child molesters. *Journal of The American Academy Of Child and Adolescent Psychiatry, 33,* 954–961.

Johansson-Love, J., & Fremouw, W. (2006). A critique of the female sexual perpetrator research. *Aggression and Violent Behavior, 11,* 12–26.

Kaufman, K. L., Wallace, A. M., Johnson, C. E., & Reeder, M. L. (1995). Comparing male and female perpetrators' modus operandi: Victims' reports of sexual abuse. *Journal of Interpersonal Violence, 10,* 322–333.

Laws, D. R., Hanson, R. K., Osborn, C. A., & Greenbaum, P. E. (2000). Classification of child molesters by plethysmographic assessment of sexual arousal and a self-report measure of sexual preference. *Journal of Interpersonal Violence, 15,* 1297–1312.

Levenson, J. S., Macgowan, M. J., Morin, J. W., & Cotter, L. P. (2009). Perceptions of sex offenders about treatment: Satisfaction and engagement in group therapy. *Sexual Abuse: A Journal of Research and Treatment, 21*, 35–56.

Lewis, C. F., & Stanley, C. R. (2000). Women accused of sexual offences. *Behavioral Sciences And The Law, 18*, 73–81.

Marziano, V., Ward, T., Beech, A. R., & Pattison, R. (2006). Identification of five fundamental implicit theories underlying cognitive distortions in child abusers: A preliminary study. *Psychology, Crime & Law, 12*, 97–105.

Matthews, J. K. (1993). Working with female sexual abusers. In M. Elliott (Ed.), *Female sexual abuse of children: The ultimate taboo* (pp. 61–78). Chichester, UK: John Wiley & Sons.

Merrill, L. L., Guimond, J. M., Thomsen, C. J., & Milner, J. S. (2003). Child sexual abuse and number of sexual partners in young women: The role of abuse severity, coping style and sexual functioning. *Journal of Consulting and Clinical Psychology, 71*, 987–996.

Messer, J., Maughan, B., Quinton, D., & Taylor, A. (2004). Precursors and correlates of criminal behaviour in women. *Criminal Behaviour and Mental Health, 14*, 82–107.

Meston, C. M., Rellini, A. H., & Heiman, J. R. (2006). Women's history of sexual abuse, their sexuality, and sexual self-schemas. *Journal of Consulting and Clinical Psychology, 74*, 229–236.

Nathan, P., & Ward, T. (2001). Females who sexually abuse children: Assessment and treatment issues. *Psychiatry, Psychology and Law, 8*, 44 55.

Nathan, P., & Ward, T. (2002). Female sex offenders: Clinical and demographic features. *The Journal of Sexual Aggression, 8*, 5–21.

O'Connor, A. A. (1987). Female sex offenders. *British Journal of Psychiatry, 150*, 615–620.

Peter, T. (2006). Mad, bad or victim? Making sense of mother–daughter sexual abuse. *Feminist Criminology, 1*, 283–302.

Ring, L. (2005). *Psychometric profiles of female sexual abusers: A preliminary analysis into the differences between sexually abusive and non-offending females.* Unpublished MSc thesis, The University of Birmingham, UK.

Russell, B. L., & Oswald, D. L. (2001). Strategies and dispositional correlates of sexual coercion perpetrated by women: An exploratory investigation. *Sex Roles, 45*(1–2), 103–115.

Saradjian, J. (1996). *Women who sexually abuse children: From research to clinical practice.* Chichester, UK: John Wiley & Sons.

Stien, P. T., & Kendall, J. (2004). *Psychological trauma and the developing brain.* New York: The Haworth Maltreatment and Trauma Press.

Strickland, S. M. (2008). Female sex offenders: Exploring issues of personality, trauma and cognitive distortions. *Journal of Interpersonal Violence, 23*, 474–489.

Tardif, M., Auclair, N., Jacob, M., & Carpentier, J. (2005). Sexual abuse perpetrated by adult and juvenile females: An ultimate attempt to resolve a conflict associated with maternal identity. *Child Abuse & Neglect, 29*, 153–167.

Tewksbury, R. (2004). Experiences and attitudes of registered female sex offenders. *Federal Probation, 68*, 30–33.

Travin, S., Cullen, K., & Protter, B. (1990). Female sex offenders: Severe victims and victimisers. *Journal of Forensic Sciences, 35*, 140–150.

Turner, K., Miller, H. A., & Henderson, C. E. (2008). Latent profile analyses of offense and personality characteristics in a sample of incarcerated female sexual offenders. *Criminal Justice and Behavior, 35*, 879–894.

Vandiver, D. M., Cheeseman Dial, K., & Worley, R. M. (2008). A qualitative assessment of registered female sex offenders: Judicial processing experiences and perceived effects of a public registry. *Criminal Justice Review, 33*, 177–198.

Ward, T., & Keenan, T. (1999). Child molesters' implicit theories. *Journal of Interpersonal Violence, 14*, 821–838.

Ward, T., & Moreton, G. (2008). Moral repair with offenders: Ethical issues arising from victimisation experiences. *Sexual Abuse: A Journal of Research and Treatment, 20*, 305–322.

Chapter 8

A REVIEW OF TREATMENT INITIATIVES FOR FEMALE SEXUAL OFFENDERS

KELLEY BLANCHETTE AND KELLY N. TAYLOR

Correctional Services Canada, Ottawa, Ontario, Canada

There is clear consensus that correctional practice should be informed by sound empirical research. While it has been repeatedly acknowledged that the evidence base supporting women's corrections is sparse relative to that for men, nowhere is it more apparent than in the area of sexual offenders. The vast majority of sex crimes are committed by men (Cortoni & Hanson, 2005; Cortoni, Hanson & Coache, 2009; Vandiver & Walker, 2002). Consequently, sexual offender assessment and intervention strategies have been developed and implemented for the male prototype, with little or no consideration of potential female-specific risk and need factors.

The dearth of knowledge pertaining to the female sexual offender imposes some significant challenges for gender appropriate assessment and intervention. For example, there is no valid and reliable actuarial measure available for specific application to female sexual offenders. There is solid evidence supporting the use of such assessments for male offenders (Rice & Harris, 2002); however, their relevance to women is dubious at best, especially in light of research suggesting that the aetiology of sexual offending varies by gender, as do the risk markers and proposed intervention strategies (Center for Sex Offender Management, 2007; Gannon & Rose, 2008). The lack of research supporting structured assessment specifically for female sexual offenders disadvantages the interventionist from the outset.

In the absence of robust research findings supporting assessment and intervention strategies for female sexual offenders, we need to reconcile what we know works for female offenders in general (Blanchette & Brown, 2006; Bloom, Owen & Covington, 2003) with the research, albeit embryonic, on female *sexual*

Note: The views expressed in this chapter are those of the authors and do not necessarily reflect those of Correctional Services of Canada. Direct correspondence to Kelley Blanchette or Kelly Taylor, National Headquarters, Correctional Service of Canada, 340 Laurier Avenue West, Ottawa, Ontario, Canada K1A 0P9 (e-mail: blanchettekd@csc-scc.gc.ca and/or taylorke@csc-scc.gc.ca).

Female Sexual Offenders: Theory, Assessment, and Treatment Edited by Theresa A. Gannon and Franca Cortoni
© 2010 John Wiley & Sons, Ltd

offenders in particular. An amalgamation of general correctional research on women with that pertaining to female sexual offenders in particular yields the following considerations for the provision of gender-informed services for female sexual offenders:

- The aetiology of female sex offending is different than that for their male counterparts – women have gendered pathways into offending in general and sexual offending in particular and therefore *gender* should be central to guiding women *out of* sexual offending (Blanchette & Brown, 2006; Gannon, Rose & Ward, 2008; Oliver, 2007);
- Female-perpetrated sexual offences are more likely to occur within the context of caregiving situations (Centre for Sex Offender Management, 2007; Grayston & DeLuca, 1999) and with an opposite-sex co-perpetrator (Grayston & DeLuca, 1999; Travin, Cullen & Protter, 1990; cited in Nathan & Ward, 2001, 2002);
- Females in the criminal justice system generally present with an interrelated set of needs: substance abuse, victimisation/traumatic history and mental health needs. The holistic approach is best to integrate multiple needs into intervention services for women (Bloom et al., 2003);
- Interventions should target deficits in important interpersonal, self-regulation (including emotion regulation) and distress tolerance skills – primary features of borderline personality disorder (BPD). Women account for the vast majority (about 75 per cent) of BPD diagnoses (American Psychiatric Association, 2000) and its prevalence is significantly more pronounced in female prison populations (Nee & Farman, 2005); and
- Correctional treatment paradigms for females should be informed, at least in part, by relational theory (Miller, 1986); interventions should assist girls and women to establish and maintain pro-social, supportive and equitable relationships.

Fortunately, some jurisdictions are modifying or tailoring sexual offender interventions to be more responsive to females; others are recognising the unique risk and need considerations for females and developing programmes from the ground up. This chapter provides an overview of the variety of services and treatment initiatives available for females who sexually offend. In brief, our descriptions were obtained through contact with an extensive network of individuals working in the domain of female sexual offenders – most notably female *child* sexual offenders – in various jurisdictions. It is anticipated that this is a relatively complete overview of gender-specific initiatives; however, this does not preclude the possibility that additional programmes, services and initiatives, specific to female sexual offenders, are actively being undertaken in jurisdictions outside of those discussed in this chapter. The chapter focuses on services provided in the UK and Canada, with a more brief discussion of developing initiatives in other jurisdictions in the USA (Texas, Colorado and New York). It will conclude with a very brief critical appraisal of current initiatives and will offer some recommendations for elements that should be incorporated into intervention paradigms for female sexual offenders.

EXISTING ASSESSMENT AND TREATMENT INITIATIVES FOR FEMALE SEXUAL OFFENDERS

Correctional Services Canada

In Canada, adult offenders sentenced to less than 2 years in prison fall under provincial jurisdiction while those sentenced to 2 years or more fall under federal jurisdiction and are the responsibility of Correctional Services of Canada (CSC). Women who sexually offend comprise a very small (less than 0.5 per cent) but visible proportion of federally sentenced sexual offenders. In recent years, at any given time, there have been about 14–20 federally sentenced female sexual offenders, dispersed across the country's vast expanse.

The *Assessment and Treatment Protocol for Women Who Sexually Offend* represents Canada's first attempt to provide a structured and gender-specific approach to the identification, assessment and treatment of women who sexually offend. The approach provides the direction and structure to ensure that the assessment and delivery of treatment and maintenance will be timely and based on sound learning principles. The treatment approach was designed for either individual or small group delivery; historically it has been more often the former. While no formal evaluation exists, the protocol is hailed to improve efficiency of treatment delivery and offer a gradual and smooth transition from prison to the community.

Staff Training

Staff training involves 1 week to review programme content and the history of the development of sexual offender treatment, research on females who sexually offend, issues surrounding assessment of women in general and sexual offenders more specifically, as well as a detailed examination of each treatment module. Opportunity for feedback and discussion are built into the staff training.

Assessment Services

Assessment is based on a timely, thorough and multi-modal approach, evaluating both sexual offender specific and general treatment needs, thereby treating each woman within a client-centred and holistic approach. Although five treatment modules are available, a comprehensive analysis of personal and crime-specific issues determine which modules best meet the needs of each offender. Thus, each woman is only referred to complete those sexual offender-specific modules matched to her identified needs.

CSC recognises the importance of assessment before any correctional plan can be formulated. While a comprehensive assessment is completed upon the offender's admission to federal custody, there is also continuous re-assessment: pre-treatment, in-treatment, post-treatment, follow-up, pre-release and post-release while under community supervision.

The comprehensive offender assessment conducted at admission generally includes (but is not limited to): (1) file reviews; (2) interviews and/or documentation from collateral contacts; (3) clinical interviews; (4) psychological/psychometric testing; (5) behavioural assessments; and (6) specialised sexual offender assessment.

File reviews include a review of information on the offender's file such as police and pre-sentence reports, victim impact statements, psychological and psychiatric reports, judge's comments/reasons for sentence, community assessment and any previous assessment or treatment reports. Any additional information on file that could be relevant to the intake assessment process is also included for consideration. The offender's caseworker (in consultation with the psychologist) conducts the file review and determines whether there is a need to include further contact with collateral sources.

Clinical interviews involve face-to-face interaction between the offender and the psychologist. They are generally semi-structured and follow a standard interview protocol, which has been developed specifically for female sexual offender assessment. The information informing the standardised structure of the clinical interview was derived from two primary sources: (1) a comprehensive review of existing female sexual offender case files; and (2) a literature review of salient factors for sexual offenders in general and female sexual offenders in particular (albeit sparse).

Psychological/psychometric tests may be used to provide information relevant to: mental ability, neuro-psychological functioning, personality, attitudes and cognitive distortions or specific treatment targets. Additional or different tests may be administered, depending on the perceived needs/deficit areas of the offender. The core battery of psychometric instruments was established according to available literature and understanding (as per file review) of issues for women who sexually offend. The psychometric evaluation takes place both pre- and post-treatment to assess changes on the treatment targets. The six standard psychometric tests include the following:

1. *Rosenberg Self-Esteem Inventory* (Rosenberg, 1965) to assess self-worth. The concept of self-worth is linked to self-efficacy, an important component in the successful implementation and maintenance of change;
2. *Miller Social Intimacy Scale* to assess the level of intimacy the client usually has in her relationship with either her romantic partner or her closest friend. Intimacy deficits are hypothesised to have a link with sexual aggression in women offenders (see Chapter 7);
3. *U.C.L.A. Loneliness Scale* (Russell, Peplau & Ferguson, 1978). In general literature, emotional loneliness is linked to interpersonal violence (e.g. Ireland & Power, 2004);
4. *Bumby Rape and Molest Scales* (1996) – These scales assess the extent of the presence of cognitive distortions that justify sexual offending. The Rape scale assesses distortions related to the sexual assault of adult victims, while the Molest scale assesses distortions that justify sexual activity with children. The Bumby scales were developed for male sexual offenders. CSC has modified the scales in the assessment, with the author's permission, to make them relevant for female offenders who have committed sexual offences;

5. *Coping Inventory for Stressful Situations* (CISS; Endler & Parker, 1999). Coping is a central concept in general self-management. The CISS provides a measure of one's ability to engage in more effective coping while reducing one's reliance on emotion-oriented or avoidance coping patterns;
6. *Paulhus Deception Scales* (1998) help to identify whether the respondent is forthright (to herself and to others) in her responses. As such, it serves as a social desirability check on the psychometric assessment to help establish the likely validity of the responses on the rest of the assessment battery.

Behavioural assessments are based on clinical observations from the psychologist and staff members as well as the woman's self-monitoring reports. In addition, structured role-play scenarios may be used to provide information on sexual fantasies/thoughts, social functioning and communication skills.

The specialised sexual offender assessment focuses on across a range of areas: family history, history and development of sexual behaviour (early role models, physical, emotional and sexual abuse history, sexual development and sexual relationships), attitudes and cognitive distortions, social competence, medical/ psychiatric history, prior violent (non-sexual) offences, prior sexual offences, current sexual offence(s) including gender and ages of victims and relationship to victims, involvement of co-offender(s) and nature of the relationship with the co-offender(s), use of alcohol and/or drugs prior to the commission of the offence, prior assessment and treatment results and compliance with post-treatment recommendations, relationships with partner and children, emotional expressiveness and emotional regulation, presence of deviant sexual fantasies/thoughts and their intensity and frequency, and other relevant information. Notably, these areas are derived primarily from the literature on sexual offenders in general.

Once the comprehensive sexual offender intake assessment process is summarised, a case-specific correctional plan is developed within 4 weeks. Issues such as duration and frequency of sexual offender therapy (in consideration of the woman's sentence length) are also determined. If there is more than one female sexual offender in a correctional facility at a given time, group therapy is the preferred option. Unfortunately, logistical problems (e.g. different treatment needs, inmate incompatibilities, security issues) often preclude that possibility, so treatment for women sexual offenders is normally delivered one-on-one.

Treatment

CSC's *Sex Offender Therapy for Women* is available at all federal women's institutions, as well as in the community for those under federal supervision.[1] It is based on cognitive-behavioural theory, though grounded in a relational context. The primary goals of treatment for women who sexually offend are to learn to identify the factors that influenced their offences, and to learn how to deal more effectively with them, in order to both reduce offending and increase the probability of leading more satisfying, pro-social lives. This approach is borrowed from

[1] At any given time, about half of Canadian federally sentenced women are incarcerated; the remainder are completing their sentences in the community under supervision (parole or statutory release).

positive psychology (Seligman, 2002; as cited in Ward & Brown, 2004), emphasising strength-based approaches to assessing and treating offenders, female offenders in particular (Sorbello, Eccleston, Ward & Jones, 2002; Van Wormer, 2001; Ward & Brown, 2004).

Programme modules were developed by a psychologist working with female sexual offenders. In conjunction with a literature review on sexual offending in general (based primarily on male offenders), a comprehensive literature review on female offender treatment (general and sexual offender), in addition to a review of female sexual offender files, informed the development of the treatment paradigm.

As noted earlier, there are five specific modules, though women are referred only to those seen as relevant to their particular needs. Together, the five modules comprise up to 70 therapeutic sessions. Each session is generally of 1 hour in length, although this may be reduced or increased in accordance with case-specific/clinical factors. Given the individualised presentation of each module, a rate of delivery of one to two sessions per week is recommended to allow for integration of treatment material and completion of homework. Below, each of the five modules is described, as outlined in the Protocol for Assessment and Treatment (CSC, 2001).

Self-management (14 sessions)   This module is designed to help each woman to understand her history and crime progression as a means of finding alternate ways to cope with factors that precipitated her offence(s). The first component of this module examines her autobiography in detail. This process allows the therapist and client to explore her early family history, education, friendships, relationships, work background, criminal history and abuse history amongst other topics. This slow process of developing understanding of the offender's background also contributes to establishment of the therapeutic alliance, an essential component of therapeutic change (Horvath & Symonds, 1991; Marshall et al., 2003).

The second component of this module examines the offence progression, focusing on the thoughts, feelings and behaviours that led up to her offence(s). Issues such as deviant arousal and fantasy, unsatisfactory relationships, cognitive distortions, lack of victim empathy, diminished ability to control alcohol and drug use, and situational factors (opportunity) may have contributed to her offence. Finally, through the detailed analysis of distal, proximal and perpetuating factors, the client is guided in the development of a plan to reduce future offending.

Deviant arousal (up to 25 sessions)   For a small proportion of women sexual offenders, deviant thoughts/fantasies may occur prior to and during offending. This is determined through self-report and self-monitoring. In this module, specific strategies for reducing and/or eliminating deviant arousal are explored. These include covert sensitisation, orgasmic reconditioning, thought-stopping and olfactory reconditioning. In all cases, an alternate and competing adult-based fantasy is developed. Successful completion of this module is also expected to enhance empathy and decrease cognitive distortions. As noted earlier, however, women only complete those modules relevant to their needs, as per the comprehensive assessment.

Cognitive distortions (11 sessions) This module examines cognitive distortions and normalises them, since they are a commonly used coping strategy (Maruna & Mann, 2006). Both common and offence-specific cognitive distortions are considered and the flaws in each are examined through discussion and guidance. Ultimately, the client will develop her own alternate ways to interpret events/behaviour. This process is referred to as cognitive restructuring and is a common element in cognitive therapies. This module should also impact on deviant arousal and intimacy difficulties. It is anticipated that at programme completion, the client will espouse fewer cognitive distortions and will have the ability to challenge those that do arise.

Intimacy, relationships and social functioning (9 sessions) Since most women who sexually offend have co-offended with a male partner, often acceding to his victim choice, resolution of relationship issues is of paramount importance.[2] In addition, the majority of women have experienced physical, sexual and emotional abuse at the hands of intimate family members and/or strangers. This module examines a range of intimate relationships, past relationships, what constitutes healthy and unhealthy relationships, coping with self-esteem deficits, jealousy/possessiveness and loneliness.

Empathy and victim awareness (10 sessions) This module involves two main phases. One focuses on the development of generalised empathy skills, while the other is specific to deficits in understanding the impact of sexual assault on victims. The development of empathic skills examines blocks to empathy, decoding others' feelings, understanding how others might interpret events, imagining how one might feel in those circumstances and showing support for others. These skills involve perception, cognition, emotion and behavioural enactment. The second component focuses on helping the client to understand how both primary and secondary victims experience sexual assault (utilising film and authentic letters from victims). The client is also asked to write a letter of responsibility (hypothetical) as well as a response from their victim to that letter. Finally, role-plays are used to give the client an opportunity to act out the part of her own victim (post-assault) as well as the friend of her victim. This module should impact on other modules such as cognitive distortions, intimacy and deviant arousal.

Evaluation of the Program Strategy for Women Sexual Offenders is hampered by the extremely small numbers (small sample sizes), lack of appropriate control or comparison group, low base rate of reoffending for female offenders in general (Gobeil & Barrett, 2008) and extremely low base rate of re-offending for female sexual offenders in particular (Cortoni et al., 2009). While CSC administers pre- and post-treatment assessments (and programme evaluation materials), no formal evaluation of the programme has been completed to date.

The *Assessment and Treatment Protocol for Women who Sexually Offend* is currently under revision. Canada's existing paradigm is relatively progressive, in that it is gender- and trauma-informed and incorporates elements of Relational Theory

---

[2] CSC's data (2001) indicate that 80 per cent of women sex offenders committed their offence(s) with a male co-perpetrator.

(Miller, 1986) and the Good Lives Model (Ward & Stewart, 2003) in its approach. However, feedback from treatment providers has clearly indicated that the module on deviant sexual arousal is not relevant for most women. Additionally, it is likely that emphasis will be placed on assertiveness training and co-dependency, given the high proportion of women who co-offend with a male partner. Finally, there is newer literature on women's pathways to crime and on the assessment and treatment of female offenders in general (Blanchette & Brown, 2006) which will be used to inform the revised approach. Consideration of these elements in the programme revision will address some of the shortcomings in the current model.

Lucy Faithfull Foundation (Birmingham and Epsom, England[3])

The Lucy Faithfull Foundation (LFF) is a child protection charity, which specialises in work around issues of sexual harm (see Chapter 10). LFF works with survivors and perpetrators of sexual abuse including adult males, adolescent males, children and families, adolescent females and adult females. Accordingly, the LFF has teams with suitable specialisations. The LFF has been working with female sexual offenders since 1993. In doing so, staff are cognisant of the existence of unique needs of female sexual offenders and are therefore dedicated to the delivery of treatment services that are gender-specific and thereby responsive to the distinctive needs of women.

The LFF serves its clients through a number of different treatment initiatives and services, including, but not limited to, the provision of: (1) assessment services; (2) treatment; (3) consultation services; and (4) staff training. The LFF is also committed to ongoing collaboration with partners working in areas pertaining to female sex offenders (e.g. researchers from the University of Birmingham as well as other academic and non-academic researchers). A wide variety of clients is typically referred to the LFF by family courts, child welfare services, the prison service, local authorities and/or other criminal justice agencies or partners.

Assessment Services

Referrals received from the family courts or child welfare services are typically related to women who may not have convictions, but where allegations have been made, where the woman has admitted to sexual offending, or where there are findings of fact in the family courts. In these instances, the required service is typically for assessment purposes. The focus of the assessment often pertains to the risk of harm that the woman may present to the children for whom she is a primary caregiver. This type of assessment is often integrated with a corresponding assessment of other significant family members, including children.

As suggested earlier in this chapter (see also Chapter 6), there is a dearth of knowledge in terms of gender-specific risk assessment. In turn, for LFF, the

[3] http://www.lucyfaithfull.org/home.aspx.

assessment focuses primarily on instructions provided by the referral agent. This type of service is typically short-term in that a standard assessment can be completed over a 6-hour period. In completing these assessments, LFF incorporates issues such as the impact of previous sexual abuse, the client's understanding of sexual abuse, her ability to protect and sustain appropriate sexual boundaries inside and outside the home, and so on. The assessment content is designed to suit the individual woman and her circumstances against a background of information from the child sexual abuse field about what constitutes risk of harm to children. A structured framework is used that includes collecting information about the woman's history, her psychological strengths and vulnerabilities, any trigger factors for past abusive behaviours and her current family circumstances including external risk and protective factors. The LFF takes an integrated approach to assessment, which includes careful consideration of other family members. Following this assessment, an analysis of the information gathered is used in evaluating the risk of harm to the child. Each assessment seeks to identify individual risk and protective factors significant to that individual case.

When required, staff from LFF attend court, in an expert witness capacity, and are asked to describe and defend their professional assessment. In the absence of gender-specific actuarial assessment tools, the challenge faced as an expert witness is intensified. The outcome of the court proceedings will normally determine whether the woman is able to take care of her children or whether the children will be removed and placed in statutory care facilities. Given ample evidence providing support for the advantages of actuarial tools over clinical judgement alone, a staff member's ability to effectively function as an expert witness would most definitely be enhanced with better resources in this regard; however, the development of actuarial tools may be negatively impacted by small numbers of woman who come to our attention. Although assessment is one function of LFF, most referrals received by LFF relate to convicted female sexual offenders who are now under the jurisdiction of the Criminal Justice System. Accordingly, treatment is a primary focus of LFF.

Treatment Programmes/Initiatives, Consultation and Training

LFF's treatment approach with female sexual offenders   The treatment approach implemented and utilised by LFF is largely cognitive-behavioural; however, the approach continues to evolve as LFF staff members integrate elements from schema therapy, dialectical behaviour therapy (Linehan, 1993) and trauma therapy. These elements have particular resonance for women who have experienced abuse histories in childhood and adulthood, a history of abusive relationships in adulthood, trauma and finally dynamics pertaining to primary attachment figures including issues of loss, emotional processing, self esteem and assertiveness. Each of these areas is critical for a treatment approach that is striving to be gender-responsive.

The model consists of an assessment module, three learning modules and a 'New Life Manual'. The concept of New Life planning is integrated from the start of the programme. The *Assessment Module* includes sections pertaining to the following: (1) an offence overview; (2) attitude to victims; (3) personal history including experiences of being parented; and (4) abuse history. The assessment module also provides an opportunity to discuss the following: (5) beliefs about children including chronologies of current children; (6) ability to meet individual needs; (7) meaning of sex to the woman; (8) relationship history; and (9) sexual fantasy.

Within the learning portion of treatment, *Module One* includes material pertaining to the following: (1) obstacles to change; (2) abuse-related fantasy; (3) positive rational thinking; and (4) offence work linking the meeting of needs with abusive behaviours, effects of sexual abuse, identification of abusive patterns and self-efficacy skills. *Module Two* focuses on three areas: (1) sexual and non-sexual relationships; (2) development of a New Life Plan; and (3) victim empathy. Finally, *Module Three* considers the following: (1) personally relevant risk factors and self-management plans; (2) goal setting, goal laddering; and (3) a review of problem-focused solutions.

The *New Life Manual* is a self-help manual used by the women while working in the programme and is designed to support the work they undertake. Although this brief description is representative of the basic treatment approach, it is important to note that, similar to the approach within Correctional Services Canada, the work with women is targeted specifically to meet their individual needs.

Importantly, as research regarding female sexual offenders emerges, the interventions used by LFF evolve and in more recent years LFF approach has been informed by the work of Eldridge and Saradjian (2000) and Ward and colleagues (e.g. Collie, Ward & Gannon, 2006; Lindsay, Ward, Morgan & Wilson, 2007; Thakker, Ward & Tidmarsh, 2006; Ward & Mann, 2004; Ward & Marshall, 2004; Ward & Stewart, 2003; Whitehead, Ward & Collie, 2007). Specifically, concepts of 'responsivity', 'readiness' and the 'good lives' are increasingly guiding programming efforts.

Although initial intervention/therapy/programming efforts offered by LFF were written as group work programmes, LFF staff members indicate that it has proven almost impossible to find clusters of compatible women to permit group work to continue in a programming environment. Even within the UK prison system, finding and maintaining groups of female sexual offenders in one location has proven unsustainable. Consequently, the programme has now been adapted to allow for individual work and follows the basic structure of assessment, formulation and intervention.

Pilot female sexual offender treatment programme   In 2000, LFF piloted a Female Sexual Offender Treatment Programme in one of the larger women's prisons in England (i.e., Her Majesty's Prison Service – Styal). The Programme was designed by Hilary Eldridge (LFF) and Jacqui Saradjian (Clinical Psychologist).

The pilot programme was designed for women who had been convicted of sexual offences against children. The overall aims of the programme were as follows:

- To facilitate the woman's acceptance and responsibility for her sexually abusive behaviour;
- To facilitate the woman gaining an understanding of her pattern of offending;
- To examine the role played by fantasy;

- To examine, where relevant, the woman's own victim issues as a child and as an adult;
- To encourage the development of intellectual and emotional empathy;
- To encourage the understanding of emotions and emotional states;
- To examine relationship issues and assist in the development of emotional intimacy skills;
- To examine sexuality and sex education; and
- To plan an abuse free 'New Life'.

The programme was delivered between January, 2000 and June, 2001 and involved both individual (78-sessions; approximately 150 hours) and group work (78 sessions), over a 10-month period (approximately 150 hours). Four women were involved in the programme, one of whom was unable to undertake the group work component due to mental health issues. Probation officers delivered the assessment and intervention modules after receiving training from the programme authors. The LFF provided consultation through the duration of the programme.

The programme was evaluated using a battery of pre- and post-test psychometric measures, selected by Richard Beckett, a Consultant Clinical Psychologists. The battery of tests included the following:

- Locus of control (e.g. Nowicki & Strickland, 1971, August; Nowicki, 1979);
- Alcohol use (MAST – Michigan Alcohol Screening Test; Selzer, 1971);
- Drug use (DAST – Drug Abuse Screening Test; Skinner, 1982);
- Sexual matters questionnaire (derived from the Multiphasic Sex Inventory; Nichols & Molinder, 1984);
- UCLA loneliness scale (Russell, 1996; Russell et al., 1978);
- Children and sex (e.g. Beckett, 1987);
- Vignettes of female offence scenarios linked to typologies (e.g. Beckett & Fisher, 1994);
- Interpersonal reactivity index (general empathy; e.g. Davis, 1980, 1983);
- Self-deception and impression management (PDS – Paulhus Deception Scales; Paulhus, 1998);
- Social response inventory (adapted by Beckett; see Keltner, Marshall & Marshall, 1981);
- Self-esteem (see Thornton, Beech & Marshall, 2004; Webster, Mann, Thornton & Wakeling, 2007);
- Millon Clinical Multiaxial Inventory (Millon, Davis & Millon, 1997; Millon, Millon, Davis & Grossman, 1997).

The battery was designed for use with women, with female norms in existence for cognitive distortions and emotional congruence (children and sex) and for the victim empathy (offence scenario vignettes) measures.

The areas measured during the pre- and post-test assessment are reflective of programme target areas and included the following: (1) affective interpersonal issues (e.g. self-esteem, assertiveness, emotional loneliness, locus of control and ability to cope with distress in others); (2) empathy; (3) cognitive distortions; and (4) depression. Results of the pre- and post-assessments indicated that the three women who completed both individual and group programming demonstrated improvements, which were both statistically and clinically significant. They demonstrated progress in all of the areas that linked to treatment targets, with the exception of changes in depression. Unfortunately, the logistics of running group programming with female sexual offenders proved difficult as a result of the very small numbers of female sexual offenders placed in institutions countrywide. However, given the programme manuals had been developed to enable both individual and group approaches, the use of the programme materials has been sustained on an individual basis. Developments in research and practice are incorporated in applying the manuals in work with women. LFF provided, and continues to provide, a combination of direct work and consultancy services to English prisons and probation based on these manuals.

Female outreach project   Following the pilot programme, the Ministry of Justice provided funding for LFF to establish a female outreach project. The project provides services to women and their supervising probation staff where no other relevant service is available. Women are referred to the project when they are in the final 6 months of a prison sentence or if they are under supervision in the community, either post-sentence or under community supervision. The services offered through this outreach project include the following: (1) one-on-one assessment and intervention work, directly with the woman; (2) consultation with probation staff while they engage in work with the woman; or (3) consultation and training to staff in residential units. Services offered aim to address areas pertaining to the support and management of implicated women.

The female outreach project also has close links with three criminal justice hostels which provide accommodation for women. This collaborative approach strives to facilitate the process of women receiving an informed and continuous flow of support, which is required if the women are to be successful in making significant changes in their behaviours and lives. Women's involvement with the project can vary from a few weeks, to several months, to a number of years. Length of involvement depends, in part, on the length of supervision specified by the Court, as well as the estimated continued value of the woman's involvement. To date, this collaboration has proven successful.

One additional function of the female outreach project is the provision of advice to staff who prepare reports for court pre-sentence procedures. Finally, when the opportunity presents itself, LFF staff attend Multi-Agency Public Protection Arrangements (MAPPA) and other professional multi-agency meetings, consequently ensuring the continuation of collaborative efforts and information sharing opportunities. As of May, 2009, the female outreach project had provided services to more than 120 women.

Other LFF Treatment Services

Female sexual offenders in the criminal justice system and staff working with them may also receive services as a result of funding initiatives from the female prison estate.[4] First, where no service is available in the prison system for a particular woman, the prison service may provide funding to allow for the completion of an assessment during the early part of the woman's sentence. Second, the prison service has also made additional funding available for the development of training packages to be used by key prison staff who are working with female sexual offenders. Finally, funding has been allocated for LFF staff to provide consultation to prison staff regarding management of high-risk female sexual offenders serving long sentences.

Notably, LFF staff continue to provide training packages, when requested, to other agencies and work in collaboration with other children's charities. Staff are also trained to engage with women who may make contact through the 'Stop It Now! UK and Ireland Helpline'. This is staffed by professionals and is designed to assist people who have concerns regarding their risk of sexual offending or another person's sexual behaviour towards children.

Finally, as well as exploring effects on children abused by women who are their caregivers, LFF has been exploring the impact of sexually harmful behaviours by mothers on their children and other family members, when the abuse has been extrafamilial. This exploration has included collaboration between an LFF 'specialist children and family worker' and an LFF worker for the woman. Together, they engage the woman's children and non-offending male partner, working on the impact and consequences of the woman's sexually harmful behaviour and building safety within the family.

The work being undertaken by LFF represents some of the most comprehensive and innovative initiatives for female sexual offenders, their families and those impacted by female-perpetrated sexual abuse. LFF's treatment philosophy aligns well with gender responsive approaches; however, and not surprisingly, not all assessment instruments being utilised within their pilot project have been validated for use with women, or with female sexual offenders specifically. Nevertheless, the implementation of standardised assessment batteries represents a best practice in terms of ensuring that research-based evidence for these types of treatment approaches is available.

United States (Texas, Colorado, New York, Illinois, California)

Our inquiries concerning gender responsive treatment initiatives for female sexual offenders produced results suggesting that only three American States (Texas, Colorado, New York) offer unique services to this group. Representatives from two additional States (Illinois and California) indicated that they had female sexual offenders as clients but were unable to provide any significant level of detail in terms of treatment and service initiatives.

---

[4] Female Prison Estate represents a collective term used to describe female prisons. In Britain, they are described as Male Prison Estates and Female Prison Estates.

Texas

In Texas, the Council on Sex Offender Treatment[5] is the state agency responsible for the licensing of treatment providers as well as setting the standards of practice for sexual offender treatment. There is a section of standards specific to female offenders and a licensed sexual offender treatment provider (LSOTP) can receive a speciality designation in female sexual offender treatment by documenting extra hours of training specific to female offenders. The community-based Counseling Institute of Texas, Inc. (CIT) provides sexual offender assessment and treatment services. The philosophy of CIT's treatment programme is that male and female sexual offenders have many similarities and therefore, benefit from being provided treatment together.

The approach taken at CIT begins with an initial evaluation and the development of a treatment plan for all offenders. Female sexual offenders are then placed in treatment groups with male sexual offenders. CIT representatives indicate that the women, through their own words and behaviours, demonstrate the same cognitive distortions, lack of victim empathy, poor judgement skills, defence mechanisms, similar sexual offences and dysfunctional histories, as the men. Testing also indicates that, similar to men, women who engage in sexual offending may also have deviant sexual arousal and interest (M. Molett, personal communication, 4th June, 2009).

Honesty is at the core of CIT's treatment focus. Accordingly, assessment begins with a determination of 'Honesty over the Offence'. Honesty is assessed through the use of the clinical polygraph and the clinical polygraph is used throughout the treatment process to assess honesty and compliance with supervision and treatment. If the polygraph test suggests that the woman is denying her offence, her version is compared to the victim's version. Following this, the offender is re-tested (via polygraph) as she is questioned about the differences between the two versions.

Once honesty about the offence has been established, the offender engages in a sex history polygraph as part of the 'Sexual History Module'. During these sessions, a list of victims and a pattern of deviant sexual behaviours is developed. The list of victims is built on the basis of offences committed as a minor and an adult. This assessment provides treatment providers with pertinent information for planning the treatment interventions, including consideration of the intensity of treatment required. Men are administered a penile plethysmograph, women are administered a female sexual arousal interest inventory (FSAII) and polygraphed to assess to their honesty in responding. The FSAII was developed by the Executive Director of CIT, Maria Molett (with permission from Dr. Richard Laws) and is founded on the male-based sexual deviance card sort (Laws, 1986). If results from the FSAII indicate deviant sexual arousal/interest, this information is then compared to the list of victims and pattern of deviant sexual behaviours that was completed as part of this module.

Through these assessments, if it is determined that no behavioural interventions are required (i.e., there is no deviant sexual arousal/interest and no deviant

[5] For additional information please refer to: http://www.dshs.state.tx.us/csot/default.shtm

history), then a cognitive focus to treatment is developed. The determination of behavioural or cognitive interventions is similar for male and female offenders. Accordingly, all treatment modules are similar for male and female offenders. More specifically, honesty, offence cycle (instant and current), thinking errors, high risk factors, victim empathy, life skills, decision making and relapse prevention comprise the treatment modules.

The CIT model is aligned with perspectives that contend that mixed-gender groups are stronger as there is less enabling and 'victim stancing'. CIT staff report that participants confront, challenge, encourage and support one another without distinction between the sexes. CIT staff also report that the women are in fact the most likely to challenge others in the group setting (as well as being encouraging). They further indicate that this approach provides an excellent opportunity to dispel stereotypes each gender has held about the other.

Notwithstanding, CIT has received reports from women indicating that initially they felt vulnerable or even victimised in a group with men as a result of previous experiences with victimisation. However, the CIT representative highlights that not all female offenders have been sexually abused, nor are they vulnerable. Comparably, she suggests that many men have been sexually abused as children by females though this abuse often goes unreported or unrecognised. Thus, professionals working with female sexual offenders need to address and challenge existing biases of treatment professionals. Furthermore, their experience indicates that as compared with men, women are typically much better organised and complete treatment at a faster pace.

In summary, it would appear that the CIT treatment philosophy and approach is, at least in part, contradictory to those being undertaken by other jurisdictions working with female sexual offenders. Despite the opportunity for a special designation in female sexual offender treatment (Texas' Council on Sexual Offender Treatments), for CIT, gender-informed strategies for women have not been endorsed as critical to treatment success.

Colorado

In the past 6 years, Wisdom Works Counseling Services (WWCS) from Colorado has treated 14 female sexual offenders. Their treatment approach is cognitive behavioural in nature and was, until recently, delivered in a group setting. Prior to a Colorado State decision to mandate same sex groups only, WWCS conducted mixed group sessions. Assessments of female sexual offenders are referred to a Colorado Sexual Offender Management Board (CSOMB) approved evaluator. WWCS representatives describe the assessment as a 'psychosexual evaluation', though no further details have been provided.

Today, the programme implemented by WWCS strives to identify a woman's path to offending while at the same time attending to her present situation and needs. The goal is to determine how the woman can best successfully function, crime-free, in her everyday life. There are four stages of treatment including the following: (1) pre-abuse cycle; (2) abuse cycle; (3) empathy letters; and (4) relapse prevention. They also use '*Choices: A Relapse Prevention Workbook for Female*

Offenders' (Steen, 2006). This workbook is used as a supplementary component of the treatment programme, contributing primarily to homework exercises.

Although the WWCS suggests that initial resistance to treatment is common, after recognising that the goal of WWCS staff is to assist the women and not work against them, the women begin to demonstrate a productive 'flow' through the programme and generally progress quite well. If the offender remains focused and works diligently on the programme, WWCS staff report that it can be completed in 24 months. However, on average it takes approximately 36 months to complete the programme. Notably, WWCS staff members indicate that the women they encounter who have served time in prison are typically the most difficult clients and most often resistant to treatment. Interestingly, this is contrary to reports by CIT staff noted earlier.

Although this brief overview provides only a superficial summary of WWCS's treatment approach, one clear and critical message is that of their attempts to identify the women's pathways to sexual offending. As identified earlier in this chapter, the aetiology of women's offending is different from that of men and the consideration of gendered pathways to criminal behaviour is essential in one's ability to successfully understand, and intervene, accordingly. In this sense, the efforts being undertaken by WWCS represent a best practice in terms of gender responsive approaches to treatment initiatives.

New York

Warren Country Probation of New York refers all of their female sexual offenders to Dr. Richard Hamill from Forensic Mental Health Associates (FMHA).[6] An initial assessment is completed at the probation office in Warren County; however, following this, the women must travel (approximately 50 miles) to Albany, New York to receive treatment through FMHA. The treatment provided by FMHA is gender-specific and although our source indicated that the Probation Office is on the verge of having enough women for group therapy, thereby justifying the delivery of treatment at the Warren County Probation Office, to date, trips to Albany are still required for the small number of female sexual offenders within this jurisdiction. At the time of this writing, Warren County Probation had four female sexual offenders on probation.

Treatment for female sexual offenders has the same underpinnings as treatment delivered to male groups. The current authors were unable to verify the precise order of treatment elements utilised with females, however the treatment programme involves the following: (1) use of the Finkelhor Model (Finkelhor, 1984); (2) exploring relationships; (3) examining the offender's thought process at the time of the offence; (4) exploring the offender's life experiences at the time of the offence; (5) examining cognitive distortions; (6) considering the issue of consent; (7) drafting apology letters for the victims; (8) considering self esteem; and (9) completing autobiographies.

A treatment element that differentiates the approaches taken for male and female groups is (similar to Colorado) the use of *'Choices: A Relapse Prevention Workbook for Female Offenders'* (Steen, 2006). Notably, in considering the possible

---

[6] Forensic Mental Health Associates, 437 Western Avenue, Albany, NY 12203.

treatment of men and women within the same treatment group, staff working with sexual offenders in this jurisdiction suggested that mixing males and females in sexual offender treatment would be counterproductive due to the 'neediness' of their clients and the strong likelihood that mixed-gender groups would lead to flirtatious behaviour and romantic relationships.

The approaches being implemented by Warren County Probation of New York highlight the vital need for services targeting female sexual offenders, and more specifically services that are appropriately geographically dispersed, thereby ensuring accessibility for women in need of these services. It is becoming increasingly apparent that these conditions are representative of the majority of jurisdictions, rather than the exception. With the small numbers of female sexual offenders, geographic restrictions will likely remain as a primary challenge in the treatment of this population.

California and Illinois

At the time of writing, Saratoga County Probation Department (SCPD) had three female sexual offenders on their caseload; two of whom were engaged in treatment with general mental health therapists, one of whom completed treatment. The offenders currently in treatment utilise the services of individual health therapists. SCPD staff indicate that female sexual offenders typically present with many mental health issues, significantly more in comparison with male sexual offenders. For this reason, the SCPD typically settles on regular mental health therapy, including disclosure of information pertaining to the offender's sexual offence history and offence history. In doing so, the therapists are tasked with addressing both mental health and sexual offence issues throughout therapy.

Unfortunately, Illinois was unable to follow-up with specific information pertaining to their assessment or treatment approaches; however, our contact did indicate that, to date, Will County Health has worked with only 12 female sexual offenders. It is anticipated that challenges experienced by this jurisdiction are similar to those experienced across the country; primarily that of very small numbers of female sexual offenders, thereby necessitating individual therapy in the community.

New and Emerging Initiatives (England, New South Wales)

Although only very limited information was available, two other jurisdictions responded to our query pertaining to existing efforts in relation to current treatment initiatives for female sexual offenders. In England, the National Offender Management Service (NOMS) is in the process of developing a Female Sexual Offender Management Programme to be amalgamated with the overall NOMS Strategy for sexual offenders. This initiative will address needs of female sexual offenders in custody and under supervision in the community; however, it is in its earliest stages of development. A psychologist from the Department of Correctional Services in New South Wales indicated that NSW currently has no treatment initiatives specific to female sexual offenders. As with many of the initiatives occurring in other jurisdictions, treatment efforts in this regard are provided one-on-one in the community.

DISCUSSION

Effectiveness of Gender-Informed Interventions

This chapter has not provided an exhaustive review of existing treatment initiatives for female sexual offenders; it is clear nonetheless that gender-informed interventions for this group are lacking. Some jurisdictions such as Canada and the United Kingdom are doing pioneer work in the area. Despite these exceptions, one could conclude that this is an international dilemma and more research is urgently required to fill the gaps in what is known about the female sexual offender and related assessment and treatment initiatives.

A second problem pertains to the (in)ability to demonstrate positive results for treatment programmes targeting female sexual offenders. Although a couple of jurisdictions are offering interventions hailed as gender-informed, it would be a significant challenge to demonstrate clear and unquestionable success for these programmes. The basis for this challenge is manifold. First, there are so few female sexual offenders that any particular intervention would likely serve fewer than a couple of dozen women a year. As such, it would take a decade to achieve a sample size large enough to support a recidivism study. This problem is further compounded by the low base rate of sexual recidivism. A meta-analysis including studies of male sexual offenders showed that the 5-year recidivism rate is about 13 per cent for sexual re-offences (Hanson & Morton-Bourgon, 2004). Cortoni et al.'s (2009) meta-analysis suggested that this rate is about 1 per cent for female sexual offenders. Taken together, these facts highlight the difficulty in demonstrating robust empirical results supporting any particular sexual offender intervention for females.

Modes of Treatment

The general research literature has underscored differences in communication between men and women (DeLange, 1995). Correctional researchers have also highlighted the necessity of dealing with gender-related impediments to treatment delivery such as male-dominated groups (Kennedy, 2004). Accordingly, a number of studies have demonstrated that women's treatment outcomes are superior when delivery is in women-only (vs. mixed-gender) format (Ashley, Marsden & Brady, 2003; Dahlgren & Willander, 1989 cited in Ashley et al., 2003; Lex, 1995).

Collectively, these studies suggest that group oriented treatment for women should *not* be mixed gender. This is true for general correctional programmes and for sexual offender programmes in particular. Recall that many female-perpetrated sexual offences include a male co-perpetrator. This lends support to the female-only group treatment model and suggests that co-therapeutic models such as that used in Texas (and, until recently, Colorado) should be reconsidered.

There are some very important practical considerations in the provision of gender-informed programming to women as well. For instance, because women are much more likely to have sole parenting responsibilities, issues such as transportation and child care (for community programming) would be important considerations (Bloom et al., 2003). The current review suggests that some jurisdictions are facing significant challenges in this regard. For instance, referrals from Warren Country Probation to Albany New York for women to engage in programming entail an approximate 50-mile commute for the participant. This would present a virtually insurmountable obstacle for any individual, let alone a single parent on limited income.

Treatment Targets

Research evidence suggests that a *holistic* approach to classification and treatment of female offenders is most promising (Ashley et al., 2003; Blanchette & Brown, 2006; Bloom et al., 2003; Covington, 2000; Covington & Bloom, 2003). Thus, effective sexual offender treatment for women would integrate multiple treatment targets into the intervention paradigm. Minimally, these would include substance abuse, trauma, mental health needs, relational difficulties and low self-esteem. Assertiveness training would be critical for those women with no deviant sexual arousal who have co-perpetrated through coercion. Conversely, where deviant sexual arousal/preferences have been assessed as a need, integration as a treatment target would be paramount. However, as noted earlier, for most female sexual offenders, this is not an identified need. Both Canada and the UK have integrated various elements into a holistic treatment model.

CONCLUSION

This review has underscored the lack of gender-informed sexual offender interventions for women. This is true despite research evidence suggesting that there are some clear differences between male and female sexual offenders. While some jurisdictions are working to address this problem, the provision of appropriate services for women will continue to be hampered by lack of research and gender-informed risk assessment tools. In addition, the small, heterogeneous and dispersed population of clients provides a significant logistical challenge. Notwithstanding that, we will continue to see advancements in the area of female sexual offender intervention as we heed the words of our esteemed colleagues (Bloom et al., 2003): *Gender Matters.*

ACKNOWLEDGEMENTS

The authors extend their deepest appreciation to the following people for providing details concerning their respective jurisdictions, organisations, treatment initiatives and emerging sexual offender-related issues:

• Doris Fortin (doris.fortin@csc-scc.gc.ca, Manager, Reintegration Programs, Correctional Services Canada)

- Sherry Ashfield (SAshfield@lucyfaithfull.org.uk, Senior Practitioner, Lucy Faithfull Foundation)
- Sheila Brotherston (SBrotherston@lucyfaithfull.org.uk, Lucy Faithfull Foundation)
- Hilary Eldridge (HEldridge@lucyfaithfull.org.uk, Lucy Faithfull Foundation)
- Maria Molett, M.A., LMFT, LPC, LSOTP (mmolett@verizon.net, Executive Director, Counseling Institute of Texas – Community Initiatives)
- Roger Mollenkamp, LPC (wisdomworkscs@msn.com, Colorado Sex Offender Management Board (CSOMB) Full Level Treatment Provider, Wisdom Works Counseling Services – Community Initiative)
- Martha DeLarm (DeLarmM@co.warren.ny.us, Probation Officer, Warren County Probation – community initiative in collaboration with St. Anne's Institute)
- Cheryl Galarneau (cgalarnequsaratoga@hotmail.com, Probation Officer, Saratoga County Probation Department)
- Patti Grosskopf (pgrosskopf@willcountyhealth.org – Will County Health)
- Caroline Stewart (Caroline.Stewart@hmps.gsi.gov.uk, Regime Development Consultant, Women and Young People's Group, Her Majesty's Prison Service – National Offender Management Service)
- Katherine Sahm (Katherine.Sahm@dcs.nsw.gov.au, Psychologist, Department of Correctional Service, New South Wales)

REFERENCES

American Psychiatric Association. (2000). *Diagnostic and statistical manual of mental disorders* (4th ed., text revision). Washington, DC: Author.

Ashley, O. S., Marsden, M. E., & Brady, T. M. (2003). Effectiveness of substance abuse treatment programming for women: A review. *American Journal of Drug and Alcohol Abuse, 29*, 19–53.

Beckett, R. C. (1987). *The children and sex questionnaire.* (Available from Richard Beckett, Room FF39, The Oxford Clinic, Littlemore Health Centre, Sanford Rd., Littlemore, Oxford, UK.)

Beckett, R. C., & Fisher, D. (1994, November). *Assessing victim empathy: A new measure. Paper presented at the 13th Annual Conference of the Association for the Treatment of Sexual Abusers,* San Francisco, USA.

Blanchette, K., & Brown, S. L. (2006). *The assessment and treatment of women offenders: An integrative perspective.* Chichester, UK: John Wiley & Sons.

Bloom, B., Owen, B., & Covington. (2003). *Gender-responsive strategies: Research, practice, and guiding principles.* Retrieved from http://www.nicic.org.

Bumby, K. M. (1996). Assessing the cognitive distortions of child molesters and rapists: Development and validation of the MOLEST and RAPE scales. *Sexual Abuse: A Journal of Research and Treatment, 8*, 37–54.

Center for Sex Offender Management. (2007). *Female sex offenders.* Silver Spring, MD: US Department of Justice.

Collie, R. M., Ward, T., & Gannon, T. A. (2006). The management of sex offenders: Introducing a Good Lives approach. In R. D. McAnulty & M. M. Burnette (Eds.), *Sex and sexuality: Vol. 3. Sexual Deviation and Sexual Offences* (pp. 179–206). Conneticut: Praeger Publishers/Greenwood Publishing Group.

Correctional Services Canada. (2001). *Women who sexually offend: A protocol for assessment and treatment.* Ottawa, ON: Correctional Services Canada. Unpublished manuscript.

Cortoni, F., & Hanson, H. K. (2005). *A review of the recidivism rates of adult female sexual offenders* (Research Report R-169). Ottawa, ON, Canada: Correctional Service of Canada.

Cortoni, F., Hanson, R. K., & Coache, M. E. (2009). *The recidivism rates of female sexual offenders are low: A meta-analysis.* Manuscript submitted for publication.

Covington, S. S. (2000). Helping women recover: Creating gender-specific treatment for substance-abusing women and girls in community corrections. In M. McMahon (Ed.), *Assessment to assistance: Programs for women in community corrections* (pp. 171–234). Arlington, VA: American Correctional Association.

Covington, S. S., & Bloom, B. E. (2003). Gendered justice: Women in the criminal justice system. In B. E. Bloom (Ed.), *Gendered justice: Addressing female offenders* (pp. 3–23). Durham, NC: Carolina Academic Press.

Davis, M. H. (1980). A multidimensional approach to individual differences in empathy. *JSAS Catalog of Selected Documents in Psychology, 10,* 85.

Davis, M. H. (1983). Measuring individual differences in empathy: Evidence for a multidimensional approach. *Journal of Personality and Social Psychology, 44,* 113–126.

DeLange, J. (1995). Gender and communication in social work education. A cross-cultural perspective. *Journal of Social Work Education, 311,* 75–81.

Eldridge, H., & Saradjian, J. (2000). Replacing the function of abusive behaviors for the offender: Remaking relapse prevention in working with women who sexually abuse children. In D. R. Laws, S. M. Hudson, & T. Ward (Eds.), *Remaking relapse prevention with sex offenders: A sourcebook* (pp. 402–426). Thousand Oaks, CA: Sage.

Endler, N., & Parker, J. D. A. (1999). *Coping Inventory for Stressful Situations (CISS).* Toronto, ON: Multi-Health Systems.

Finkelhor, D. (1984). *Child sexual abuse: New theory and research.* New York: Free Press.

Gannon, T. A., & Rose, M. R. (2008). Female child sexual offenders: Towards integrating theory and practice. *Aggression and Violent Behavior, 13*(6), 442–461.

Gannon, T. A., Rose, M. R., & Ward, T. (2008). A descriptive model of the offense process for female sexual offenders. *Sexual Abuse: A Journal of Research and Treatment, 20,* 352–374.

Gobeil, R., & Barrett, M. R. (2008). *Rates of recidivism for women offenders* (Research Report R-192). Ottawa, ON: Correctional Service of Canada.

Grayston, A. D., & DeLuca, R. V. (1999). Female perpetrators of child sexual abuse: A review of the clinical and empirical literature. *Aggression and Violent Behavior, 4,* 93–106.

Hanson, R. K., & Morton-Bourgon, K. (2004). *Predictors of sexual recidivism: An updated meta-analysis* (User Report 2004–02). Ottawa, ON: Public Safety Canada.

Horvath, A. O. and Symonds, B. D. (1991). Relation between working alliance and outcome in psychotherapy: A meta-analysis. *Journal of Counseling Psychology, 38,* 139–149.

Ireland, J. L., & Power, C. L. (2004). Attachment, emotional loneliness, and bullying behaviour: A study of adult and young offenders. *Aggressive Behavior, 30,* 298–312.

Keltner, A. A., Marshall, P. G., & Marshall, W. L. (1981). Measurement and correlation of assertiveness and social fear in a prison population. *Corrective and Social Psychiatry, 27,* 41–47.

Kennedy, S. M. (2004). A practitioner's guide to responsivity: Maximizing treatment effectiveness. *Journal of Community Corrections, XIII*(7–9), 22–30.

Laws, D. R. (1986). *Sexual deviance card sort.* Tampa, FL: Florida Mental Health Institute. Unpublished manuscript.

Lex, B. W. (1995). Alcohol and other psychoactive substances dependence in women and men. In M. V. Seeman (Ed.), *Gender and psychopathology* (pp. 311–357). Washington, DC: American Psychiatric Press.

Lindsay, W. R., Ward, T., Morgan, T., & Wilson, I. (2007). Self-regulation of sex offending, future pathways and the Good Lives Model: Applications and problems. *Journal of Sexual Aggression, 13,* 37–50.

Linehan, M. M. (1993). *Cognitive behavioral treatment of borderline personality disorder.* New York: The Guilford Press.

Marshall, W. L., Fernandez, Y. M., Serran, G. A., Mulloy, R., Thornton, D., Mann, R. E., et al. (2003). Process variables in the treatment of sexual offenders: A review of the relevant literature. *Aggression and Violent Behaviour, 8,* 205–234.

Maruna, S., & Mann, R. (2006). Fundamental attribution errors? Re-thinking cognitive distortions. *Legal and Criminological Psychology, 11,* 155–177.

Miller, J. B. (1986). *What do we mean by relationships?* Work in Progress No. 33. Wellesley, MA: Stone Center, Working Paper Series.

Millon, T., Davis, R., & Millon, C. (1997). *MCMI-III manual* (2nd ed.). Minneapolis, MN: National Computer Systems.

Millon, T., Millon, C., Davis, R., & Grossman, S. (1997). *MCMI-III (Million Clinical Multiaxial Inventory-III).* Minnesota, US: Pearson Assessments.

Nathan, P., & Ward, T. (2001). Females who sexually abuse children: Assessment and treatment issues. *Psychiatry, Psychology and Law, 8,* 44–55.

Nathan, P., & Ward, T. (2002). Female sex offenders: Clinical and demographic features. Journal of Sexual Aggression, 8, 5–21.

Nee, C., & Farman, S. (2005). Female prisoners with borderline personality disorder: Some promising treatment developments. *Criminal Behaviour and Mental Health, 15,* 2–16.

Nichols, H. R., & Molinder, I. (1984). *Multiphasic sex inventory manual.* (Available from Nichols and Molinder, 437 Bowes Drive, Tacoma, WA 98466)

Nowicki, S. (1979). Sex differences in independence-training practices as a function of locus of control orientation. *Journal of Genetic Psychology, 135,* 301–302.

Nowicki, S., & Strickland, B. R. (1971, August). *A locus of control scale for children. Paper presented at the 79th Annual Convention of the American Psychological Association,* Washington, DC.

Oliver, B. E. (2007). Preventing female-perpetrated sexual abuse. *Trauma, Violence, and Abuse, 8,* 19–32.

Paulhus, D. L. (1998). *Paulhus Deception Scales (PDS).* Toronto, ON: Multi-Health Systems.

Rice, M. E., & Harris, G. T. (2002, June). *Actuarial assessment of risk among sex offenders.* Paper Presented at the New York Academy of Sciences, Washington, DC.

Rosenberg, M. (1965). *Society and the adolescent self-image.* Princeton, NJ: Princeton University Press.

Russell, D. (1996). The UCLA Loneliness Scale (Version 3): Reliability, validity, and factor structure. *Journal of Personality Assessment, 66,* 20–40.

Russell, D., Peplau, L. A., & Ferguson, M. L. (1978). Developing a measure of loneliness. *Journal of Personality Assessment, 42,* 290–294.

Selzer, M. L. (1971). The Michigan alcoholism screening test: The quest for a new diagnostic instrument. *The American Journal of Psychiatry, 127,* 1653–1658.

Skinner, H. A. (1982). The drug abuse screening test. *Addictive behaviours, 7,* 363–371.

Sorbello, L., Eccleston, L., Ward, T., & Jones, R. (2002). Treatment needs of female offenders: A review. *Australian Psychologist, 37,* 196–205.

Steen, C. (2006). *Choices: A relapse prevention workbook for female offenders.* Brandon, VT: Safer Society.

Thakker, J., Ward, T., & Tidmarsh, P. (2006). A reevaluation of relapse prevention with adolescents who sexually offend: A Good-Lives Model. In H. Barbaree & W. Marshall (Eds.), *The juvenile sex offender* (2nd ed., pp. 313–335). New York: Guilford Press.

Thornton, D., Beech, A., & Marshall, W. L. (2004). Pretreatment self-esteem and posttreatment sexual recidivism. *International Journal of Offender Therapy and Comparative Criminology, 48,* 587–599.

Travin, S., Cullen, K., & Protter, B. (1990). Female sex offenders: Severe victims and victimizers. *Journal of Forensic Sciences, 35,* 140–150.

Vandiver, D. M., & Walker, J. T. (2002). Female sex offenders: An overview and analysis of 40 cases. *Criminal Justice Review, 27,* 284–300.

Van Wormer, K. (2001). *Counseling female offenders and victims: A strengths-restorative approach.* New York: Springer.

Ward, T., & Brown, M. (2004). The good lives model and conceptual issues in offender rehabilitation. *Psychology, Crime & Law, 10,* 243–257.

Ward, T., & Mann, R. (2004). Good lives and the rehabilitation of offenders: A positive approach to sex offender treatment. In P. Linley & S. Joseph (Eds.), *Positive psychology in practice* (pp. 598–616). New Jersey: John Wiley & Sons.

Ward, T., & Marshall, W. L. (2004). Good lives, aetiology and the rehabilitation of sex offenders: A bridging theory. *Journal of Sexual Aggression, 10*, 153–169.

Ward, T., & Stewart, C. A. (2003). The treatment of sex offenders: Risk management and good lives. *Professional Psychology: Research and Practice, 34*, 353–360.

Webster, S. D., Mann, R. E., Thornton, D., & Wakeling, H. C. (2007). Further validation of the short self-esteem scale with sexual offenders. *Legal and Criminological Psychology, 12*, 207–216.

Whitehead, P. R., Ward, T., & Collie, R. M. (2007). Time for a change: Applying the Good Lives Model of rehabilitation to a high-risk violent offender. *International Journal of Offender Therapy and Comparative Criminology, 51*, 578–598.

Chapter 9

USING THE POLYGRAPH WITH FEMALE SEXUAL OFFENDERS

PEGGY HEIL AND DOMINIQUE SIMONS

Colorado Department of Corrections, CO, USA

DAVID BURTON

Smith College, Northampton, MA, USA

Criminal justice data indicate that convicted female sexual offenders are rare (about 5 per cent of all sexual offenders; Cortoni & Hanson, 2005; Cortoni, Hanson & Coache, 2009). However, societal disbelief of female perpetrators inhibits reporting and limits knowledge of the incidence and characteristics of women who commit sexual offences. Although most women who come to the attention of authorities for sexual crimes do not have extensive documented histories, it is impossible to know whether criminal justice records contain accurate information on the extent of their offending histories. Studies of male sexual offenders using the polygraph have shown that they typically have greater offending histories than found in official records (Ahlmeyer, Heil, McKee & English, 2000; English, Jones, Pasini-Hill, Patrick & Cooley-Towell, 2000; Heil, Ahlmeyer & Simons, 2003; O'Connell, 1998). The extent to which similar findings are also found in female offenders is unknown. The authors were only able to locate one unpublished paper by Wolfe (1995) that referenced polygraph testing with female sexual offenders. Unfortunately, the women were only polygraph tested on their current offence, not their entire history of sexual offending behaviour. This chapter, however, presents recent polygraph-related research with female sexual offenders. Specifically, the chapter provides a brief overview of polygraph testing, presents new research findings on the offence patterns and developmental histories of female sexual offenders participating in treatment with polygraph testing, and compares female sexual offence patterns and histories with those reported by male sexual offenders. The chapter concludes with practice recommendations for polygraph-assisted work with female sexual offenders.

Female Sexual Offenders: Theory, Assessment, and Treatment   Edited by Theresa A. Gannon and Franca Cortoni
© 2010 John Wiley & Sons, Ltd

POLYGRAPH TESTING WITH MALE SEXUAL OFFENDERS

Research on adult male sexual offenders has indicated that only 0.7 per cent of non-contact sexual offences and 3 per cent of offenders' self-admitted contact sexual offences are identified in official records (Abel, Becker, Cunningham-Rathner, Mittelman & Rouleau, 1988). Recent studies that utilise guaranteed confidentiality, anonymous survey or treatment with polygraph testing have shown that many male offenders have a long history of offending that includes diverse victim types and offences (e.g. Abel et al., 1988; Emerick & Dutton, 1993; English, Jones, Patrick & Pasini-Hill, 2003; Heil et al., 2003; O'Connell, 1998; Simons, Heil & English, 2004; Weinrott & Saylor, 1991; Wilcox, Sosnowski, Warberg & Beech, 2005). These findings remain consistent across research methods and populations (i.e. parole, incarcerated, probation, unsupervised). Specifically, these studies have shown increases in the identified number of victims and offences, decreases in the age of onset of offending behaviours, increases in the prevalence of crossover offences (i.e. assaulting individuals from different relationship categories, genders or age groups) and increases in known paraphilic behaviours.

Using polygraph testing combined with treatment, Heil et al. (2003) examined offence patterns of 223 incarcerated and 266 paroled sexual offenders. This study demonstrated that the average number of identified *victims* in official records (2 victims for incarcerated offenders, 1 for paroled offenders) increased, after polygraph testing, to 18 and 3, respectively. Similarly, after polygraph testing, the average number of identified *offences* in official record increased from 12 for incarcerated and 3 for paroled offenders to 137 and 14, respectively. Of note, the majority of the polygraph tests (70 per cent) were deceptive within both populations. In the majority of these studies, the mean age of onset of sexual offending was prior to age 18; most studies found a mean age of onset in early adolescence (i.e. 12 years of age). These studies also revealed a lengthy time period between onset of sexual offending and criminal justice detection. Adult offenders have successfully hidden their sexual offending behaviours in an average range of 6–16 years, dependent upon the study. In addition, the majority of studies report a mode of three types of admitted paraphilias or sexual offending behaviours per offender, although a substantial number of offenders have more than three.

Studies that use the polygraph have also shown that male sexual offenders engage in crossover sexual offending at higher rates than reported in studies that do not use the polygraph (e.g. Guay, Proulx, Cusson & Ouimet, 2001; Marshall, Barbaree & Eccles, 1991; Smallbone & Wortley, 2004). Offenders who sexually assault both children and adults (i.e. age crossover) ranged from 29 to 73 per cent (Simons et al., 2004; Wilcox et al., 2005). Of note, 71 per cent of the sexual history polygraphs were scored deceptive in the study that reported the lowest rate (Wilcox et al., 2005) whereas the study with the highest rate included only individuals with non-deceptive sexual history polygraphs (Heil & Simons, 2008; Simons et al., 2004). In addition, polygraph studies report a high percentage of official record-identified rapists who admit to child victimisation. Studies range from 32 to 64 per cent, with the majority at 50–60 per cent (Abel & Osborn, 1992; English et al., 2000; Heil et al., 2003; O'Connell, 1998; Wilcox et al., 2005). Findings with respect to gender crossover (i.e. victimising both males and females) are relatively consistent across studies and range from 20 to 43 per cent (Abel & Osborn, 1992; English et al., 2000; Heil et al., 2003). The majority of offenders who assault males have also assaulted females (63–92 per cent), but not the reverse (23–37 per cent). With respect to relationship crossover, studies have shown that 64–66 per cent of incest offenders report sexually assaulting non-relative children (Abel et al., 1988; English et al., 2000; Heil et al., 2003). Taken together, these research findings support the use of the polygraph to obtain sexual offence patterns that would otherwise remain unknown.

Basic Overview of Polygraph

Polygraph testing measures physiological responses when individuals are asked specific questions. Specifically, the polygraph measures galvanic skin responses, blood pressure, pulse rate, blood volume and breathing. When individuals fear detection, they frequently have autonomic nervous system reactions; these are measured by the polygraph. Therefore, polygraph can be a useful tool in helping sexual offenders become less secretive about past and current behaviours. Polygraph testing can support sexual offender treatment and supervision by increasing disclosures of the types and frequency of prior sexual offending behaviour (Ahlmeyer et al., 2000; English et al., 2000; Heil et al., 2003; O'Connell, 1998), detecting and deterring high-risk behaviours and re-offence (Grubin, Madsen, Parsons, Sosnowski & Warberg, 2004; Harrison & Kirkpatrick, 2000) and increasing successful parole completion rates (Abrams & Ogard, 1986). Generally, five types of polygraph tests are used in sexual offender treatment and supervision to achieve the above objectives.

Instant Offence and Sexual History Disclosure Exams

The first type of polygraph test generally used in sexual offender treatment and supervision is the *instant offence disclosure exam*, which is a specific type of *single issue exam*. This exam focuses on the details of the sexual offence that brought the offender under criminal justice supervision and treatment. Another commonly used test is the *sexual history disclosure exam*. During treatment, offenders record their history of sexual offending behaviour prior to the exam. This exam probes whether the offender has fully disclosed the frequency and range of their prior sexual offending behaviours, including the numbers and types of victims and offences. As one polygraph exam typically includes only three to four relevant questions, more than one test may be required to address the range of possible sexual offending behaviours. Common questions for male offenders include the following: *'After your age of 18, have you had physical sexual contact with anyone under the age of 15; Before your age of 18, have you had physical sexual contact with anyone under the age of 15; Have you ever physically forced anyone to have sexual contact with you?'*. The sexual history disclosure exam helps treatment providers and supervising officers determine preferred and secondary victim pools, develop individualised treatment plans, identify risk factors, develop relevant relapse prevention plans and select essential supervision conditions.

Maintenance and Monitoring Exams

A third type of test is the *maintenance exam*. This exam focuses on behaviour during a recent time period (e.g. since starting treatment, since your last polygraph exam, during the last 6 months). Questions focus on high-risk behaviours such as substance abuse, unauthorised contact with children or pornography use. This exam includes questions on multiple-risk behaviours that are of specific concerns for the offender. If there are significant reactions indicative of deception, the focus of the next test is narrowed to the single issue of greatest concern; single issue exams appear to have higher accuracy rates than multiple issue exams (National Academy of Sciences, 2003). Maintenance exams query recent behaviour not only to provide early intervention if the offender engages in high-risk behaviour but also to discourage high-risk behaviours based on a greater likelihood of detection. *Monitoring exams* are similar to maintenance exams as both types of exams focus on recent behaviour. However, the monitoring exam questions pertain to new sexual offences rather than high-risk behaviours. As with maintenance exams, the monitoring exam is designed to detect re-offence early on and, more importantly, to prevent re-offence.

Maintenance and monitoring polygraphs help therapists evaluate whether an offender is applying treatment concepts and avoiding high-risk offending behaviours. Tanner (2001) researched 396 polygraph case files of probationers who were participating in sexual offender treatment and supervision. These probationers had also received at least one maintenance test. Within this sample, 39 per cent of the offenders acknowledged alcohol or drug use, 41 per cent acknowledged viewing sexually explicit material, 29 per cent reported masturbating to deviant fantasies and 20 per cent disclosed unauthorised contact with a minor while in treatment and supervision. A significant portion of the probationers admitted that they were still engaging in sexual offending behaviour. Specifically, 13 per cent had sexual contact with a minor, 17 per cent had masturbated in public, 3 per cent had forced someone to have sex and 6 per cent had committed voyeurism. In total, 82 per cent acknowledged new high-risk behaviour and/or offence behaviour, with 41 per cent acknowledging new sexual crimes while participating in sexual offence-specific treatment and specialised supervision. While these findings are disturbing, other studies have found that regular maintenance/monitoring testing diminishes ongoing high-risk behaviours.

Several studies have detected a deterrent effect through the use of maintenance/monitoring testing (Abrams & Ogard, 1986; Grubin et al., 2004; Harrison & Kirkpatrick, 2000). For example, Harrison and Kirkpatrick (2000) studied the deterrent effect of maintenance/monitoring exams through anonymous survey of 28 offenders in community treatment. The following percentage of survey participants reported that they refrained from the listed high-risk behaviour due to polygraph testing: 36 per cent – substance use, 36 per cent – frequenting adult book stores, 57 per cent – masturbation, 57 per cent – grooming behaviours and 27 per cent – sexual touching of children. In an earlier study, Abrams and Ogard (1986) found that 69 per cent of probationers (i.e. general offenders that included some sexual offenders) who were polygraph tested successfully completed probation versus only 26 per cent of probationers who were not polygraph tested during supervision. This study lends further support for the deterrent effect of polygraph. Taken together, these studies suggest that maintenance/monitoring testing effectively decreases high-risk behaviour and re-offence.

Specific Issue Exam

The final type of test that is typically used in sexual offender treatment is the *specific issue exam*. Exam questions are focused on a specific event or concern. The instant offence disclosure test is a type of specific issue exam, which is used when an offender is denying the offence or significant aspects of the offence. Specific issue tests focus exclusively on one type of high-risk behaviour or an alleged behaviour; as such, these tests have the highest mean accuracy rate (National Academy of Sciences, 2003).

Many treatment providers have concerns about the accuracy of polygraph testing. After reviewing available research, the National Academy of Sciences (2003) found an average accuracy rate of 80 per cent for a well-executed screening test (similar to a multiple issue test) and a median accuracy rate of 89 per cent for a single-incident test. Some jurisdictions require examiners to use computer-scoring programs along with hand scoring. Computerised scoring has been shown to significantly improve the accuracy for detecting deception; studies typically report accuracy rates ranging from 72 to 100 per cent; these accuracy rates vary according to which scoring algorithm is used (Gordon et al., 2006). Likewise, recent findings of an improved objective scoring system (i.e. *Objective Scoring System, version 3*) have reported significant increases in accuracy (i.e. overall decision accuracy, fewer inconclusive results, sensitivity to deception, specificity to truthfulness, fewer false negative and false positive results) in comparison to traditional hand-scoring techniques (Nelson, Handler & Krapohl, 2007). Although polygraph testing is not 100 per cent accurate, the accuracy rates are similar to many of the assessment instruments that are used in sex offender treatment, typically yielding receiver operating characteristic (ROC) curves (a statistic utilised to assess the quality of the discriminating power of a test) between 0.80 for a well-executed screening test and 0.89 for a single-incident exam (National Academy of Sciences, 2003). These results compare favourably with the average accuracy rates of actuarial risk assessment instruments (ROC $\approx$ 0.70; Knight & Thornton, 2007). Accuracy rates of polygraph exams are also influenced by the base rate of deception within the population of interest. Researchers have estimated that 90 per cent of convicted sexual offenders are dishonest regarding their offence history (Maletzsky, 1991), which suggests that post-conviction polygraph testing may be useful for this population (Madsen, 2009; see Heil & English, 2009, and Wilcox, 2009, for further information on polygraph testing practices).

FEMALE SEXUAL OFFENCE AND DEVELOPMENTAL HISTORIES USING POLYGRAPH TESTING

Female Sexual Offence Histories Using Polygraph Testing

Simons, Heil, Burton and Gursky (2008) examined the high-risk behaviours and offence patterns of 74 Colorado Department of Corrections (CDOC) incarcerated adult female sexual offenders and 22 community female sexual offenders on probation. Of the community sample, 19 were polygraph tested, but only 43 incarcerated sexual offenders were polygraph tested. Sexual offence characteristics of these 62 female sexual offenders, including age of onset, crossover offences, number of victims and number of offences were obtained from official records (i.e. pre-sentence investigation reports, sexual offence-specific evaluations) and admissions during treatment combined with polygraph testing. High-risk behaviours (e.g. substance abuse, domestic violence, group sex, pornography use) of the 96 female sexual offenders were obtained through official records.

All participants received cognitive-behavioural treatment. The community sample averaged 1.25 treatment sessions per week (1 hour per session) whereas the incarcerated female sample averaged two treatment sessions per week (2 hours per session). Polygraph testing was conducted by experienced polygraph examiners using standardised sex history disclosure questions. The offence characteristics of the 62 polygraph-tested female offenders were then compared to the results of 222 incarcerated male sexual offenders, all of whom received over 6 months of cognitive-behavioural treatment 4 days per week, for approximately 2 hours per day. To maximise the accuracy of their offence histories, only male offenders who had non-deceptive polygraph results were included in the study (Simons et al., 2004).

Of the entire sample ($n = 96$), almost half (48 per cent) of the female offenders were convicted of sexual assault on a child, 34 per cent were convicted of sexual assault, 17 per cent were convicted of child exploitation and 1 per cent were convicted of incest. There were no significant differences among the female populations (i.e. incarcerated and community) with respect to current sexual offence conviction. Within the male incarcerated sexual offender sample, 67 per cent were convicted of child sexual assault, 27 per cent were convicted of sexual assault and 6 per cent had convictions for both child and adult sexual offences. With respect to demographics, the female sexual offenders were comparable to male sexual offenders in education (12 years), ethnicity (primarily Caucasian) and average number of children (three). Male sexual offenders were more likely to be older (i.e. average age 36), divorced or single as compared to female offenders, who were more likely to be younger (i.e. average age 31) and married.

The offence patterns of the polygraph-tested male ($n = 222$) and female sexual offenders ($n = 62$) are reported in Table 9.1. Offender disclosures during treatment with polygraph testing revealed similarities and differences among the populations. Most notably, both male and female offenders have more extensive offence histories, including crossover offending, than otherwise indicated in their official records. As a group, female sexual offending patterns were less extensive than male offence patterns, although 56 per cent of the female incarcerated sample had deceptive polygraph results in comparison to the male sexual offenders and community female sexual offenders. For these offenders, deceptive results were 0 and 5 per cent, respectively. It should not be assumed that female sexual offenders are more likely to obtain deceptive results on a polygraph examination in comparison to males. As mentioned earlier, only male offenders who had non-deceptive polygraph results were included in the study, but all women who had been polygraph tested were included in this study, regardless of whether deception was indicated.

Table 9.1 Comparison of victims, offences and crossover

	Male Offenders (n = 222)		Female Incarcerated Offenders (n = 43)		Female Community Offenders (n = 19)	
	Official Record	Self-Report Polygraph	Official Record	Self-Report Polygraph	Official Record	Self-Report Polygraph
Victims (mean)	2.09	29.98*	1.16	3.74*	1.63	2.58*
Offences (mean)	11.32	218.35*	33.07	44.41*	5.37	13.26*
Age crossover (%)	4	73*	9	21*	0	11*
Gender crossover (%)	8	37*	26	59*	0	11*
Relationship crossover (%)	16	87*	12	30*	5	21*
Relative victims (%)	44	83*	56	61	15	26*
Bestiality (%)	0	56*	0	23*	0	32*
Age of onset (mean)	36.25	12.31*	29.91	25.67	32.00	28.74
Co-offender only (%)	9	0*	35	12*	21	21
Alone only (%)	91	91	56	49	79	79
Alone and co-offender (%)	0	9*	9	39*	0	0

Note: Percentages and means are presented. Males selected for this study all had non-deceptive polygraphs. Forty-three incarcerated female offenders and 19 female community offenders were polygraph tested with a non-deception rate of 44 and 95%, respectively.
*$p < 0.05$.

Incarcerated female sexual offenders reported significantly more offences than those in the community, but these groups were comparable in the number of victims. While age crossover (i.e. offending against children and adults) and relationship crossover (i.e. offending against individuals from more than one relationship) were evident among all groups, they were significantly less prevalent among the female offenders. Interestingly, the incarcerated women were more likely than the female offenders in the community and male sexual offenders to report victims of both genders. Similar to male sexual offenders, female offenders who report child victims were more likely than those with adult victims to engage in bestiality. Finally, incest offending was more prevalent among male and female incarcerated sexual offenders; only 26 per cent of female community sexual offenders reported sexual assault of a family member. Instead, these offenders were more likely to sexually assault adolescent males.

From the polygraph examination, it was found that the majority of male sexual offenders committed offences during adolescence while official records indicate a much later onset. Unlike the male sexual offenders, the reports of age of onset of sexual offending among the female populations did not significantly decrease after polygraph examination. These discrepancies among the male and female sexual offender population may be due to the high deception rate within the incarcerated sample and the misperception of inappropriate sexual behaviour among community sexual offenders. Indeed, studies have shown that female sexual offenders (particularly adolescents) often do not perceive their offending as abusive; they often offend alone, in the course of babysitting and are motivated by curiosity (Fromuth & Conn, 1997; Kubik, Hecker & Righthand, 2002; Mathews, Hunter & Vuz, 1997). Alternatively, it could be that female sexual offenders simply start offending at a later age compared to males.

As expected, the most apparent difference between male and female sexual offending is the presence of a co-offender. According to official record, 35 per cent

Table 9.2   Incarcerated co-offending females' ($n = 17$) sequence of solo and co-offending behaviours as identified in official records versus admissions during treatment with polygraph testing

Official Record	Polygraph	
	Alone Before Co-offender	Alone After Co-offender
Solo* ($n = 4$)	1	3
Male coerced ($n = 3$)	3	0
Male accompanied ($n = 5$)	3	2
Group coerced ($n = 1$)	0	1
Solo and co-offenders ($n = 4$)	4	0

Note: 65% committed a sexual offence alone before committing an offence with a co-offender.
*These offenders were only known to have committed a sexual offence alone in official records. They admitted that they engaged in other sexual offences as a co-offender during polygraph testing.

of the incarcerated female offenders and 21 per cent of the community female offenders committed their sexual offences in company of a co-offender. The co-offenders were most likely to be a spouse (59 per cent) or an acquaintance (22 per cent). Following the polygraph exam, only 12 per cent of incarcerated females reported sexually assaulting strictly with a co-offender ($n = 5$) and 39 per cent disclosed both solo and co-offending ($n = 17$). Within the community female sexual offenders, none of the females reported committing both solo and co-offences. However, the community female sexual offenders were more likely to engage in indirect sexual co-offending (e.g. procuring victims or assisting co-offenders) in comparison to incarcerated female offenders.

Previous studies have indicated that female offenders may initially be coerced into offending but later offend alone (Saradjian, 1996). However, as Table 9.2 indicates, after polygraph testing, of the 17 incarcerated women who reported both solo and co-offending, 65 per cent admitted they had committed sexual assaults alone prior to co-offending. Further, of the three incarcerated females who, according to official records, had been coerced into the offending by a male accomplice, all three admitted that they had actually sexually assaulted alone prior to co-offending. These findings suggest that it should not be assumed that a woman whose offences appear coerced has not offended alone.

In addition to sexual offence histories, our research examined offence-related issues. Many researchers postulate that female offenders sexually assault due to fear of their significant other because they are victims of domestic violence (e.g. Hunter & Mathews, 1997). According to official records, only 23 per cent of the female sexual offenders in our sample were victims of domestic violence. Interestingly, however, almost 69 per cent of the entire sample acknowledged childhood sexual activities with family members. In addition, 76 per cent of the women reported substance abuse issues and 29 per cent reported having perpetrated non-sexual child abuse. Finally, many of the females reported high rates of pornography use (85 per cent), group sex (56 per cent), bondage/sadism/masochism (39 per cent), prostitution (35 per cent) and coprophilia/urophilia (13 per cent). These latter findings suggest that many of the female sexual offenders lived highly sexualised lifestyles in which sexual behaviour may have served as a coping mechanism or a substitute for emotional connection.

In summary, female sexual offence histories appear less extensive than male sexual offence histories. However, some differences may be due to the higher rates of deception among the incarcerated female population and the use of polygraph questions designed for male sexual offenders. Polygraph questions designed for males do not address co-offending or indirect offending. Differences among the incarcerated and community sample of female offenders may also be accounted for by treatment intensity and the format of the sexual history questionnaire. After 6 months of psycho-educational treatment, the incarcerated female sample was required to write out narrative responses to sexual history questions and to complete a chart that summarised their victim and offence disclosures. The community sample strictly filled out the summary chart upon entering treatment, without significant education about the definitions of sexual abuse. As a result of these differences, the incarcerated sample may have been more cognisant of the wide range of activities that constitute sexual offending. In addition, women were more likely to co-offend than male offenders. After polygraph testing, these co-offences were seldom described as coercive and the majority of women sexually assaulted alone either before or after the co-offence. These patterns emphasise the importance of helping women build a conceptual framework for healthy sexuality and boundaries as a component of offence-specific treatment.

Developmental Experiences of Female Sexual Offenders

The female sexual offender literature suggests that female sexual offenders have experienced more dysfunctional childhoods in comparison to male sexual offenders. Female sexual offenders are more likely to be physically and sexually abused, to witness domestic violence by female perpetrators and to report neglect (Johansson-Love & Fremouw, 2006; Mathews et al., 1997).

Regarding psychopathology, female sexual offenders are more likely than males to attempt suicide and to report post-traumatic stress disorder (PTSD) symptoms (Hunter, Lexier, Goodwin, Browne & Dennis, 1993; Mathews et al., 1997). Both male and female sexual offenders report childhood depression, anxiety and low self-esteem. Similar to male sexual offenders (Simons, Wurtele & Durham, 2008), female sexual offenders admit to masturbating to their own abuse experiences, masturbating to thoughts of younger children and fantasising about deviant sexual acts prior to the offence (Hunter et al., 1993).

Among male sexual offenders, recent studies have also shown that different types of childhood experiences may be associated with different types of sexual offending behaviours (e.g. Jespersen, Lalumière & Seto; 2009; Lee, Jackson, Pattison & Ward, 2002; Simons, 2007; Simons, Wurtele et al., 2008; Simons, Wurtele & Heil, 2002). Specifically, adult male offenders who sexually assault children exhibit childhood histories characterised by heightened sexuality (i.e. sexual abuse, early exposure to pornography, early onset and frequent masturbation and bestiality), whereas adult male offenders who sexually assault adults report childhood histories that appear more indicative of violence (i.e. witnessing domestic violence, emotional abuse, physical abuse and cruelty to animals). To date, developmental studies of female sexual offending have not differentiated among different types of female offenders. Further, research has not directly examined factors such as early exposure to pornography, early masturbation, bestiality and parental attachment among women.

As a second component of their research, Heil and her colleagues examined the developmental experiences of 30 incarcerated and 12 community female sexual offenders and compared their histories to those of male sexual offenders (Heil & Simons, 2008; Simons, Tyler & Heil, 2005). Only female sexual offenders who provided consent to complete a childhood experiences questionnaire were included in this component of the study. Developmental experiences (e.g. sexual abuse, physical abuse, emotional abuse, domestic violence, masturbation, parental attachment, psychiatric disorders and bestiality) were recorded from a behavioural checklist (i.e. *Childhood Experiences Questionnaire*; Simons, Wurtele et al., 2008). Sexual offence characteristics were obtained from criminal history records and admissions from treatment and polygraph testing.

The developmental experiences of male and female sexual offenders are presented in Table 9.3. As seen in the table, similar to the indiscriminant male offenders, the majority of female sexual offenders reported both violent and sexualised childhoods. The majority had been sexually abused with high frequency by multiple perpetrators at a young age. Interestingly, females reported starting to masturbate later than male offenders (i.e. during adolescence instead of childhood) and with less frequency, but like male offenders who abuse children, they were more likely to report masturbating to their abuse experiences and to other deviant fantasies during adolescence. On the other hand, while many female offenders had been exposed to pornography before age 10, early exposure was significantly more prevalent among male sexual offenders. Interestingly, the prevalence of early exposure to pornography (i.e. before age 10) was higher among community female offenders than incarcerated females. Similar to male offenders, females reported engaging in bestiality during adolescence, but the prevalence rates were significantly lower than those of the males.

With respect to violent experiences, the majority of female sexual offenders reported physical abuse, emotional abuse and witnessing domestic violence. Although the frequency of physical abuse experience among female sexual offenders was less than the rapists and indiscriminant male offenders, they were more likely to have been abused by both male and female perpetrators (Simons, Tyler & Heil, 2005). In addition, female sexual offenders were more likely than male offenders to report witnessing violence perpetrated by a female; rapists and indiscriminant offenders more often witnessed violence by a male perpetrator.

In comparison to male sexual offenders, female offenders reported more severe attachment deficits and more psychiatric symptoms during childhood. Interestingly, female sexual offenders were more likely to report insecure attachment to parents that could not be classified as anxious or avoidant, which suggests disorganised attachment. During childhood, female offenders were more likely to endorse psychiatric symptoms consistent with social phobia, major depressive disorder and PTSD. Social phobia (77 per cent) and PTSD (73 per cent) were significantly more prevalent among incarcerated female sexual offenders.

Table 9.3 Comparison of childhood experiences for rapists, child sexual abusers, indiscriminant offenders and female sexual offenders

	Male Offenders			Female Offenders	
	Child Sexual Abusers ($n = 81$)	Rapists ($n = 60$)	Indiscriminant* ($n = 74$)	Incarcerated ($n = 30$)	Community ($n = 12$)
Sexual abuse (%)	65_a	42_b	46_b	87_c	67_a
Mean (SD)	18.46 $(18.51)_a$	2.50 $(4.79)_b$	12.61 $(15.32)_c$	52.20 $(22.21)_d$	13.41 $(8.25)_c$
Average age at abuse	7.34 $(4.66)_a$	11.32 $(2.78)_b$	6.57 $(6.12)_a$	8.00 $(3.81)_a$	9.67 $(4.69)_a$
Multiple perpetrators (%)	34_a	17_b	51_c	81_d	25_a
Physical abuse (%)	54_a	68_a	66_a	63_a	42_a
Mean (SD)	6.67 $(7.81)_a$	16.32 $(15.62)_b$	16.42 $(15.54)_b$	10.42 $(8.50)_a$	8.13 $(8.51)_a$
Emotional abuse (%)	61_a	72_a	64_a	70_a	42_b
Mean (SD)	12.64 $(11.68)_a$	19.28 $(16.40)_b$	17.36 $(15.94)_{ab}$	18.06 $(17.21)_b$	21.82 $(28.92)_b$
Domestic violence (%)	53_a	77_b	87_c	63_a	67_b
Mean (SD)	9.22 $(11.25)_a$	19.78 $(13.79)_b$	26.22 $(16.60)_c$	31.37 $(19.80)_c$	37.30 $(23.43)_c$
Exposure to pornography (%)	62_a	57_a	64_a	33_b	58_a
Mean (SD)	11.14 $(10.22)_a$	5.15 $(5.95)_b$	15.82 $(15.87)_c$	6.70 $(9.89)_b$	4.92 $(2.96)_b$
Masturbation (%)	62_a	5_b	58_a	38_c	33_c
Mean (SD)	26.44 $(11.07)_a$	11.67 $(6.54)_b$	28.74 $(9.94)_a$	2.00 $(2.21)_c$	1.58 $(2.94)_c$
Masturbation to abuse (%)	51_a	19_b	68_c	42_a	25_b
Masturbation to deviant fantasies (%)	55_a	12_b	76_c	35_d	25_d
Bestiality (%)	59_a	30_b	81_c	20_b	13_b
Social phobia (%)	52_a	35_b	$43\%_b$	77_c	58_a
Major depressive disorder (%)	67_a	43_b	$51\%_b$	70_a	58_b
PTSD (%)	33_a	10_b	47_c	73_d	58_c
Secure attachment (%)	11_a	4_b	0_b	0_b	0
Anxious attachment (%)	62_a	20_b	26_c	33_c	33_c
Avoidant attachment (%)	27_a	76_b	43_c	30_a	38_c
Unclassified attachment (%)	0_a	0_a	31_b	37_b	29_b

Note: Mean represent frequency of experiences. Means or percentages in the same row that do not share the same subscript differ at $p < 0.05$ using the appropriate statistical procedures. Early masturbation is defined as before age 11. Early exposure to pornography is before age 10.

*Indiscriminant male offenders consist of individuals who sexually assault both adults and children.

In summary, females frequently reported violent and sexualised childhoods that contributed to insecure attachments and a distorted sense of self and others. Compared with community female offenders, incarcerated females appear to have more extensive abuse histories with multiple perpetrators and more severe attachment disorders. This finding may be explained through the aetiological explanations provided in female typologies. Community female offenders were more likely to sexually assault adolescent males exclusively (i.e. teacher/lover) in comparison to female incarcerated offenders; studies indicate that females within this typology are less likely to have experienced childhood maltreatment (Matthews, Mathews & Speltz, 1991). Further research is needed to determine whether developmental experiences differ among female offender typologies.

RECOMMENDATIONS FOR POLYGRAPH PRACTICE WITH FEMALE SEXUAL OFFENDERS

As discussed above, research findings demonstrate the importance of a thorough assessment of the developmental history and offence patterns of female sexual offenders (Simons, Heil et al., 2008). Polygraph testing appears beneficial in obtaining more complete information regarding female offence patterns, which may then be used to create individualised treatment interventions and self-management plans.

Sexual History Disclosure Polygraph Examinations

Carefully established polygraph procedures (Colorado Sexual offender Management Board Standards, 2004) produce the most beneficial information. Most treatment programmes that use polygraph testing have developed areas of inquiry that inform sexual offender treatment and supervision strategies. Unfortunately, these have been developed through experience with male offenders and their validity with female offenders has not yet been established. Typical two-part sexual history exams for males include the following questions:

Part I
1. Since your age of 18, have you had physical sexual contact with anyone under the age of 15?
2. Before your age of 18, did you ever have physical sexual contact with anyone 4 or more years younger?
3. Other than what we talked about[1], have you had physical sexual contact with any family members?

Part II
1. Have you ever physically forced or threatened anyone to have sexual contact with you?

---

[1]This portion of the question is intended to exclude any abuse the offender experienced by family members. These issues would be discussed in the pretest.

2. Have you ever had physical sexual contact with anyone who was asleep or unconscious?
3. Have you ever had physical sexual contact with an animal?

Polygraph research with women suggests that these questions are relevant to female offenders (Simons, Heil et al., 2008). Nonetheless, there are some areas where female offending patterns differ from male patterns. A particularly significant difference is co-offending; questions designed for men do not explore this issue. Another difference is female involvement in childcare. Bunting (2007) noted that female abuse can involve intrusive activities that are guised as childcare such as vaginal exams, enemas and watching a child dress or bathe beyond the age when assistance is necessary. Research has shown that both female offenders and their victims often perceive these incidents as normative or not abusive (Bunting, 2007; Hetz, Simons & Durham, 2004; Simons, 2007; Simons, Tyler & McCullar, 2005). Inquiries with respect to sexual arousal during childcare activities may also neglect other offending patterns. For example, it has been the experience of the authors that many women sexually abuse their children out of anger with the intent of hurting the child, not due to sexual arousal. This finding has received some support in the literature, as researchers note that some female offenders sexually assault to seek revenge due to perceived jealousy or rejection (Gannon, Rose & Ward, 2008; Nathan & Ward, 2002). On another note, due to societal acceptance, many female offenders fail to perceive exhibitionism as a problematic sexual behaviour (Deering & Mellor, 2007; Lawson, 1993; Rosencrans, 1997). Finally, polygraph questions designed for male offenders do not capture information regarding female offenders who indirectly participate in a sexual offence (i.e. procuring victims or assisting). Thus, new polygraph questions need to be developed to address issues specifically related to women.

The following clinical example illustrates how questions designed for men overlook co-offending and indirect sexual offending. A female sexual offender who had sexually abused her own children scored 'no deception indicated' when asked sexual history questions about sexual abuse of other children or physically forcing or threatening anyone over the age of 15 into having sexual contact (i.e. questions that assess direct sexual contact). Thus, this individual was deemed as having a non-deceptive sexual history. Therapists devised treatment plans based on the disclosures of direct contact only. During treatment, after the individual disclosed additional information regarding her offence cycle, the therapist became concerned that there were other abusive incidents of a different nature. In the next sexual history polygraph exam, this woman was asked 'Other than what you disclosed, did you ever threaten or force anyone else into doing something sexual?'. This question encompasses both indirect and direct sexual offending. She scored 'deception indicated' and she eventually admitted that she had threatened 40 women friends and acquaintances she met in bars to have sexual contact with a male co-offender (i.e. an indirect offence). In exchange for procuring victims, she received money, clothes or drugs. This example demonstrates how traditional questions based on male offending patterns fail to address female co-offending patterns and indirect sexual offending.

Given the above, to accurately define the wide range of female offending behaviours, it is recommended that the following areas be defined for the woman during her pre-test examination to obtain more accurate results:

1. Physical contact with their children's genitals: includes finger or object insertions in the vagina or rectum, sexual arousal to physical contact and injury to the sexual organs (e.g. biting, pinching, twisting).
2. Voyeurism activities: includes age of the child when the woman stopped bathing or dressing the child, or observing the child bathe or dress.
3. Exhibitionism: includes allowing sexual organs to be viewed in public.

To address indirect co-offending patterns, it is recommended that the following questions be included in female sexual history disclosure examinations:

1. Did you ever help or assist anyone to forcibly have sexual contact with another person?
2. Since your age of 18, did you help or assist anyone to have sexual contact with someone under the age of 15?

Maintenance Examinations

Maintenance questions should be developed from the offender's risk factors. Although empirically validated risk factors for sexual offending among women have not yet been established (Cortoni, 2010), factors that were related to the offending behaviour for the specific woman should be monitored. Research though indicates some areas of particular relevance. For example, several researchers (Fromuth & Conn, 1997; Hunter et al., 1993; Nathan & Ward, 2002) have found a significant portion of female sexual offenders acknowledge deviant sexual arousal/interest. Hunter and Mathews (1997) determined that some juvenile offenders appeared to develop deviant arousal patterns based on their own childhood victimisation. Similarly, Simons, Heil et al. (2008) established that many women masturbated to their childhood abuse prior to developing deviant sexual interests. Consequently, in addition to factors relevant in a given case (e.g. substance abuse), it seems appropriate during maintenance polygraphs to ask questions about masturbation to sexual abuse experiences, children in general and their known victim pools, specifically, and use of force. This information may assist clinicians to employ appropriate treatment interventions.

In their review of female sexual offender recidivism rates, Cortoni, Hanson and Coache (2009) concluded that risk assessments should be based on general female offender risk factors such as antisocial attitudes and associates, substance abuse, problematic relationships and emotional dyscontrol. Although polygraph testing cannot assess attitudes, intentions and emotions, it can query contact with antisocial peers and behaviours associated with problematic relationships (e.g. perpetrating domestic violence). These may therefore be important areas to explore during maintenance testing to improve the management of these women.

CONCLUSIONS

In summary, polygraph can be a useful tool when used in conjunction with treatment and collateral contacts to determine the extent of female sexual histories and to monitor current risk behaviours. Polygraph testing with women may be particularly useful given societal reluctance to report and to acknowledge female sexual offending. Admissions during treatment with polygraph may also supplement the lack of information provided in official records.

Although this chapter presents new polygraph research on the offence patterns of female offenders, the majority of incarcerated women in this study remained reluctant to disclose the full extent of their offence histories, as indicated by the high prevalence of deceptive polygraph results. In addition, these new research findings were based on the results of polygraph questions formulated for male sexual offenders. Further questions about co-offending, indirect offending and clear definitions of female perpetrated abuse remain necessary to understand female offence patterns. As professionals are more inclined to be dismissive of female perpetrated offences, the use of polygraph may be a crucial component of effective assessment, treatment and supervision of female sexual offenders. Most importantly, future research using polygraph testing may enhance our understanding of female sexual offences and developmental histories.

ACKNOWLEDGEMENTS

The authors thank Melissa Gursky, Sarah Marlow and John Davis at Redirecting Sexual Aggression, Roberta Bolton at the Colorado Department of Corrections and Jeff Jenks at Amich and Jenks Inc. for their contributions, expertise and willingness to collaborate in research to advance knowledge and understanding of female sexual offending.

REFERENCES

Abel, G. G., Becker, J. V., Cunningham-Rathner, J., Mittelman, M. S., & Rouleau, J. L. (1988). Multiple paraphilic diagnoses among sexual offenders. *Bulletin of the American Academy of Psychiatry and the Law, 16*, 153–168.

Abel, G. G., & Osborn, C. A. (1992). The paraphilias: The extent and nature of sexually deviant and criminal behavior. In J. M. W. Bradford (Ed.), *Psychiatric clinics of North America* (Vol. *15*, pp. 675–687). Philadelphia, PA: W.B. Saunders Company.

Abrams, S., & Ogard, E. (1986). Polygraph surveillance of probationer. *Polygraph, 15*, 174–182.

Ahlmeyer, S., Heil, P., McKee, B., & English, K. (2000). The impact of polygraphy on admissions of victims and offenses in adult sexual offenders. *Sexual Abuse: A Journal of Research and Treatment, 12*, 123–138.

Bunting, L. (2007). Dealing with a problem that doesn't exist? Professional responses to female perpetrated child sexual abuse. *Child Abuse Review, 16*, 252–267.

Colorado Sexual offender Management Board. (2004). Standards for polygraphy. *Colorado sexual offender management board standards and guidelines for the assessment, evaluation, treatment and behavioral monitoring of adult sexual offenders* (pp. 99–102). Denver, CO: Colorado Department of Public Safety.

Cortoni, F. (2010). Female sexual offenders: A special sub-group. In K. Harrison (Ed.), *Dealing with high-risk sex offenders in the community: Risk management, treatment and social responsibilities* (pp. 159–173). Devon, UK: Willan Publishing.

Cortoni, F., & Hanson, R. K. (2005). *A review of the recidivism rates of adult female sexual offenders* (Research Report 2005 N° R-169). Ottawa, Ontario: Correctional Service of Canada, Research Branch.

Cortoni, F., Hanson, R. K., & Coache, M. E. (2009). Les délinquantes sexuelles: Prévalence et récidive (Female sexual offenders: Prevalence and recidivism). *Revue Internationale de Criminologie et de Police Technique et Scientifique, LXII*, 319–336.

Cortoni, F., Hanson, R. K., & Coache, M. E. (2009). *The recidivism rates of female sexual offenders are low: A meta-analysis.* Manuscript submitted for publication.

Deering, R., & Mellor, D. (2007). Female-perpetrated child sexual abuse: Definitional and catergorisational analysis. *Psychiatry, Psychology and Law, 14*, 218–226.

Emerick, R. L., & Dutton, W. A. (1993). The effect of polygraphy on the self-report of adolescent sexual offenders: Implications for risk assessment. *Annals of Sex Research, 6*, 83–103.

English, K., Jones, L., Pasini-Hill, D., Patrick, D., & Cooley-Towell, S. (2000). *The value of polygraph testing in sexual offender management.* Final research report submitted to the National Institute of Justice for grant number D97LBVX0034. Denver, CO: Colorado Division of Criminal Justice, Office of Research and Statistics.

English, K., Jones, L., Patrick, D., & Pasini-Hill, D. (2003). Sexual offender containment: Use of the postconviction polygraph. In R. A. Prentky, E. Janus, & M. Seto (Eds.), *Sexually coercive behavior: Understanding and management* (pp. 411–427). New York: Annals of the New York Academy of Science.

Fromuth, M. E., & Conn, V. E. (1997). Hidden perpetrators: Sexual molestation in a nonclinical sample of college women. *Journal of Interpersonal Violence, 12*, 456–465.

Gannon, T. A., Rose, M. R., & Ward, T. (2008). A descriptive model of the offense process for female sexual offenders. *Sexual Abuse: A Journal of Research and Treatment, 20*, 352–374.

Gordon, N. J., Mohamed, F. B., Faro, S. H., Platek, S. M., Ahmad, H., & Williams, J. M. (2006). Integrated zone comparison polygraph technique accuracy with scoring algorithms. *Physiology & Behavior, 87*, 251–254.

Grubin, D., Madsen, L., Parsons, S., Sosnowski, D., & Warberg, B. (2004). A prospective study of the impact of polygraphy on high-risk behaviors in adult sexual offenders. *Sexual Abuse: A Journal of Research and Treatment, 16*, 209–222.

Guay, J., Proulx, J. Cusson, M., & Ouimet, M. (2001). Victim-choice polygmorphia among serious sexual offenders. *Archives of Sexual Behavior, 30*, 521–533.

Harrison, J. S., & Kirkpatrick, B. (2000). Polygraph testing and behavioral change with sexual offenders in an outpatient setting: An exploratory study. *Polygraph, 29*, 20–25.

Heil, P., Ahlmeyer, S., & Simons, D. (2003). Crossover sexual offenses. *Sexual Abuse: A Journal of Research and Treatment, 15*, 221–236.

Heil, P., & English, K. (2009). Sexual offender polygraph testing in the United States: Trends and controversies. In D. Wilcox (Ed.), *The use of the polygraph in assessing, treating and supervising sexual offenders: A practitioner's guide.* Chichester, UK: John Wiley & Sons.

Heil, P., & Simons, D. (2008). Multiple paraphilias: Prevalence, etiology, assessment, and treatment. In D. R. Laws & W. T. O'Donohue (Eds.), *Sexual deviance: Theory, assessment, and treatment* (2nd ed., pp. 527–556). New York: Guildford Press.

Hetz, N., Simons, D., & Durham, R. L. (2004, October). *Societal beliefs regarding child sexual abuse: An explanation for the underreporting of male victimization.* Poster presented at the 23rd Annual Association for the Treatment of Sexual Abusers Research and Treatment Conference in Albuquerque, New Mexico.

Hunter, J. A., Lexier, L. J., Goodwin, D. W., Browne, P. A., & Dennis, C. (1993). Psychosexual, attitudinal, and developmental characteristics of juvenile female sexual perpetrators in a residential treatment center. *Journal of Child and Family Studies, 2*, 317–326.

Hunter, J. A., & Mathews, R. (1997). Sexual deviance in females. In D. R. Laws & W. O'Donohue (Eds.), *Sexual deviance: Theory, assessment, and treatment* (pp. 465–480). New York: Guildford Press.

Jespersen, A. F., Lalumière, M. L., & Seto, M. C. (2009). Sexual abuse history among adult sexual offenders and non-sexual offenders: A meta-analysis. *Child Abuse & Neglect, 33*, 179–192.

Johansson-Love, J., & Fremouw, W. (2006). A critique of the female sexual perpetrator research. *Aggression and Violent Behavior, 11*, 12–26.

Knight, R. A., & Thornton, D. (2007). *Evaluating and improving risk assessment schemes for sexual recidivism: A long-term follow-up of convicted sexual offenders* Final Report, NCJ 217618, http://nij.ncjrs.gov/publications.

Kubik, E. K., Hecker, J. E., & Righthand, S. (2002). Adolescent females who have sexually offender: Comparisons with delinquent adolescent female offenders and adolescent males who sexually offend. *Journal of Child Sexual Abuse, 11*, 63–83.

Lawson, C. (1993). Mother–son sexual abuse: Rare or underreported? A critique of the research. *Child Abuse & Neglect, 17*, 261–269.

Lee, J. K. P., Jackson, H. J., Pattison, P., & Ward, T. (2002). Developmental risk factors for sexual offending. *Child Abuse & Neglect, 26*, 73–92.

Madsen, L. (2009). The accuracy of polygraphy in the treatment and supervision of sexual offenders. In D. Wilcox (Ed.), *The use of the polygraph in assessing, treating and supervising sexual offenders: A practitioner's guide*. Chichester, UK: John Wiley & Sons.

Maletzky, B. M. (1991). *Treating the sexual offender*. Newbury Park, CA: Sage.

Marshall, W. L., Barbaree, H. E., and Eccles, A. (1991). Early onset and deviant sexuality in child molesters. *Journal of Interpersonal Violence, 6*, 323–336.

Mathews, R., Hunter, J. A., & Vuz, J. (1997). Juvenile female sexual offender: Clinical characteristics and treatment issues. *Sexual Abuse: A Journal of Research and Treatment, 9*, 187–199.

Matthews, J. K., Mathews, R., & Speltz, K. (1991). Female sexual offenders: A typology. In M. Q. Patton (Ed.), *Family sexual abuse: frontline research and evaluation* (pp. 199–219). Newbury Park, CA: Sage.

Nathan, P., & Ward, T. (2002). Female sexual offenders: Clinical and demographic features. *Journal of Sexual Aggression, 8*, 5–21.

National Academy of Sciences. (2003). *The polygraph and lie detection*. Washington, DC: The National Academic Press.

Nelson, R., Handler, M., & Krapohl, D. (2007, August). *Development and validation of the objective scoring system, version 3*. Poster presentation at the annual meeting of the American Polygraph Association, New Orleans, LA.

O'Connell, M. A. (1998). Using polygraph testing to assess deviant sexual history of sexual offenders (Doctoral dissertation, University of Washington, 1998). *Dissertation Abstracts International, 49*, MI 48106.

Rosencrans, B. (1997). *The last secret: Daughters sexually abused by mothers*. Brandon, VT: The Safer Society Press.

Saradjian, J. (1996). *Women who sexually abuse children: From research to clinical practice*. New York: John Wiley & Sons.

Simons, D. A. (2007). Understanding victimization among sexual abusers. In D. S. Prescott (Ed.), *Knowledge to practice: Practical applications in the treatment and supervision of sexual abusers*. Oklahoma City: Wood 'N' Barnes.

Simons, D., Heil, P., Burton, D., & Gursky, M. (2008, October). *Developmental and offense histories of female sexual offenders*. Symposium presented at the 27th Annual Association for the Treatment of Sexual Abusers Research and Treatment Conference, Atlanta, GA.

Simons, D., Heil, P., & English, K. (2004, October). *Utilizing polygraph as a risk prediction/treatment progress assessment tool*. Paper presented at the Association for the Treatment of Sexual Abusers, 23rd Annual Research and Treatment Conference, Albuquerque, NM.

Simons, D., Tyler, C., & Heil, P. (2005, November). *Childhood risk factors associated with crossover offending*. Poster presented at the 24th Annual Association for the Treatment of Sexual Abusers Research and Treatment Conference in Salt Lake City, Utah.

Simons, D., Tyler, C., & McCullar, B. (2005). *Annual polygraph results of disclosures made by sexual offenders in treatment*. Paper presented at the meeting of the Colorado Department of Corrections Sexual Offender Treatment Program, Canon City, CO.

Simons, D., Wurtele, S. K., & Heil, P. (2002). Childhood victimization and lack of empathy as predictors of sexual offending against women and children. *Journal of Interpersonal Violence, 17,* 1291–1307.

Simons, D. A., Wurtele, S. K., & Durham, R. L. (2008). Developmental experiences of child sexual abusers and rapists. *Child Abuse & Neglect, 32,* 549–560.

Smallbone, S. W., & Wortley, R. K. (2004). Onset, persistence, and versatility of offending among adult males convicted of sexual offenses against children. *Sexual Abuse: A Journal of Research and Treatment, 16,* 285–298.

Tanner, J. (2001). Incidence of sexual offender risk behavior during treatment. (Available from www.kbsolutions.com)

Weinrott, M. R., & Saylor, M. (1991). Self-report of crimes committed by sexual offenders. *Journal of Interpersonal Violence, 6,* 286–300.

Wilcox, D., Sosnowski, D., Warberg, B., & Beech, A. (2005). Sexual history disclosure using the polygraph in a sample of British sexual offenders in treatment. *Polygraph, 34,* 171–181.

Wilcox, D. T. (2009). *The use of the polygraph in assessing, treating and supervising sexual offenders: A practitioner's guide.* Chichester, UK: John Wiley & Sons.

Wolfe, G. (1995). *Women who commit sex crimes.* Unpublished manuscript, Northwest Treatment Associates, Seattle, WA.

Chapter 10

WORKING WITH FEMALE SEXUAL OFFENDERS: THERAPEUTIC PROCESS ISSUES

SHERRY ASHFIELD, SHEILA BROTHERSTON AND HILARY ELDRIDGE

The Lucy Faithfull Foundation, Birmingham, UK

IAN ELLIOTT

The Lucy Faithfull Foundation & University of Birmingham, Birmingham, UK

Although the body of empirical literature relating to female sexual offenders has increased significantly, many areas require further research if knowledge pertaining to this group of offenders is to increase (Gannon & Rose, 2008). However, it is important that this quest for further empirical evidence does not replicate mistakes made by other disciplines in the past. For example, Marshall et al. (2003) argue that a significant 'error' in relation to the male sexual offending discipline has been the lack of attention to therapeutic process variables. Researchers in male sexual offending now know that attention to such process issues holds key significance for successful treatment outcomes (Beech & Fordham, 1997; Levenson & Prescott, 2009; Marshall & Eccles, 1995).

This chapter considers the importance of process issues for female sexual offenders (focussing particularly on females who sexually abuse children), using experience from work within The Lucy Faithfull Foundation (LFF). The LFF offers flexible, and usually individualised, treatment designed specifically to meet the needs of females who have been convicted in criminal courts of sexual offences, but who are unable to access a service from other agencies. Further information on the services provided by LFF may be found in Blanchette and Taylor (see Chapter 8). This chapter draws on LFF experience and empirical work with female sexual offenders and offenders, more generally, to show how therapeutic processes can be effectively integrated into practice. First we discuss the problems in the therapeutic process, as we see them, and then we consider the role gender has to play in therapeutic processes. Finally we identify factors which we believe hold particular significance for positive therapeutic processing with female sexual offenders.

Female Sexual Offenders: Theory, Assessment, and Treatment Edited by Theresa A. Gannon and Franca Cortoni
© 2010 John Wiley & Sons, Ltd

THERAPEUTIC PROCESS ISSUES IDENTIFIED BY FEMALE SEXUAL OFFENDERS AND PRACTITIONERS

For many practitioners, translating theory into practice presents a number of difficulties. Ford (2006) suggests that although the scale of research literature on female sexual offenders has increased substantially, professionals in this area still hold no consistent approach to gender differences. Miller (2003) identifies two opposing approaches: *gender-biased* approaches rooted in stereotypical beliefs which portray women as very different to men and *gender-blind* approaches based on an assumption that all abusers are alike and gender is irrelevant. Typically, gender-biased approaches focus their attention on the woman's personal history of victimisation to the exclusion of any exploration or focus on her own abusive behaviours. Gender-blind approaches regard women's individual victim experiences as simply an 'excuse', and regard males and females as 'all the same' (Koonin, 1995). This chapter seeks to identify the value of moving forward from these approaches to one that is gender responsive. In this chapter, we use the term *gender responsive* to refer to a therapeutic approach that acknowledges the impact of gender without resorting to stereotypes of either women or of offenders.

Despite debates regarding methodologies used to measure the scale of female sexual abuse (Hislop, 2001) the fact remains that the number of females who come to the attention of authorities in relation to their sexually abusive behaviour is much lower than their male counterparts (Bunting, 2005; Cawson, Wattam, Brooker & Kelly, 2002; Ford, 2006; Grayston & De Luca, 1999). For example, Prison Service figures (England and Wales) suggest that 31 female sexual offenders were sentenced in 2005, with this number increasing in 2009 to 56 (Stewart, 2009). Bunting (2005) has highlighted the severe lack of training provision available to practitioners in the UK and notes the most common preventative barrier to training as being 'the pressure of competing training priorities and female sex offending not being identified as a priority training need' (p. 54).

Professionals contacting LFF for consultancy or training report feelings of anxiety and loss of confidence when asked to interview a female sexual offender. At this point some practitioners report a sense of resorting, almost in desperation, to approaches that are gender-biased or gender-blind. The result is one where female sexual offenders frequently recount negative experiences in their encounters with professionals. Women who we work with at LFF often relate examples of professionals sharing their lack of knowledge and experience with them. These women also report that hearing such disclosures from professionals increases their sense of vulnerability and fear. Others relate how such disclosures confirm their sense of being 'doubly deviant' as women (Carlen, 1983). In other words, not only did these women feel that they had committed acts that were perceived to be deviant but they also felt that they had committed acts which even professionals did not expect women to commit.

We have found that female sexual offenders often report professionals *not listening* to what they say. In most instances it appears that the lack of listening relates not to the words the woman speaks but the intrinsic meanings she is seeking to convey. This appears to have particular relevance for women who are engaged in disputes regarding the location or care of their children where the woman is subjected to a plethora of multi-agency assessments. The women we have worked with also identify feeling unheard regarding the impact of their behaviours on others. In this context, their apparent emotionless response to victims appears to be interpreted by professionals as 'evidence' of their deviancy. For many women, however, the feelings of shame and guilt associated with being a sexual offender at the early stages of detection are so strong they become intolerable. Thus, one means of surviving is simply to close down from all emotional affect.

Marshall et al. (2003) draw attention to Horvath's premise (2000) that it is not so much what the practitioner *does* but the client's perception of the practitioner's behaviour that determines treatment outcomes (see also Bennun, Hahlweg, Schindler & Langlotz, 1986; Saunders, 1999). The perceptions reported back to us by female sexual offenders suggest that in order to engage effectively and therapeutically with this group, professionals need to reassess their personal belief systems and the degree to which these inform professional practice.

ACKNOWLEDGING GENDER IN THERAPY FOR FEMALE OFFENDERS

As much of the research relating to female sexual offenders is innately linked to research regarding male sexual offenders, it is important also to consider learning that can be gleaned from other sources including factors relating to women who engage in other forms of illegal activities. Covington (2002), writing regarding female non-sexual offenders, identifies acknowledging gender differences as a critical element of any therapeutic engagement. The impact of gender stereotypes has already been highlighted as a factor implicated in professional responses to females who sexually abuse (e.g. Denov, 2001; Hetherton, 1999). However, in this context the focus has been on links between stereotypes and perceptions of harm or risk rather than implications for treatment provision. Covington (2002) suggests that the failure to respond to female offenders in a holistic manner leads to gaps in policy planning and ultimately service provision.

In order to address this issue, increasing attention has been given to the concept of gender responsiveness and its relevance for treatment provision and engagement. Bloom (2006) provides a definition of gender responsiveness as 'creating an environment through site selection, staff selection, programme development, content and material that reflects an understanding of the realities of the lives of women and girls and that addresses and responds to their strengths and challenges' (p. 4). The Center for Sex Offender Management USA highlights the importance of ensuring that the features inherent in a gender responsive approach are translated across to include female sexual offenders (Giguere & Bumby, 2007). Later in the chapter, we will look at what this means for therapeutic processes.

Gender responsiveness in this chapter relates to its relevance to female sexual offenders yet we would suggest its relevance for male sexual offenders should not be overlooked. Although there may be similar elements which need addressing the experiences of both sexes in society will remain significantly different. It is difficult from a gender responsive perspective to see how the needs of both genders could be adequately responded to in a mixed gender groupwork setting. Kelly (2008) suggests that research from education indicates that in mixed gender groups, males are more influential than females and more concerned with issues of power and status (Levine & Moreland, 1990). Koppenhaver and Shrader (2003) and Greenfield, Trucco, McHugh, Lincoln and Gallop (2007) identify how single gender groups lead to better long term treatment outcomes for women with substance abuse and psychiatric disorder histories. Many female sexual offenders come into treatment with extensive abuse histories (Giguere & Bumby, 2007) which are potentially gender-related, while others have co-offended within the context of ongoing abuse by a recent male partner. In these circumstances, the potential for mixed group programmes to lead to further abusive relationships cannot be discounted. All of these factors, we would suggest, contraindicate mixed gender groupwork for sexual offenders.

In the section that follows, we examine five individual elements identified in research relating to non-sexual female offenders as essential elements of a gender responsive approach (Bloom & Covington, 2000; Bloom, 2004, 2006; Covington, 2002; Miller, 1984). These themes are also apparent in other disciplines where the importance of gender responsiveness as a 'fundamental element of any criteria for inclusion' is recognised (UN-HABITAT, 2001, p. 16). It is important to bear in mind that a gender responsive approach which seeks to respond to the individual woman will, if authentic, also seek to respect and explore her individual culture and heritage.

Relationships – Personal and Therapeutic

Miller's (1976) Relational Theory has importance for increasing our understanding of the differences in development between males and females. Miller suggested that although a desire for separation and autonomy may be a primary developmental progression for males, it holds less significance for females, as they are motivated to a greater degree by a desire for connections with others. Miller (1984) developed the argument further by suggesting that mutual, empathic and empowering relationships are particularly necessary for women to promote positive psychological growth. This is not to suggest that healthy relationships are not important for men but the significance and impact of relationships, particularly abusive relationships, would appear to be greater for women.

Covington (2002) suggests that relational theory is especially important when one examines the importance of reoccurring themes of relationships and family in the lives of female offenders. In our experience, female sexual offenders are certainly no exception. Indeed, the existence and dynamic of the relationship with a male co-defendant has been identified as one of the significant differences between female sexual offenders and their male counterparts (McCarty, 1986; Mathews, Matthews & Speltz, 1989; Nathan & Ward, 2002; Saradjian, 1996). Furthermore, Eldridge, Elliott and Ashfield (2009) highlight the significance of poor parental relationships and attachments as significant developmental factors in their sample, with relationship problems (e.g. violent relationships) featuring as a significant trigger to perpetration of sexual abuse (see also Gannon, Rose & Ward, 2008).

Effective interpersonal skills and a good level of social support have also been identified as significant protective factors for female sexual offenders (Eldridge et al., 2009). This suggests that although relationship variables may be part of the vulnerabilities, or risk, displayed by female sexual offenders, such factors may also be protective.

In order to create change in their lives, women need to experience relationships which do not repeat histories of loss, neglect and abuse. This clearly has implications for the practice of practitioners seeking to engage with female sexual offenders. Bloom (2006) suggests that it is important that women learn about and experience healthy relationships with staff as part of the intervention process. Yet her study of correctional professionals identified a perception that female offenders are more difficult to work with than their male counterparts. Similar attitudes have been identified by Van Voorhis and Presser (2001). Experience at LFF suggests that this is linked to more complex needs associated with female offenders and a perception that female sexual offenders will require more time and resources. This suggests there may be an additional gender hurdle in relation to female sexual offenders that needs to be addressed by organisations if staff/offender relationships are to provide the right environment for positive growth and development.

Trauma and Mental Health

Other aspects identified as affected by gender are trauma and mental health (see Chapter 5). Identifying the key aspects of Trauma Theory in relation to women, Bloom (2004) notes that trauma can occur on multiple levels. Bloom also suggests that organisations may need to adjust the behaviour of staff to ensure they are equipped to support and facilitate female survivors in the management of their trauma symptoms. The relevance of a trauma-informed response in relation to females who engage in sexual abuse is clearly apparent. Bunting (2005) identifies one of the most consistent findings in relation to female sexual offenders as the high incidence of sexual/physical/emotional abuse experienced during childhood. Giguere and Bumby (2007) suggest that female sexual offenders' victimisation histories are more common, more severe and more longstanding than their male counterparts. Furthermore, research and clinical work suggests that early abuse is often followed by abusive relationships with adult partners (Eldridge et al., 2009; Gannon et al., 2008).

Briere (1996) identifies the need to acknowledge the significance of gender in trauma therapy and the impact of gendered violence and abuse in women's lives. He outlines some of the power dynamics and the transferences that can occur as the historical view the client holds of male/female, female/female interactions become evident. For those seeking to engage with female sexual offenders, the significance of the role of gender in the woman's experiences of violence may need to be considered at the point at which decisions are being made regarding practitioner allocation. Experience suggests that for some women, the expectation that they will disclose male-perpetrated abuse to a male practitioner in the early stages of their contact with professional services leaves them feeling overwhelmed and revictimised. Similar care needs to be taken in cases where there are suspicions that the primary offender has been a female. It is equally important to consider the impact of sex role socialisation not only in relation to clients' responses but also practitioners' responses.

Although a causal link between female sexual abuse and mental health has not been directly established (Bunting, 2005) there is some evidence that mental health problems may be common among female sexual offenders (Elliott, Eldridge, Ashfield & Beech, 2007; Grayston & De Luca, 1999; Mayer, 1992). Elliott et al. (2007) found that 42 per cent ($n = 18$) of their sample were receiving antidepressant medication at the time of their offence. This suggests the merit of ensuring that basic information about medication regimes, signs of deterioration in personal presentations and contacts within the mental health system are recorded. Failure to do this may result in women who are experiencing poor mental health being labelled as 'resistant' or 'difficult'. The potential for medication levels to impact on cognitive processing suggests that regular monitoring of significant changes in drug regimes is imperative for responsive treatment approaches.

Children

Covington (2002) identifies the nature of the relationship women have with their children as another feature which sets them apart from their male counterparts. Quoting a range of statistics from the US Bureau of Justice Statistics (1999) she identifies how an estimated 70 per cent of female offenders have young children. Figures for England and Wales show similar patterns with the Griffin Society quoting figures of 66 per cent (Chapman, 2002). One of the aspects of female sexual offenders often overlooked is the frequency with which they too are primary carers for dependent children. Experience engaging with Children and Families Services suggest that decision-making in relation to contact with children can also be influenced by gender-biased or gender-blind approaches. Some women are viewed solely as victims, despite their abusive behaviours, and inappropriately assessed as presenting no risk of harm to children in the home. For others, limited evidence of risk is construed to infer they are too dangerous to have any form of contact, even when supervised.

For many female offenders, their identity as a mother, even if they have abused the trust in this position, forms a crucial part of their view of self. Female sexual offenders report feeling the lack of any 'right' to grieve the loss of removed children and struggle to identify roles they will hold in the future now the pivotal role of 'mother' is no longer available. Women who have patterns of multiple pregnancies may be at risk of further pregnancies, despite their apprehension and conviction. The court systems (in England and Wales) mean it is not unusual for female offenders to find they are involved in two separate court processes simultaneously: a family based court system focusing on the needs (and potential removal) of their children and a criminal justice system dictating punishment and level of supervision. Lack of liaison between these two systems can result in women being requested to engage in work in one system which undermines work required by the other. Matthews (1998) has identified the need for female sexual offenders to receive empathic support for their own pain before they can develop empathy for the pain of others. Thus, for female sexual offenders who have experienced loss and separation from their children, a supportive and informed response from professionals is necessary long after the initial sentencing process has ended.

Covington (2002) highlights how the invisibility of women within the criminal justice system also leads to the invisibility of their children and identifies the need for a gender responsive system to also consider the needs of children. Experiences related by children of female sexual offenders to LFF practitioners appear to indicate a high level of secondary stigma. Even when birth children were not the victims of their mothers' abusive behaviours the level of stress and trauma they experience appears to show similarities to behaviours associated with primary victims.

Peter (2008) describes the sense of increased betrayal and shock identified by victims who have been sexually abused by mothers and the degree to which their survival mechanisms reflect many stereotypical views of gender. She identifies a lack of anger or expectation regarding their male non-abusing parents' failure to protect them and suggests that 'fathers are not held to the same stringent standards as mothers' (Peter, 2006, p. 290). It appears that stereotypical views may also reflect the mechanisms other children of female offenders use to make sense of their mothers' behaviours and illustrate the potential for unhelpful thinking to develop. Johnston (1995) identified separation, enduring trauma and inadequate quality of care as pertinent factors for the children of mothers who had been imprisoned and reflected that these factors would continue to affect their development as they passed through the various developmental stages. Although the number of female sexual offenders experiencing custody may remain a tiny percentage of the female prison population, there is no reason to suppose that these factors are not pertinent for their children too. Unfortunately, little attention has been given to consideration of the needs and wider safeguarding issues experienced by children of female sexual offenders.

Community Reintegration

The significance of a continuum of care that can connect women back into the community after custody is identified as another integral aspect of a gender responsive strategy (Bloom, 2006; Covington, 2002). Covington argues that professionals should recognise the importance of community integration as early as possible in the process if additional services to help the woman re-establish with her family and community are to be identified. Saradjian (1996) comments on the lack of supports available to female sexual offenders and on the need for support systems that can sustain the women through the treatment process until they feel confident to meet their own needs more effectively. Wrap-around supports of this nature have significant implications for resource allocation and require high levels of co-ordination and consistency.

One of the most positive means of achieving relevant support systems for female sexual offenders can be the use of gender-specific residential units. In England and Wales, units of this nature often have close links with the National Offender Management Service (NOMS) and are known as 'Approved Premises (APs)'.

Placements form an integral part of the supervision process as ordered by the courts, but experience shows that many women value the benefits of access to supportive staff. This environment also enables women to access groupwork programmes relating to assertiveness, self esteem, experiences of domestic violence and parenting skills in a manner that is not often available to them in the wider community. Ensuring appropriate employment and training opportunities for female sexual offenders often raises significant difficulties. For example, opportunities presented to these women are often based on gender stereotypes and include contact with children. APs are often able to support women as they deal with the difficult issues of disclosure of their sexual offending to prospective employers.

Strengths-Based Approaches

Van Wormer and Boes (1998), reviewing the treatment of females in custody, highlighted how gender-blind approaches in policies often led to the extreme disempowerment of women and suggested professionals need to provide interventions that would utilise previous 'undetermined reservoirs of mental, physical, emotional, social and spiritual abilities that can be mobilised in time of need' – an approach based on strengths and possibilities rather than the past and problems (p. 6).

The concept of a strengths-based approach is now integrated into many disciplines (Eldridge et al., 2009; Rapp & Goscha, 2006; Saleebey, 1997; Van Wormer & Davis, 2003; Ward, Mann & Gannon, 2007). This provides a positive emphasis to practice that is associated with increased effectiveness (Miller, Duncan & Hubble, 1997). LFF takes a strengths-based approach to treatment with the New Life programme (see Chapter 8), highlighting the need to value each woman's positive qualities and help her recognise that although she has done harm, she is a worthwhile human being capable of change (Eldridge & Saradjian, 2000). Focusing on strengths and positive qualities has the potential to increase motivation to change in female sexual offenders who, we would argue, are particularly susceptible to holding a negative view of their abilities and skills and experiences of intense shame. Thus, while a strengths-based approach is likely to be useful for all types of offenders, we believe that the use of such approaches with female sexual offenders is particularly pertinent.

IMPORTANT FACTORS IN THERAPEUTIC PROCESS WITH FEMALE SEXUAL OFFENDERS

Marshall et al. (2003) draw on professional experience and evidence from a wide range of psychotherapeutic fields to help identify the characteristics of therapists which facilitate or work against change. They identify characteristics they believe hold particular relevance for therapeutic interventions with male sexual offenders in a groupwork context. These include the therapist–client relationship (or *therapeutic alliance*) and the key features of the practitioner that increase the strength of this alliance such as *active collaboration* with the client, *confidence, genuineness, support, directiveness, flexibility, appropriate self-disclosure* and *recognition and reward for small aspects of progress*. Sorbello, Eccleston, Ward and Jones (2002) highlight the issue that although attention has been given to identifying gender differences that may have significance for programme content, attention should also be given to gender differences that may affect the therapeutic process.

Given the low numbers of female sexual offenders, the majority of interventions offered tend to be on an individual basis (see Chapter 8). Experience working on a one-to-one basis with female sexual offenders suggests that many of the core features Marshall et al. (2003) identify also hold significance for female offenders, provided work takes place within a gender responsive and strengths-based framework. Using Marshall et al's review, key publications in the therapeutic domain and our own experiences of working with female sexual offenders, we hypothesise that the following 10 factors are key to the process of positive engagement and progress with female sexual offenders.

Therapeutic Alliance

Marshall et al. (2003) refer to the therapeutic alliance or the therapist–client relationship as the 'glue' for facilitating effective treatment. They suggest that the success of this alliance is dependent on two discrete elements: (1) the therapist's behaviour; and (2) the client's perception of that behaviour. Our previous discourse regarding professional relationships indicates the role that gender responsiveness has to play in this alliance. Most important, for example, is ensuring that the female sexual offender perceives that she is heard, respected, valued and supported. It is also critically important that she believes in the practitioner's knowledge and ability to work effectively in the area of female sexual offending.

The disparity between offenders' perceptions and practitioners' perceptions of the relationship they have developed is often particularly interesting in relation to female sexual offenders. Some female practitioners in their desire to create a therapeutic alliance will strive to develop a relationship based on friendship, that is, a 'girl's together' approach. Although the practitioner will report having a positive relationship with the female client, the client's actual experience is more likely to be one of confusion and anxiety. When this dynamic occurs, female sexual offenders describe feeling uncomfortable disclosing some of the more difficult aspects of their behaviour to the practitioner due to concerns that the practitioner may perceive it as 'letting them down'. This appears to relate to the disparity female sexual offenders perceive between the 'nice' woman the practitioner takes for coffee and the awful reality of her abusive behaviours.

Our experience suggests that female sexual offenders are particularly sensitive to perceived slights and nuances, including reading lateness on the part of their supervisor or last minute changes of appointments as indications of rejection. This may be influenced by messages received through personal histories that are often associated with disregard and abuse. Consequently, practitioners seeking to engage with female sexual offenders may need to pay particular care to the messages they convey, even regarding the most routine behaviours.

Establishing a strong therapeutic alliance is a delicate task, which is likely to be influenced by a whole host of factors. Below we describe the range of factors that we believe will have an impact on the development of the overall therapeutic alliance.

Establishing Emotional Bonds and Collaboration

Marshall et al. (2003) describe empathy as the ability of the therapist to attempt to understand and relate to the feelings of the client. Approaching a female sexual offender from a gender responsive perspective allows practitioners to understand some of the elements she is likely to have in her personal history. One of the key concerns for many female sexual offenders is the degree to which they feel 'doubly deviant' through their offending by virtue of being female. Such feelings may lead to a sense of being the only woman who has ever committed sexual offences. It is at this stage that the confidence and knowledge of the practitioner becomes significant. Use of statements such as, 'other women who have behaved in a similar way talk about feeling scared and alone' immediately conveys to the woman messages that she is not the only one and that the practitioner has some understanding of the issues that she is experiencing.

McCormack (2007) commenting on critical elements of strengths-based approaches highlights the importance of establishing a vocabulary that focuses on strengths rather than deficits, pointing out the negative impact of both a societal culture and a professional culture that looks for problems or weaknesses rather than strengths. This has particular resonance in relation to female sexual offenders where gender-biased responses particularly focus on perceived weaknesses, rather than strengths. The strengths-based focus needs to begin at an early stage in the engagement process and can be facilitated by establishing a personal care and support plan to help the woman engage. It may be triggered by questions exploring how 'we', that is, the woman and her practitioner, will know if she is struggling with the inherent stress associated with addressing difficult issues. This enables the practitioner to explore with the woman vocabulary she uses in the session. An example might be encouraging the woman to identify the vocabulary she will use to show distress. Sometimes a woman may say 'I'll be OK'. This leaves an opportunity for the practitioner to say something like 'When I've worked with other women, their "OK" can sometimes be another way of saying, "I don't want to talk about it" – what might you say if you didn't want to talk about something?' The aim is to establish a shared vocabulary in this early session to facilitate future work. The concept of learning from other women is a key component of LFF work and includes introducing women to the *New Life Manual* (Eldridge, Saradjian, Brotherston & Ashfield, 2000). This workbook was developed from clinical practice with female sexual offenders and provides anonymised, composite examples of other women's abusive patterns and self-management plans which women can use privately on a self-help basis outside of structured sessions with their practitioner.

Establishing the meaning of language is also helpful when exploring an appropriate vocabulary for discussing sexual experiences and behaviours. For many women, the word 'masturbation' is a term they associate with male behaviour.

Consequently, they may not necessarily see such a term as being appropriate for use by women. Similarly, women will often deny using 'sexual fantasy' but will speak of 'sexy daydreams'. It is important throughout this process to confirm that despite any discomfort the woman might feel, key issues like 'victims' and 'abuse' will be named for what they are. To do otherwise would be to introduce an element of collusion into the therapeutic process.

Van Wormer (2002) identifies the importance of positive collaboration rather than confrontation as a means of validating an individual's worth and experiences. Ford (2006) examines traditional confrontational techniques associated with sexual offender treatment and questions the degree to which they may simply reinforce notions of powerlessness and victimisation for female offenders. Although at present there is no research reviewing the impact of such approaches for women, individual feedback from female offenders who have experienced these techniques indicates an increase in their sense of being disregarded as well as a reluctance to disclose any information on the premise that everything they say, in their opinion, is viewed by practitioners with hostility and suspicion.

Introducing the Possibility of Change and Realistic Shared Goals

Martin, Garske and Davis (2000) identify agreement regarding treatment goals as a significant aspect of any therapeutic alliance. One of the notions incorporated into the early interactions between practitioners and female sexual offenders should be the concept that change is possible. McCormack (2007) outlines how using strengths-based approaches shifts the client from a recipient of treatment into an 'active collaborator'. Motivational statements can be used from the first meeting. An effective way to establish the concept of change can include practitioners explaining how their desire to engage with the woman is based on their belief that she has the strengths and potential to work towards a positive 'New Life' in the future. Given that many female sexual offenders have experienced high levels of abuse, it is important that practitioners emphasise the potential for the 'New Life' to be free from abuse for her as well as for others. For many women the desire to experience a life that is abuse-free for them may start as their primary motivation to engage. This facilitates exploration of the safety of the therapeutic alliance before making further disclosures regarding their own patterns of abuse.

Examples of motivational statements that can foster this objective are as follows:

- We believe that with support you can make sense of how you came to be here (i.e. convicted of or believed to have committed sexual offences);
- We believe change is possible but recognise that it may be difficult for you to imagine. Today it may feel out of your control but we believe you can make it;
- We know change is difficult and will take time and effort from all of us; and
- We believe that you can make good choices and work towards a positive new life.

One of the exercises that has proved popular with women relates to exploring the faces or 'masks' we all present to the world, often to protect ourselves when we feel vulnerable and are frightened by the possibility of change (adapted from Geese Theatre Group's work). Asking women what masks they present when experiencing difficult emotions allows them to identify behaviours which may be unhelpful and which have layers of meaning. It also develops further the notion of a shared language that the practitioner can use to help the woman when her behaviour suggests the work has hit a block.

Examples of masks identified include the following:

- Brick wall: Arms folded, stern features;
- Joker: Makes light of everything;
- Poor me: Plays the victim at every opportunity – too vulnerable to be challenged;
- Rescuer: Helps others with problems to avoid her own;
- Angry woman: Verbally aggressive, sarcastic – may threaten physical violence;
- Little girl: Behaves and talks in childlike way, has temper tantrums, sulks;
- Angel: Always helpful, especially to staff. Too innocent to do anything wrong or harmful;
- Blah Blah: Talks incessantly, gives convoluted answers to avoid the truth; and
- Anonymous: Rarely speaks except when prompted, hides in a crowd.

Directiveness – Confirming Appropriate Boundaries

Sanderson (2008), writing in relation to survivors of domestic violence, identifies how the loss of a sense of control through their experiences makes it critical for engagement with them to have clear boundaries. She describes how safety is only established through the consistent and reliable behaviour of the therapist and suggests that if internal and external safety is not apparent, attempts to engage in therapeutic work are likely to fail.

For many female sexual offenders previous aspects of their lives, including their sexual behaviour, may have been chaotic and lacking in boundaries. Thus an element of directiveness in the therapeutic engagement is positive. Although women may initially resist this, on reflection they identify boundaries as an integral part of making them feel safe and secure. Some of these boundaries will be very specific and reflect their legal status as offenders under statutory supervision. These are likely to relate to contact with children, access to computers and reporting requirements. Others will relate to limits of confidentiality and liaison with other agencies. However some may be specific to issues identified as relevant for the individual woman. For some women this might lead to contracts regarding appropriate clothing to wear to sessions (i.e. items which are not sexually explicit), for others it may relate to displaying respect through not resorting to verbal or physically abusive behaviours. Female sexual offenders need to know that their practitioner can differentiate between them as individuals and their abusive behaviour. They also need to have confidence in the practitioners' ability to manage their own emotions when supporting them to deal with difficult issues. For example, one woman we worked with who had chosen a particular practitioner to accompany her on a final contact visit with her child prior to adoption commented: 'I chose Jane as I knew she wouldn't cry – I didn't have to worry about making sure she was OK'.

Establishing the Importance of Openness and Honesty

The importance of establishing a culture of openness and honesty as integral to the therapeutic relationship has been accepted by a range of therapeutic traditions (Byrne, 2001; Rogers, 1951) and appears to hold particular significance for establishing a sense of genuineness and authenticity in relation to the therapist's responses (Bryant-Jefferies, 2006; Scuka, 2005). Given that sexual abuse occurs in a context of secrecy, where respect for the rights of others are excluded, we believe it is particularly important that practitioners establish a relationship built on genuineness, openness and respect. This will mean establishing with the woman an understanding that treating her with respect may mean sharing observations or information with her that she may prefer not to hear. An example of how to incorporate this into practice is to ensure that reports prepared on her are disclosed to her for discussion before being shared with other professionals. This may mean that practitioners need to ensure that the language they use when writing is accessible to the individual woman. The women we have worked with report experiencing professional encounters where, in order to avoid triggering their distress or anger, practitioners have become secretive in their interactions leading to unpleasant 'surprises'. In order to develop a sense of trust and security with the women, practitioners need to be willing to demonstrate openness, honesty and consistency.

Appropriate Use of Personal Disclosure

Literature relating to therapeutic processes suggests that personal disclosure by therapists can have benefits such as strengthening the therapeutic alliance, increasing a sense of equality, reinforcing authenticity and empathic resonance and inviting further disclosure (Bugental, 1987; Farber, 2006; Vinogradov & Yalom, 1989). Farber (2006) suggests that self-disclosure can reinforce and model more effective ways of functioning for clients but cautions that the motivation for disclosure needs to relate to meeting the needs of the client, not the therapist. Marshall et al. (2003) identified the role self-disclosure can play in a group setting with male sexual offenders in relation to disclosure about unhelpful thinking patterns, e.g. 'I know when I get angry I tend to start thinking the whole world is against me'.

If female sexual offenders are to learn about how to develop and maintain more positive relationships, practitioners need to understand the significance of appropriate disclosure. Whilst the practitioner should not divulge significant personal details about children or personal contact information, it may be helpful to have discussions about hobby details or food preferences – general snippets of information which make each of us individuals. Connections with others are significant to female sexual offenders, so practitioners who remain too detached run the risk of being viewed as rejecting and judgemental. Other appropriate disclosures might relate to examples of coping behaviours which are helpful (e.g. 'When I feel anxious I take deep breaths'), or normalising difficult situations which the woman is experiencing (e.g. 'I was really nervous when I went for my first job interview too').

Use of Therapeutic Stories and Mirroring

The use of therapeutic stories in work with children is recognised as important in reducing feelings of isolation, developing problem-solving skills and mirroring positive solutions (Friedber & McClure, 2002). Adult literature also highlights how use of therapeutic stories can change negative emotional affect (Parker & Wampler, 2006), reduce resistance to new ideas and appeal to internal resources for problem solving (Barker, 1996). Reducing the sense of isolation and shame experienced by female sexual offenders should be an integral part of the therapeutic process. One means of doing this is to relate anonymised stories from other women who have experienced similar situations. An example might be relaying techniques other women have used to deal with similar stressful situations or sharing achievements they have made;

> Sonia was convicted of co-offending against children with her boyfriend Paul. Walking down a busy street with her niece Sally aged 3, she sees Paul coming towards her. In the past she has been afraid of Paul and has never disobeyed him. Sally feels a sense of panic. Sally recognises her sense of panic but tells herself, 'relax, he can't hurt me now. I'm different, I'm strong. If he follows me I'll walk into the nearest shop. If necessary I'll tell the shopkeeper this man is pestering me and I'll make sure I stay with other people'. (*New Life Manual LFF*, p. 92)

Many female sexual abusers have co-offended with male partners and run the risk of engaging in further dangerous relationships due to poor self worth and fear of being alone. Processing their anxieties and sharing stories of other women who have felt similarly but managed to avoid a 'love's illusion' route to re-abuse, can help them make plans for an abuse-free life of their own (Eldridge & Saradjian, 2000).

Dewhurst and Neilson (2008) comment on how stories of change help to mirror change as well as influence our ability to see possibilities. The practitioner might say 'Other women who have committed offences similar to you have told me how talking about their abusive behaviour is very difficult, but they feel as if a weight has been lifted from their shoulders when they do'. This will only work if it can be done authentically as female sexual offenders will quickly identify attempts to appear empathic that are insincere. If practitioners have no previous experience with female sexual offenders they may have experience with female non-sexual offenders or women with other problematic behaviours.

Mirroring is a useful technique to assist women in identifying and developing appropriate emotional responses, as for many female sexual offenders emotional processing is limited. These women often have one favoured or safe emotional term they employ to describe a range of emotional experiences. A woman might use a term like 'worked up' to describe anxiety, anger or frustration. Some women have an even narrower language for emotions, in which 'worked up' can describe both positive and negative emotions, and may need help in identifying, naming and regulating emotions. Responding to a description of an event the woman has experienced a practitioner might suggest (or *mirror*) how they might feel if a similar experience had happened to them; 'If I was still waiting for my benefit cheque to come through three weeks after release I would probably feel very angry. I might also feel frustrated that there didn't seem to be anything I could do to speed it up'.

Recognising Survival Strategies for What They Are

Giguere and Bumby (2007) identify the high proportion of female sexual offenders who have severe histories of abuse. Gilbert (1989) suggests that stressful experiences which women have endured reinforce feelings of low self-worth and can present as a fundamental threat to survival, thus triggering a survival response. In their eagerness to get to the 'truth' professionals can mislabel women's survival strategies as resistance or denial. For some women, denial of abuse in childhood is the only means they have available to continue to function; it may not be effective but it is better than no response (Dewhurst & Neilson, 2008). Eldridge and Saradjian (2000) highlight the functions different behaviours can hold for female sexual offenders in terms of meeting fundamental or perceived needs. For some women, resisting the label of offender is to avoid comparisons with their own abuser. Attempting to dismantle these survival strategies before new skills are learned is unhelpful. Thus, the practitioner's acceptance that they will continue to emerge at times of significant stress is vital. In cases of self-harm, initial goals may be to reduce the rate and impact of the behaviours rather than eradicate them completely.

There are many coping strategies that have been used to help deal with emotional regulation (Linehan, 1993). One strategy is to develop a vocabulary to enable the woman to talk about her emotions and gain comfort from it. For many women, simple techniques like learning to identify physical sensations, associated thought patterns and behaviours for emotions can prove very effective in assisting them to believe they can learn to take control of emotions previously perceived as overwhelming. Other distress tolerance skills are distraction or positive self-soothing behaviours like visualisation or physical exercise.

Recognition of Progress

Marshall et al. (2003) identify how cognitive behavioural literature emphasises the importance of recognising and rewarding client progress as a means of encouraging further progress. Experience working with female sexual offenders indicates that progress is often slower than practitioners anticipated. Given that much of the treatment provision for men is groupwork orientated and work with women is likely to be individual, it is difficult to assess the degree to which gender differences affect progress.

The slow pace of the work can lead practitioners to feel despondent and lose sight of the length of the journey the woman needs to take. This can translate into a sense of impatience which can reinforce the woman's sense of worthlessness and powerlessness. Consequently, being alert to small but significant changes the woman has made and sharing evidence of change with her is important. Although regular review meetings, which the woman attends, should form part of the management strategy; more immediate therapeutic tasks can also prove effective.

Introducing homework tasks that can be agreed with the woman as achievable can prove a useful means of ensuring regular, positive feedback. When goals are owned by the woman, her motivation to work towards them increases. One task that has proved popular with female sexual offenders is the completion of a 'good decisions diary'. A good decision for an individual woman may be to choose fruit instead of chocolate if improving health is her goal, similarly walking instead of taking a bus may relate to fitness goals. Over time, the nature of the goals and identified good decisions may change to more complex issues. Women find re-reading their diaries useful as they act as personal reminders of the progress they have made, particularly at times of increased stress or crisis when faith in their ability to change is faltering. We have also found it important to share positive comments from other professionals with the woman so she can incorporate these into her diary and increase her overall perception of worth and ability to change.

Flexibility

The ability to demonstrate flexibility is highly significant to the enhancement of the therapeutic relationship (Martin & Pear, 1992). Kottler, Sexton and Whiston (1994) suggest that therapists must be able to adapt their styles to not only fit the needs of different clients but also the variation in need individual clients may present during different parts of therapy. Worrell and Remer (2002) identify how women often hold diverse identities which may necessitate different responses and suggest that the key to empowering women may be to facilitate them to achieve increased flexibility in their problem solving abilities.

Given that many women who come into treatment bring complex lives as well as their abusive behaviour, it is important that practitioners have the knowledge and capacity to identify a response appropriate to the woman's particular needs. It is not unusual when working with female sexual offenders to find that the presenting needs at any given time may be influenced by external factors relating to relationships or family court proceedings and an overly prescriptive approach is unlikely to leave the woman feeling supported or validated. This is not to suggest that structure and core elements of a treatment programme should be disregarded, but there should be an acceptance that a gender responsive approach must be holistic and responsive to the woman's needs. Sometimes practitioners describe feeling under pressure to get to the 'offence work' to fit alongside time scales set at the early assessment stage. Although these may function as useful reminders of the need to review progress, each woman can only respond at a pace that is appropriate to her individual needs.

CONCLUSIONS

Eldridge et al. (2009, p. 226) suggest that an advantage of assessment and treatment of female sexual offenders being relatively undeveloped is that there is 'no excuse for repeating the mistakes made with male offenders'. This chapter has sought to illustrate the possibilities that exist for female sexual offender treatment when a strengths-based approach is informed by gender awareness. In particular, we have put forward 10 main factors which we believe are critical for engaging female sexual offenders in therapy and for motivating them to change. While the majority of these factors clearly overlap with factors identified as being important in the male sexual offending literature, there are some factors that are clearly female-specific. The benefits that can follow for female sexual abusers and their workers are most important in the wider context of safeguarding children and vulnerable people.

Although the notion of adapting Marshall's research on therapeutic processes with male sexual offenders for use with female sexual offenders may appear attractive, in reality this is likely to encounter a range of difficulties. Most notably, the high level of availability of male groupwork programmes has made the identification of male subjects for therapeutic process research relatively easy. Certainly in England and Wales, the small numbers of females who come to attention in local communities would render observation of group processes impossible. Indeed, identifying individual work to observe could also prove difficult, given the limited range of treatment options currently available.

Finally, although research into effective treatment for male sexual offenders cannot be overlooked, the increased growth in specific research relating to female sexual offenders may mean that the time has arrived to move away from continual comparisons with male sexual offenders and look instead to alternative research relating specifically to the needs of women. If we are to be truly gender responsive in our engagement with female sexual offenders we need to be willing to identify them as *women* who are sexual offenders not *offenders* who happen to be women.

REFERENCES

Barker, P. (1996). *Psychotherapeutic metaphors*. New York: Brunner.

Beech, A., & Fordham, A. S. (1997). The therapeutic climate of sex offender treatment programmes. *Sexual Abuse: A Journal of Research and Treatment, 9*, 219–237.

Bennun, I., Hahlweg, K., Schindler, L., & Langlotz, M. (1986). Therapist's and clients' perceptions in behaviour therapy: The development and cross-cultural analysis of an assessment instrument. *British Journal of Clinical Psychology, 27*, 145–150.

Bloom, B. E. (2004, March). *A theoretical framework for gender responsive strategies in corrections*. Paper presented at the Annual Meeting of the American Sociological Association, San Francisco, CA. Retrieved 18th January 2009, from http://www.allacademic.com/meta/p108747_index.html.

Bloom, B. E. (2006, November). *gender responsive strategies: Research, practice, and guiding principles for women offenders*. Keynote presentation at the Excellence in Justice Symposium of Ohio State University, Columbus, OH. Retrieved 21st January 2009, from http://www.drc.state.oh.us/web/iej_seminars.htm.

Bloom, B. E., & Covington, S. (2000, November). *Gendered justice: Programming for women in correctional settings*. Paper presented at the 52nd Annual Meeting of the American Society of Criminology, San Francisco, CA. Retrieved 18th January 2009, from http://www.centerforgenderandjustice.org/pdf/11.pdf.

Briere, J. (1996). *Therapy for adults molested as children* (2nd ed.). New York: Springer.

Bryant-Jefferies, R. (2006). *Counselling for death and dying*. Oxford: Radcliffe.

Bugental, J. F. T. (1987). *The art of the psychotherapeutic*. New York: W. W. Norton & Co.

Bunting, L. (2005). *Females who sexually offend against children: Responses of the child protection and criminal justice systems*. NSPCC Policy Practice Research Series. London: NSPCC.

Bureau of Justice Statistics. (1999). *Women offenders*. Washington, DC: US Department of Justice.

Byrne, E. (2001). *Transactional analysis in psychotherapy*. London: Souvenir Press.

Carlen, P. (1983). *Women's imprisonment: A study in social control*. London: Routledge.

Cawson, P., Wattam, C., Brooker, S., & Kelly, G. (2002). *Child maltreatment in the United Kingdom: A study of the prevalence of child abuse and neglect*. London: NSPCC.

Chapman, R. (2002, January). *Resettlement issues facing female lifers*. Griffin Society Research Briefing. Retrieved 18th January 2009, from http://www.thegriffinssociety.org/Research_Briefing_2002_01.pdf.

Covington, S. S. (2002, January). *A woman's journey home: Challenges for female offenders and their children*. Working paper presented at the National Policy Conference of the U.S. Department of Health and Human Services: The Urban Institute, Washington DC. Retrieved 23rd January 2009, from http://aspe.os.dhhs.gov/hsp/prison2home02/Covington.pdf.

Denov, M. S. (2001). A culture of denial: Exploring professional perspectives on female sex offending. *Canadian Journal of Criminology, 43*, 303–329.

Dewhurst, A. M., & Nielson, K. (2008, November). *Therapeutic engagement of women who have been mandated to participate in Therapy*. Paper presented at the Centre for State and Legal Studies, Athabasca University, Canada. Retrieved 26th April 2009, from http://auspace.athabascau.ca:8080/dspace/bitstream/2149%20/1758/1/Karen%20Nielsen_paper.ppt.

Eldridge, H., Elliott, I. A., & Ashfield, S. (2009). Assessment of women who sexually abuse children. In M. C. Calder (Ed.), *Sexual abuse assessments: Using and developing frameworks for practice* (pp. 213–227). London: Russell House Publishing.

Eldridge, H. J., & Saradjian, J. (2000). Replacing the function of abusive behaviours for the offender: Remaking relapse prevention in working with women who sexually abuse children. In D. R. Laws, S. M. Hudson, & T. Ward (Eds.), *Remaking relapse prevention with sex offenders: A sourcebook* (pp. 402–426). Thousand Oaks, CA: Sage.

Eldridge, H. J., Saradjian, J., Brotherston, S., & Ashfield, S. (2000). *Lucy Faithfull Foundation assessment and intervention programme for women who sexually abuse children* [Treatment Manual]. (Enquiries to The Lucy Faithfull Foundation, Bordesley Hall, The Holloway, Alvechurch, Birmingham, B48 7QA, UK)

Elliott, I. A., Eldridge, H. J., Ashfield, S., & Beech, A. R. (2007, April). *An exploratory investigation into risk factors, protective factors and treatment need in the clinical assessment histories of a sample of female sex offender*. Paper presented at the 5th Tools to Take Home Conference, Coventry.

Farber, B. A. (2006). *Self disclosure in psychotherapy*. New York: Guildford Press.

Ford, H. (2006). *Women who sexually abuse children*. Chichester, UK: John Wiley & Sons.

Friedber, R., & McClure, J. M. (2002). *Clinical Practice of cognitive therapy with children and adolescents*. New York: Guildford Press.

Gannon, T. A., & Rose, M. R. (2008). Female child sexual abusers: Towards, integrating theory and practice. *Aggression and Violent Behaviour, 21*, 194–207.

Gannon, T. A., Rose, M. R., & Ward, T. (2008). A descriptive model of the offence process for female sexual offenders. *Sexual Abuse: A Journal of Research and Treatment, 20*, 352–374.

Giguere, R., & Bumby, K. (2007). *Female sex offenders* [Policy and Practice Brief]. Center for Sex Offender Management, USA. Retrieved 12th February 2009, from http://www.csom.org/pubs/female_sex_offenders_brief.pdf.

Gilbert, P. (1989). *Human nature and suffering*. London: Lawrence Erlbaum Associates.

Grayston, A. D., & De Luca, R. V. (1999). Female perpetrators of child sexual abuse: A review of the clinical and empirical literature. *Aggression and Violent Behaviour, 4*, 93–106.

Greenfield, S. F., Trucco, E. M., McHugh, R. K., Lincoln, M., & Gallop, R. (2007). The woman's recovery group study: A stage 1 trial of women-focused group therapy for substance use disorders versus mixed gender drug counselling group. *Drug and Alcohol Dependence, 90*, 39–47.

Hetherton, J. (1999). The idealization of women: Its role in the minimization of child sexual abuse by females. *Child Abuse & Neglect, 23*, 161–174.

Hislop, J. (2001). *Female sex offenders: What therapists, law enforcement and child protective services need to know*. Ravensdale, WA: Issues Press.

Horvath, A. O. (2000). The therapeutic relationship: From transference to alliance. *Journal of Clinical Psychology*, *56*, 163–173.

Johnston, D. (1995). Effects of parental incarceration. In C. Grobel & D. Johnston (Eds.), *Children of incarcerated parents* (pp. 59–88). New York: Lexington Books.

Kelly, P. (2008). Achieving desirable groupwork outcomes through the group allocation process. *Team Performance Management*, *14*, 22–38.

Koonin, R. (1995). Breaking the last taboo: Child sexual abuse by female perpetrators. *Australian Social Work Journal*, *30*, 195–210.

Koppenhaver, G., & Shrader, C. B. (2003). Structuring the classroom for performance: Co-operative learning with instructor-assigned teams. *Decision Sciences: Journal of Innovative Education*, *1*, 1–21.

Kottler, J. A., Sexton, T. L., & Whiston, S. C. (1994). *The heart of healing: Relationship in therapy*. San Francisco, CA: Jossey-Bass.

Levenson, J., & Prescott, D. (2009). Treatment experiences of civilly committed sex offenders: A consumer satisfaction survey. *Sexual Abuse: A Journal of Research and Treatment*, *21*, 6–20.

Levine, J. M., & Moreland, R. L. (1990). Progress in small group research. *Annual Review of Psychology*, *41*, 585–634.

Linehan, M. M. (1993). *Skills training manual for treating borderline personality disorder*. New York: Guildford Press.

Marshall, W. L., & Eccles, A. (1995). Cognitive-behavioural treatment of sex offenders. In V. B. Van Hasselt & M. Hersen (Eds.), *Sourcebook of psychological treatment manuals for adult disorders* (pp. 295–332). New York: Plenum Press.

Marshall, W. L., Fernandez, Y. M., Serran, G. A., Mulloy, R., Thornton, D., Mann, R. E., et al. (2003). Process variables in the treatment of sexual offenders: A review of the relevant literature. *Aggression and Violent Behaviour*, *8*, 205–234.

Martin, D. J., Garske, J. P., & Davis, M. K. (2000). Relation of the therapeutic alliance with outcome and other variables: A meta-analytic review. *Journal of Consulting and Clinical Psychology*, *68*, 438–450.

Martin, G., & Pear, J. (1992). *Behaviour modification: What it is and how to do it*. Englewood Cliffs, NJ: Prentice-Hall.

Mathews, R., Matthews, J. K., & Speltz, K. (1989). *Female sexual offenders: An exploratory study*. Orwell, VT: Safer Society Press.

Matthews, J. K. (1998). An 11 year perspective of working with female sexual offenders. In W. L. Marshall, Y. M. Fernandez, S. M. Hudson, & T. Ward (Eds.), *A sourcebook of treatment programmes for sexual offenders* (pp. 259–272). New York: Plenum.

Mayer, A. (1992). *Women sex offenders*. Holmes Beach, FL: Learning Publications.

McCarty, L. (1986). Mother–child incest: Characteristics of the offender. *Child Welfare*, *65*, 447–458.

McCormack, J. (2007). *Recovery and strength based practice* (SRN Discussion Paper Series: Report No. 6). Scottish Recovery Network. Retrieved 19th January 2009, from http://www.scottishrecovery.net/content/mediaassets/doc/SRN%20Discussion%20-Paper%206%20Strengths.pdf.

Miller, D. L. (2003, October). *Research approaches and treatment protocols with female sexual perpetrators: Going beyond gender-biased and gender-blind approaches*. Paper presented at the 22nd Annual Conference of the Association for the Treatment of Sexual Abusers (ATSA), St. Louis, MO.

Miller, J. B. (1976). *Towards a new psychology of women*. Boston, MA: Beacon Press.

Miller, J. B. (1984). *The development of women's sense of worth*. Work in progress, No. 96. Stone Center Working Paper Series. Retrieved 18th January 2009, from http://www.wellesley.edu/JBMTI/pdf/Previews/wp22preview.pdf.

Miller, S. D., Duncan, B. L., & Hubble, M. A. (1997). *Escape from Babel: Towards a unifying language for psychotherapy practice*. New York: Norton.

Nathan, P., & Ward, T. (2002). Female sex offenders: Clinical and demographic features. *Journal of Sexual Aggression*, *8*, 5–21.

Parker, T. S., & Wampler, K. (2006). Changing emotions: The use of therapeutic storytelling. *Journal of Marital and Family Therapy*, *32*, 155–166.

Peter, T. (2006). Mad, bad or victim? Making sense of mother–daughter sexual abuse. *Feminist Criminology*, 1, 283–302.

Peter, T. (2008). Speaking about the unspeakable: Exploring the impact of mother–daughter sexual abuse. *Violence Against Women*, 14, 1033–1053.

Rapp, C. A., & Goscha, R. (2006). *The strengths model: Case management with people with psychiatric disorders* (2nd ed.). New York: Oxford.

Rogers, C. (1951). *Client-centered therapy*. Boston, MA: Houghton-Mifflin.

Saleebey, D. (1997). *The strengths perspective in social work practice* (2nd ed.). New York: Longmans.

Sanderson, C. (2008). *Counselling survivors of domestic abuse*. London: Kingsley.

Saradjian, J. (1996). *Women who sexually abuse children: From research to clinical practice*. Chichester, UK: John Wiley and Sons.

Saunders, M. (1999). Clients' assessments of the affective environment of the psychotherapy session: Relationship to session quality and treatment effectiveness. *Journal of Clinical Psychology*, 55, 597–605.

Scuka, R. F. (2005). *Relationship enhancement therapy: Healing through deep empathy and intimate dialogue*. Boca Raton, FL: CRC Press.

Sorbello, L., Eccleston, L., Ward, T., & Jones, R. (2002). Treatment needs of female offenders: A review. *Australian Psychologist*, 37, 198–205.

Stewart, C. (2009, April). *Female sex offenders: Managing risk and need*. Presentation at the Spring Conference of the National Organisation for the Treatment of Abusers (NOTA), London, UK.

UN-HABITAT. (2001). *Local crime prevention toolkit*. United Nations. (Available from http://www.unhabitat.org/categories.asp?catid=9)

Van Voorhis, P., & Presser, L. (2001). *Classification of women offenders: A national assessment of current practices*. Washington, DC: National Institute of Corrections.

Van Wormer, K. (2002, January). *Restorative justice and social work, Social Work Today*. Retrieved 12th January 2009, from http://www.restorativejustice.org.uk/International_RJ/pdf/RJ&Social_Work.pdf.

Van Wormer, K., & Boes, M. (1998, June). *Social Work, corrections, and the strengths approach*. Paper presented at the National Social Work Conference of the Canadian Association of Social Workers, Edmonton, Canada. Retrieved 21st January 2009, from http://www.uni.edu/vanworme/canada.html.

Van Wormer, K., & Davis, D. R. (2003). *Addiction treatment: A strengths perspective*. Florence, KY: Wadsworth Publishing.

Vinogradov, S., & Yalom, I. (1989). *Concise guide to group psychotherapy*. Washington DC: American Psychological Association.

Ward, T., Mann, R. E., & Gannon, T. A. (2007). The good lives model of offender rehabilitation: Clinical implications. *Aggression and Violent Behavior*, 12, 87–107.

Worrell, J., & Remer, P. (2002). *Feminist perspectives in therapy: Empowering diverse women*. New York: Wiley.

Chapter 11

DEVELOPMENTS IN FEMALE SEXUAL OFFENDING AND CONSIDERATIONS FOR FUTURE RESEARCH AND TREATMENT

THERESA A. GANNON

University of Kent, Kent, UK

MARIAMNE R. ROSE

Royal Holloway, University of Kent, Kent, UK

FRANCA CORTONI

Université de Montréal, Quebec, Canada

Consideration of the possible future directions for the female sexual offender literature requires some examination of historical trajectories and contemporary research and treatment. In this sense then, the chapter contributors within this book have done much of the hard work for us. Not only do the preceding chapters outline historical and current knowledge regarding the theory, research, assessment and treatment of female sexual offenders, but these chapters also helpfully highlight some of the gaps, problems and issues in need of future consideration. In this chapter, we highlight some of the key developments that have been made regarding female sexual offending over the past two decades with reference to the research discussed in the previous chapters. Following this, again with reference to previous chapters, we outline core areas within the literature, which we believe require future research consideration and core areas of need in relation to the future assessment and treatment of female sexual offenders.

KEY DEVELOPMENTS IN FEMALE SEXUAL OFFENDING

There is no doubt whatsoever that we know more about female-perpetrated sexual abuse now than we did two decades ago. This is also true for male-perpetrated

Female Sexual Offenders: Theory, Assessment, and Treatment   Edited by Theresa A. Gannon and Franca Cortoni
© 2010 John Wiley & Sons, Ltd

sexual abuse. What is interesting about female-perpetrated sexual abuse, however, is that our knowledge of this topic is inextricably entwined with social attitudes towards women and the subsequent effects of such attitudes on detecting and labelling cases of female sexual offending (see Chapter 2). In other words, the willingness (or lack thereof) of society and professionals to label a behaviour as sexual offending when it is perpetrated by women affects which female sexual offenders come to our clinical and research attention as well as the acceptability of conducting research and services in this area. Thus, in recent years, as recognition of the issue of sexual offending by women has increased (Cortoni, Hanson & Coache, 2009), so too have research and treatment efforts with this population.

Theoretical Developments

It would not be unreasonable to conclude that the literature on female sexual offenders has been, and still is, largely atheoretical. Unlike the male sexual offending literature, there are no multifactorial comprehensive theories of female sexual offending to date (Cortoni & Gannon, in press; Gannon & Rose, 2008). Instead, over the past two decades, female sexual offender researchers have concentrated almost exclusively on the proliferation of typologies using demographic information, offence details, clinical observations, quantitative sources or some combination of these factors (Adshead, Howett & Mason, 1994; Faller, 1987; Mathews, Matthews & Speltz, 1989; Sandler & Freeman, 2007; Syed & Williams, 1996; Vandiver & Kercher, 2004). Presumably, theory development in the area of female sexual offending has been severely hindered by the paucity of research conducted with this population.

Recently, however, there has been some attempt to remedy this situation. Gannon and her colleagues (Gannon, Rose & Ward, 2008, 2010) constructed an *offence chain theory* of the female sexual offence process (known as the *Descriptive Model of the Offence Process for Female Sexual Offenders* or DMFSO) using 22 female sexual offenders' offence narratives. In short, offence chain theory involves developing a theory – inductively – from offenders' own accounts about the sequence of occurrences leading up to their offence. This qualitative method of generating theory (known as *Grounded Theory*; Strauss & Corbin, 1998) has been successfully implemented with male sexual offenders and emphasises *how* and *why* offending occurs, as well as *offence style patterns* useful for relapse prevention (Ward, Louden, Hudson & Marshall, 1995). The final DMFSO (described and illustrated in detail by Harris in Chapter 3) explains the sequence of lifetime behavioural, contextual, cognitive and affective factors that serve to facilitate and maintain female sexual offending against either children or adults.

Following completion of the DMFSO, each female offender's progression throughout the model was assessed by two independent raters. Gannon et al. found evidence for two main types of female sexual offender who appeared to show similarly distinct patterns of behaviour (or pathways) as they progressed through the model. *Directed-Avoidant* female offenders offended typically against children and were characterised by *avoidant* offence goals (i.e. they wished to avoid sexually offending) and *negative* affect. These women tended to offend in order to achieve intimacy with their male co-perpetrator, or because they feared repercussions from their co-perpetrator for *not* engaging in the abuse. As the label suggests, these women were *directed* to partake in the abuse by their male co-perpetrator, who pre-planned the sexual abuse and directed the woman to fulfil particular roles. Conversely, *Explicit-Approach* female sexual offenders were either abusers of adults or children. These women seemed to explicitly plan their offences in pursuit of various goals (e.g. sexual gratification, intimacy with victim, revenge) and experienced positive affect throughout the model (e.g. excitement, satisfaction). A further possible subtype of offender was noted (*Implicit-Disorganised*) who engaged in little organised planning and sudden impulsive offending associated with either positive or negative affect.

To our knowledge, the DMFSO is the only available theoretical framework for describing offence processes in female sexual offenders. A key strength of this theory is that it has been developed from *female* sexual offenders themselves and so does not attempt to fit females to pre-existing male theories (see Chapter 3). Because the DMFSO is female-specific, it may well help to engage female sexual offenders in therapy since the pathways are likely to resonate with female experience. As noted in the previous chapter (see Chapter 10), because therapeutic knowledge about sexual offending is male-dominated, female-specific knowledge is likely to play a valuable role in both the creation and maintenance of a strong therapeutic alliance. There is also potential for the DMFSO to guide the treatment of female sexual offenders, including the formulation of varying treatment plans for the different noted subtypes of offenders. A key issue, however, is the fact that the model requires further validation of these subtypes since the current DMFSO was developed using the experiences of very few female sexual offenders. Nevertheless, this model represents theoretical development and shows that although females may hold similar offence patterns to males (i.e. avoidant or approach goals), the factors associated with these goals are gender-specific (e.g. the presence of male coercive co-perpetrators).

Research Developments

Recidivism Rates

One key – and very recent – research development with female sexual offenders concerns the establishment of recidivism rates with this population (see Chapter 6). In the male sexual offending literature, basic recidivism rates have been established for some time now and these provide a benchmark for the evaluation of future risk (Hanson & Bussière, 1998; Hanson & Morton-Bourgon, 2004). For an average follow-up period of 5–6 years, meta-analytic research shows that male sexual offenders hold recidivism rates of 13.7 per cent for new sexual offences, 25 per cent for violent offences (including those of a sexual nature) and 36.9 per cent for any offence type (Hanson & Morton-Bourgon, 2004). It is only relatively recently, however, that researchers have begun to pay attention to the recidivism rates of female sexual offenders (e.g. Broadhurst & Loh, 2003; Cortoni & Hanson, 2005; Cortoni et al., 2009; Freeman & Sandler, 2008; Sandler & Freeman, 2009; Vandiver, 2007).

Cortoni and Hanson (2005) provided what can be described as the first overall review of available studies detailing female recidivism patterns (total $n = 380$). For an average follow-up period of 5 years, Cortoni and Hanson reported low base rates of sexual recidivism for female sexual offenders (1 per cent), 6 per cent for violent offences (including those of a sexual nature) and 20 per cent for any offence type. However, because meta-analysis was not adopted, it was impossible to establish whether variability across studies was significant. Thus, in a later study, Cortoni et al. (2009) not only updated their review such that it included an aggregated total of 1,414 female sexual offenders, but also adopted a meta-analysis approach. In this study, Cortoni et al. defined *recidivism* as 'being charged, convicted, or incarcerated for a new offence' (p. 6[1]), with *violent* recidivism being defined as a new charge, conviction or incarceration for violence (inclusive of sexual offences), and *any* recidivism being defined as any new charge, conviction or incarceration. Thus, rather than being mutually exclusive, the recidivism categories are *cumulative*. For an average follow-up period of 6.5 years, and when one significant outlying study was removed (Vandiver, 2007), Cortoni et al. – similarly to Cortoni and Hanson (2005) – reported low base rates of sexual recidivism (1.5 per cent), violent offences (including those of a sexual nature, 6.5 per cent) and any type of recidivism (20.3 per cent). Cortoni and Hanson and Cortoni et al. report that the female recidivism figures (for all categories) were *significantly* lower than that reported for male sexual offenders.

Establishment of the base rate of recidivism for female sexual offenders represents a significant achievement since such figures are crucial for current and future development of risk assessment practices for female sexual offenders. As Cortoni et al. have pointed out, current knowledge of the extremely low base rates of new sexual offences for female sexual offenders renders male risk assessment tools (validated for males) useless, since they will typically *overestimate* the risk of female sexual offenders. Clearly, such results highlight our need to understand risk – and other elements associated with female sexual offending – using research, knowledge and tools *specifically* developed for use with female sexual offenders. As yet, the research literature is still too immature for us to *precisely* pinpoint risk factors for sexual offending in females (although see Chapter 6 for some guidance and tentative conclusions on these issues). However, it is likely that the research conducted by Cortoni and colleagues will prompt research designed to further our understanding of both the static and dynamic risk factors relevant to female sexual offending.

Treatment Needs

As noted above – and in Chapter 6 – although the dynamic risk factor literature is well established for male sexual offenders, we know very little about the dynamic risk factors of female sexual offenders. Unlike the male sexual offending literature (see Beech, Craig & Browne, 2009), to date, no research has identified a group of dynamic risk factors which, when altered, lead to reductions in sexual or other types of recidivism for female sexual offenders. However, our

---

[1] Note, this is the submission page number and will change when the article is finally in print.

understanding of the *likely* treatment needs of female offenders has evolved slowly from various pieces of research, which have noted deficits or vulnerabilities seemingly over-represented in female sexual offenders. Clinical accounts and systematic research reviews have been used, not only to pinpoint key areas for research, but also to supplement – and make sense of – the knowledge obtained via research (Denov & Cortoni, 2006; Eldridge & Saradjian, 2000; Ford & Cortoni, 2008; Gannon & Rose, 2008; Grayston & De Luca, 1999; Nathan & Ward, 2002). As noted by Ford (see Chapter 7), the research literature to date appears to suggest that female sexual offenders (typically female child sexual offenders) hold a number of treatment needs that, on the surface, appear similar to male sexual offenders' needs. These are *offence-supportive cognition* (including victim empathy), *inappropriate sexual interests*, *intimacy deficits* and *emotional regulation* or *coping deficits*. Treatment needs that appear to have become closely associated with female sexual offenders rather than their male counterparts are *mental health problems* (see Chapter 5), *male dependency* (see Chapters 3 or 7) and *previous victimisation* (both child and adult victimisation, see Chapter 7). Ford provides an in-depth evaluation of each of these likely treatment needs in Chapter 7 and so we summarise and synthesise this evaluation, alongside our own observations in the sections that follow.

Offence-supportive cognition (including victim empathy) In terms of offence-supportive cognition, until relatively recently there was almost no research conducted with female sexual offenders on this particular issue (see Green & Kaplan, 1994 or Saradjian, 1996 for exceptions). However, some empirical research – both quantitative and qualitative – has emerged more recently (e.g. Beckett, 2008; Beech, Parrett, Ward & Fisher, 2009; Gannon, Hoare, Rose & Parrett, in press; Gannon & Rose, 2009; Kubik & Hecker, 2005; Strickland, 2008). For example, Beckett (2008) has argued that female sexual offenders illustrate similarly high levels of offence-supportive cognitions and victim empathy deficits as male sexual offenders measured using questionnaires originally developed and validated for males (i.e. the *Children and Sex Questionnaire*, Beckett, 1987, and the *Victim Empathy Questionnaire*; Beckett & Fisher, 1994). Other research suggests that female sexual offenders misperceive social information such that they *underestimate* the negative impact of child sexual abuse (Kubik & Hecker, 2005), and *overestimate* the hostility of adult males (Beech, Parrett et al., 2009; Gannon et al., in press; Gannon & Rose, 2009).

In a recent study, Beech, Parrett et al. (2009) interviewed 15 female child sexual offenders from the UK about their offences and then attempted to categorise their offence-supportive statements into predetermined schema categories developed from the male child sexual offender literature (i.e. Ward & Keenan's *implicit theories*, 1999). Like males, female child sexual offenders were found to hold beliefs about the world being *dangerous*, children being *sexual*, sex being *harmless* and sexually abusive actions being *uncontrollable*. Unlike males, female child sexual offenders did not appear to believe themselves to be *entitled* to abuse children. Interestingly, however, in a follow-up study using some of the same offenders, Gannon et al. (in press) found that although many female child sexual offenders' cognitions could be 'fitted' into pre-existing male schema categories, the *flavour* of female's offence-supportive cognitions appeared to be very different. For example, Gannon et al. noted that female sexual offenders generally appeared to believe, not that abuse was harmless per se, but that *female-perpetrated* abuse was less harmful in comparison with *male-perpetrated* abuse. Interestingly, Gannon et al. did not find evidence for an overall sexualisation of children as suggested by Beech, Parrett et al., although they did find evidence of female sexual offenders (1) believing *men* to be controlling and dangerous; and (2) believing that men were *entitled* to behave inappropriately (i.e. sexually) towards women and children. Consequently, Gannon et al. argued that, for some female sexual offenders, basic disturbances of early sex-role stereotyping (Bem, 1981) play a role in the development of extreme sexual stereotyping that supports sexually inappropriate behaviour with children. It should be noted that the research specifically focussing on the victim empathy deficits of female sexual offenders is particularly scant. So too is the research on cognition generally in adolescent female sexual offenders. Here, what has been conducted tends to have been adapted from self-report measures with males (e.g. Kubik & Hecker, 2005).

Inappropriate sexual interests In terms of inappropriate sexual interests, the research on female sexual offenders is extremely underdeveloped in relation to the literature on male sexual offenders. The majority of studies that examine female sexual offenders' sexual interests or fantasies have generally been based on case studies or self-report data during clinical practice (Cooper, Swaminath, Baxter & Poulin, 1990; Davin, 1999; Mathews et al., 1989; Saradjian, 1996), although there are others studies, using more implicit measures, that are of relevance (Gannon & Rose, 2009; Gannon, Rose & Williams, 2009). In one clinical self-report study, Saradjian (1996) asked female child sexual offenders and non-sexual offending females about masturbatory habits, fantasies and sexual thoughts. Neither female child sexual offenders nor the comparison group reported highly prevalent levels of masturbatory fantasies about children. Nevertheless, female child sexual offenders did report having sexual thoughts about children. Interestingly, Saradjian reported that of the small number of male-coerced females who reported masturbating to sexual fantasies about children ($n = 4$), none reported masturbating to such fantasies *prior* to engaging in coerced sexual abuse. However, all of these women subsequently went on to sexually abuse children autonomously.

These findings are interesting, especially when one considers the polygraph results reported in Chapter 9. Here, Heil, Simons and Burton report that, following implementation of the polygraph, females who, from official record, were initially believed to have been coerced to offend by a male disclosed having offended by themselves before co-offending. These results *suggest* that sexual fantasies and thoughts could play more of an aetiological role in female-perpetrated abuse than currently estimated. However, it should be noted that implicit research with female child sexual offenders has been unable to establish any inappropriate cognitive links between children and sex (Gannon et al., 2009).

Generally, the self report/clinical literature suggests that the consulting professional should carefully assess female sexual offenders for the presence of inappropriate sexual interests, since a small proportion of females – including adolescents – appear to hold inappropriate sexual interests at some level (Green & Kaplan, 1994;

Hunter, Lexier, Goodwin, Browne & Dennis, 1993; Nathan & Ward, 2002; Sarad-jian, 1996; Simons, Tyler & Heil, 2005). However, a particularly challenging aspect is ascertaining exactly what level of sexual interest exists, how this should be measured in females and the role that this sexual interest actually played in the abusive behaviour. As noted by Rousseau and Cortoni (see Chapter 5), Chivers and colleagues (Chivers, Rieger, Latty & Bailey, 2004; Suschinsky, Lalumière & Chivers, 2009) have suggested that women's sexual arousal may be qualitatively different from men's, that is, less indicative of fixed sexual interests. This highlights the importance of keeping gender differences in mind as knowledge in this area develops.

Intimacy and social skills deficits   The exploration of intimacy and social skills deficits in female sexual offenders has not specifically been researched to any great degree. Instead, as outlined by Ford (see Chapter 7), the general literature typically *alludes* to female sexual offenders' apparent difficulties in this area. For example, female sexual offenders generally report their developmental relationships with caregivers as being adversarial and/or characterised by physical, sexual or emo-tional abuse (Allen, 1991; Gannon et al., 2008, 2010; Green & Kaplan, 1994; Saradjian, 1996). Given that adversarial early attachment experiences are hypothesised to impact upon an individual's ability to interact effectively with adult partners (Bartholomew, 1990; Bowlby, 1969, 1973), it is perhaps unsurprising to see reports of female sexual offenders' adversarial adult relationships (e.g. Gannon et al., 2008, 2010; Saradjian, 1996) and self-reported social inadequacies (Strickland, 2008).

Connected with this, researchers have found that female sexual offenders gen-erally report sexually offending against children to obtain intimacy and emotional fulfilment either with the victim themselves, or with their co-perpetrator (Gannon et al., 2008; Saradjian, 1996). Thus, for some women, sexually abusive behaviour may occur as an inappropriate means of gaining intimacy either because social skills are impoverished, because the environmental context does not foster inti-macy, or both. Interestingly, research shows that female sexual offenders appear socially isolated and lacking friends in the period leading up to and around the time of their offending (Gannon et al., 2008; Saradjian, 1996). Clearly, not only could such emotional loneliness function to increase the likelihood of a woman seeking out intimacy inappropriately, but it could also enable male sexual offenders to target such women and groom them as co-perpetrators. Finally, similarly to the other treatment areas described, the research and knowledge regarding the inti-macy deficits and social skills of adolescent female sexual offenders is particularly impoverished although research suggests evidence of similarly adverse early at-tachment relationships (Bumby & Bumby, 1997; Tardif, Auclair, Jacob & Carpentier, 2005; Vick, McRoy & Matthews, 2002) and subsequent fear of intimacy (Hunter & Mathews, 1997).

Emotional regulation or coping deficits   The emotional regulation or coping deficits of *male* sexual offenders have been researched fairly substantively (Cortoni & Marshall, 2001; Feelgood, Cortoni & Thompson, 2005; Serran & Marshall, 2006). However, this is one area of potential treatment need for female sexual offenders that is also under-researched to date. Available research suggests that female sexual offenders – relative to non-offenders – report more stressful experiences and inadequacy in coping with such experiences (Saradjian, 1996). Research also suggests that around the time of the offence, female sexual offenders' lives are particularly turbulent, and stressful, and that women feel generally out of control (Beech, Parrett et al., 2009; Gannon et al., 2008). Thus, female sexual offenders may hold inadequately developed coping abilities that compromise their ability to deal with negative experiences and the negative affect associated with these experiences (i.e. anger, depression, anxiety). One mechanism by which female-perpetrated abuse may occur is via perceived stress-release in the form of sexual soothing or *sexual coping* (Cortoni & Marshall, 2001; Saradjian, 1996). In the male sexual offending literature, it seems that both *inappropriate* and *appropriate* sexual activities may form part of a sexual coping style (Cortoni & Marshall, 2001). However, whether this is true also for female sexual offenders is largely unknown and requires further examination. Gannon and Rose (2008) have noted that emotional regulation in female sexual offenders – like their male counterparts – will be strongly affected by limited brain functioning such as brain injuries or intellectual impairment (see Faller, 1987). It is also likely that limited brain functioning – in the form of intellectual impairment – may well lead to offending behaviour at a particularly young age and this could in part explain the high levels of learning disability reported by Frey (see Chapter 4) in adolescent female sexual offender samples (see Hunter et al., 1993 and Tardif et al., 2005 for individual studies). Finally, in recent years, professionals in the *male* sexual offending literature have begun to realise that it is not just *negative* affective states that are associated with sexual offending, and that positive affective states such as excitement can also play a seemingly facilitatory role (Ward & Hudson, 2000; Ward et al., 1995; Yates, Kingston & Hall, 2003). The research with female sexual offenders is only beginning to develop in this area, although Gannon et al. (2008, 2010) have illustrated that some female sexual offenders do experience strong positive affect throughout their offence chain (e.g. anticipatory excitement or satisfaction) which is likely to both facilitate and maintain sexually abusive behaviour. What is unclear, however, is the extent to which such positive affect – as experienced by female sexual offenders – is associated with inappropriate sexual interests.

Dependency   Perhaps one of the most widely noted – yet controversial – treatment needs associated with female sexual offenders revolves around the issue of male coercion and the associated *dependency* of male-coerced female sexual offenders. There is no doubt that female sexual offenders are different from male sexual offenders since, in addition to abusive experiences throughout childhood, they are often additionally victimised by males throughout their adult lives (Gannon et al., 2008; O'Connor, 1987). As Ford (see Chapter 7) rightly notes, what is important here is our understanding of when a woman who co-perpetrates with a male becomes categorised as having been *coerced* into that abuse (i.e. is the female simply male-*accompanied* or male-*coerced?*). Clearly, this is a difficult issue to ascertain, especially when so much of our research relies on female sexual offenders' self-reports; these are likely to be subject to impression management strategies. In Chapter 9 of this book, Heil, Simons and Burton provide data showing that perhaps all is not what it seems when it comes to female co-perpetration/coercion. Here, the authors report that, for females who were officially recorded as having offended under male-coercion ($n = 3$), all of these women later admitted having offended by themselves *before* having been coerced by a male when subjected to polygraph examination. To our knowledge, this is the first piece of research examining this issue, although previous research has highlighted that coerced females may subsequently begin offending of their own volition (Gannon et al., 2008). The available clinical literature and research evidence does, however, indicate that women identified as having been coerced into their sexual offending show traits of dependence, and passivity, as well as a general fearfulness of adult men (Beech, Parrett et al., 2009; Gannon et al., in press; Green & Kaplan, 1994; Nathan & Ward, 2001).

In relation to adolescent female sexual offenders (see Chapter 4), the research literature appears to suggest that these females are most likely to offend unaccompanied (see Fehrenbach & Monastersky, 1988; Kubik & Hecker, 2005; Tardif et al., 2005), although this does not preclude the possibility that these females hold passive traits since the literature suggests that these may be apparent in adolescents who hold low self-esteem and identity confusion (Hunter & Mathews, 1997). In summary, some important issues remain to be addressed in this domain. In particular, how researchers should universally define the concepts of male-coerced vs. male-accompanied abuse and the prevalence of *genuine* male-coerced female sexual abuse.

Mental health problems   A similarly controversial area of treatment need highly associated with female sexual offenders regards *mental health problems* (see Chapter 5). A brief examination of the research and clinical literature appears to suggest that female sexual offenders are highly likely to experience mental health problems (Faller, 1995; Green & Kaplan, 1994) and this, of course, suggests that mental health problems may well play an aetiological role in offending. However, researchers have increasingly started to question – and research – the premise that mental health deficits are over-represented in apprehended female sexual offenders (Fazel, Sjöstedt, Grann & Langström, 2008; Ford, 2006; Johansson-Love & Fremouw, 2006; Miller, Turner & Henderson, 2009). The key problems with the literature examining female sexual offenders' mental health are methodological. First, some studies do not incorporate adequate comparison groups, making it impossible to assess the significance of the prevalence rates observed for female sexual offenders (e.g. Faller, 1995; O'Connor, 1987). Second, studies use wholly different definitions and measurements of mental health problems (i.e. some use diagnostic information while others do not). Third, because mental health problems are often assessed using self-report methods, it is likely that women may *overstate* their problems to impression manage (Miller et al., 2009). Fourth, it is likely that only the most serious – and consequently *disordered* – cases of female-perpetrated sexual offences are reported or acted upon by authorities (Fazel et al., 2008; Ford, 2006). Finally, it is also likely that professionals are more likely to pathologise female sexual offenders due to deeply ingrained stereotypes regarding women (Peter, 2006).

In the most recent – and perhaps methodologically advanced – study on this topic to date, Fazel et al. (2008) examined 93 female sexual offenders from Sweden and compared their mental health issues with (1) those of the female community population ($n = 20,597$); and (2) those of a female violent offender comparison group

($n = 13,452$). Although, psychosis (measured via clinical diagnoses) appeared to be particularly prevalent in the female sexual offending group relative to the community females (7.5 per cent vs. 1.4 per cent, respectively), there were no substantial differences between female sexual offenders and the violent offender comparison group. In other words, it appeared as if the female sexual offenders were no different to other violent female offenders on mental health deficits. Clearly, however, this issue is in need of further investigation using rigorous, standardised research.

Previous victimisation   A final area of potential treatment need highly associated with female-perpetrated sexual abuse is *previous victimisation*. As noted previously, a whole host of researchers and clinical professionals have noted the high prevalence of developmental – and adult – trauma experienced by female sexual offenders, typically at the hands of males (Allen, 1991; Gannon et al., 2008; Green & Kaplan, 1994; Lewis & Stanley, 2000). Generally, the research literature has suggested that female sexual offenders, relative to their male counterparts, experience abuse more frequently and severely (Allen, 1991; Miccio-Fonseca, 2000; Pothast & Allen, 1994). For example, Allen (1991) found that significantly more female sexual offenders, relative to male sexual offenders, reported having experienced physical abuse at the hands of their parents (e.g. being slapped or hit with something). Furthermore, a recent study by Wijkman and Bijleveld (2008) has demonstrated that having experienced violence from a partner, school bullying and physical abuse was associated with the numbers of sexual offences perpetrated by women.

In recent research using a combination of questionnaires, behavioural checklist, official records and the polygraph (Heil & Simons, 2008; Simons et al., 2005), Heil, Simons and Burton (see Chapter 9; Table 9.3) found that incarcerated female sexual offenders ($n = 30$) experienced more sexual abuse during childhood by multiple offenders, relative to various male sexual offenders. In addition, these women also experienced more sexual abuse compared with female sexual offenders within the community ($n = 12$). Thus, more research is required to understand the relationship between early victimisation and later offending among women and whether various subtypes of female sexual offenders can be differentiated on victimisation histories according to their offence characteristics (see Chapter 9).

Treatment Developments

Because our knowledge of female sexual offenders and their associated treatment needs is only just developing, it is easy to overlook the significant gains that have been made over the past two decades (particularly the last decade) in relation to our understanding of treatment for female sexual offenders. As noted in Blanchette and Taylor's review of female sexual offender service provision (see Chapter 8), some relatively established assessment and treatment services have been developed in the UK (i.e. the Lucy Faithfull Foundation), Canada (Correctional Service of Canada) and the USA (e.g. Wisdom Works Counseling Services). Two decades ago, such programmes were simply unheard of and so the provision of such treatment for females is a remarkable achievement. In the UK, for example, the *Lucy Faithfull Foundation* – a child protection charity – have been developing their work with female sexual offenders over the past 16 years while the Correctional Service of Canada implemented its national strategy for the assessment and treatment of incarcerated female sexual offenders in 2002.

Given the development of knowledge in rehabilitation and treatment generally (e.g. the Good Lives Model; Ward & Gannon, 2006; Dialectical Behaviour Therapy; Linehan, 1993), and information regarding gender-responsive approaches (i.e. Trauma; Bloom, 2004), the Lucy Faithfull Foundation have moulded and amended their treatment for female sexual abusers to reflect major developments in the field. In 2000 (see Chapter 8), the Lucy Faithfull Foundation provided a group programme for female sexual offenders in prison, although programme provision became compromised by the very small numbers of incarcerated female sexual offenders, a problem that appears to hamper many attempts at programme provision for female sexual offenders. However, the Lucy Faithfull Foundation continues to provide treatment using the materials from this programme, which covers the treatment needs outlined earlier in this chapter (i.e. *cognition or schemas, sexual arousal, relationships* and *self management,* as well as human need fulfilment).

A critical issue for this programme, like others, is the lack of female-specific resources and measures available. The Lucy Faithfull Foundation currently uses a series of questionnaire assessments that, although initially developed with males (e.g. *The children and sex questionnaire,* Beckett, 1987) have now been implemented with females (Beckett, 2008). This highlights one of the significant challenges for treatment with female sexual offenders in the future. That is, should we adapt and validate tools previously developed with male sexual offenders for use with females? Or, should we begin developing tools specifically for use with female sexual offenders? Clearly, this is one area that will undoubtedly evolve one way or the other over the forthcoming decades.

The Correctional Service of Canada (see Chapter 8) similarly run a gender-responsive assessment and treatment initiative for female sexual offenders who are serving a federal sentence (i.e. a sentence of 2 years or more). Like the Lucy Faithfull Foundation, the Correctional Service of Canada typically runs one-to-one treatment services because of the problems of implementing a group treatment for few women who hold differing needs. The therapy is cognitive-behavioural in orientation and is based on the available literature regarding female offender issues (i.e. the general female offender and sexual offender populations) as well as the male sexual offending literature. Elements of the Good Lives Model (Ward & Gannon, 2006) and Relational theory (Miller, 1986) are also used. Treatment consists of modules examining *cognitions, deviant arousal, intimacy and social functioning, victim awareness* and *self-management* and women are assigned to modules deemed to fit their underlying treatment needs based upon pre-assessment. Like the Lucy Faithfull foundation, the Correctional Service of Canada is providing innovative and groundbreaking services for a group of offenders previously overlooked. In doing so, however, it is facing similar challenges regarding female group work provision and female-specific assessments (Ford & Cortoni, 2008).

Blanchette and Taylor's summary of treatment provision for female sexual offenders in the USA (see Chapter 8) show that there are a number of female-specific treatment services being implemented for female sexual offenders and that there are also some significant variations across states (e.g. Texas, Colorado & New York).

For example, the Counseling Institute of Texas, Inc. (CIT) works on the fundamental philosophy that female sexual offenders hold similar treatment needs to those of males. Thus, CIT treats female sexual offenders alongside their male counterparts. Women treated by CIT are also assessed throughout treatment using the polygraph to facilitate honesty. On the other hand, however, treatment services in Colorado – Wisdom Works Counseling Services – have moved away from treating female sexual offenders alongside their male counterparts, instead favouring female-specific treatment and their programme is not polygraph-assisted. We think it is highly probable that the variation in treatment provision across states and countries is very likely due to the fact that knowledge of female sexual offenders' treatment needs is only just gaining momentum. Thus, a good deal of the preliminary literature is still very much open to individual clinical interpretation (Gannon & Rose, 2008). Nevertheless, we believe that treatment initiatives are set to develop in a more cogent manner as research in this area expands. Blanchette and Taylor (see Chapter 8) document other promising programme developments in Australia (Department of Corrective Services, New South Wales) and the UK (National Offender Management Service). Furthermore, Frey (see Chapter 4) notes the evident increase in treatment programmes being developed for adolescent female sexual offenders – and this despite the absence of key empirical research investigating the treatment needs of this group. It is critical, then, that research into female sexual offending is both promoted and supported so that these and other developing initiatives become evidence-based.

A critical issue associated with the infancy of treatment service provision for female sexual offenders is the difficulty in demonstrating *treatment effectiveness*. As Blanchette and Taylor (see Chapter 8) have pointed out, due to the low numbers of women who receive treatment and the overall low rate of sexual recidivism by female sexual offenders, it is likely to take some significant time before we are able to demonstrate treatment effectiveness for this population, including which elements are necessary for its effectiveness. Thus, in the absence of such information, it is critical that treatment providers base their programmes, as much as possible, on the emerging 'What Works' literature for female offenders in general (see Blanchette & Brown, 2006; Sheehan, McIvor & Trotter, 2007). That is, treatment should strive to adhere to the risk, need and responsivity principles of effective interventions with offenders (Andrews & Bonta, 2007) taking care to do so in a gender-informed manner (Blanchette & Brown, 2006). This, we believe, will not only involve conceptualising and synthesising current research knowledge in a female-informed manner, but going back to the drawing board and developing *female-specific* assessment procedures associated with relevant treatment programmes.

In Chapter 10, Ashfield, Brotherston, Eldridge and Elliott outline their overview of female-specific process issues that they believe are essential for successful therapy with female sexual offenders. These process issues seem sensible and gender-informed. However, as the authors of this chapter themselves acknowledge, it may take some time, or even be unrealistic, to assume that research on the process issues of female sexual offenders will be executed in the same manner as has been done with males. Quite simply, at present, there are neither the numbers of female sexual offenders, nor the number of standardised groups available to support rigorous therapeutic process research with female sexual offenders. Thus, as Ashfield,

Brotherston, Eldridge and Elliott (see Chapter 10) have rightly argued, it is time to view female sexual offending as a topic within its own right, rather than constantly looking for similarities with male sexual offenders. This will, we are sure, minimise the possibility of female sexual offender treatment getting 'off track' or pursuing what might ultimately turn out to be 'blind alleys'.

FUTURE DIRECTIONS FOR RESEARCH AND TREATMENT WITH FEMALE SEXUAL OFFENDERS

In drawing this book to a close, we would like to make a number of recommendations for future research and treatment of female sexual offenders. These are based on preceding chapters and our discussions within this chapter.

We believe that a crucial shift needs to occur in terms of the development of gender-informed theory, research, assessment and treatment with female sexual offenders. For example, although it is much harder to devise assessment practices from the ground up with female sexual offenders, we believe that this option is far preferable than assessing female sexual offenders using male-derived practices. Put simply, male-derived assessments have typically been developed from research and clinical experience with *males*. Thus, implementing such assessments with females is likely to miss vital elements of the female sexual offenders' treatment needs, hindering our ability to develop female-specific knowledge in this area. Consequently, we believe it is far more preferable to develop our knowledge of female sexual offending from the bottom upwards rather than continually impose male-specific theory and models to female sexual offenders. Thus, policy makers and other professionals thinking about devising research and clinical practices, or those already implementing them, should carefully examine whether these practices are gender-informed.

A particularly prominent area of neglect in terms of gender-informed practices with female sexual offenders revolves around the absence of actuarial or dynamic risk assessment tools. It might seem tempting in the absence of any female-specific tools to simply adapt what is available with men for use with women. We advise strongly against such procedures. As Cortoni and colleagues' research has shown, female sexual offenders offend at vastly different – and reduced – rates than their male counterparts. Thus, in addition to refraining from utilising actuarial risk tools devised for males, we also advise against assuming that the dynamic risk factors for females are exactly the same as those illustrated in men. Currently, the contemporary research literature suggests that although there may be some very basic similarities, the actual meaning of each factor varies greatly depending on whether the offender is male or female. Related to this, it is crucial that we conduct research to examine which of the hypothesised treatment needs for female sexual offenders, when altered, lead to reductions in later offending. Current research suggests that females who offend sexually will more often re-offend with non-sexual crimes; thus, further research should look at this relationship and how best we can reduce non-sexual offending in women who come to our attention for sexual offences.

There are further important caveats in our research knowledge that currently impede our ability to provide evidence-based treatment with female sexual offenders. In short, research on female sexual offenders appears to have been concentrated in particular areas (e.g. typologies, offence-related cognitions, mental health deficits) while other areas of likely importance have been neglected. These are the prevalence and measurement of inappropriate sexual arousal, intimacy issues, psychosocial issues (in particular dependency issues and attachment styles) and emotional regulation and coping skills. In addition, there is a crucial need for the development of an empirically informed theoretical understanding of how trauma and previous victimisation interact with the above noted factors to culminate in sexual offending. A further area that requires more research is the influence of male coercion on female-perpetrated sexual offending. It seems, as discussed in this book (see Chapter 9), that we may be currently overestimating this aspect among female sexual offenders. However, further research is required to substantiate preliminary conclusions. Finally, the overall patterns of criminal offending of female sexual offenders (e.g. presence of other types of child abuse, relationships between prostitution-related activities and sexual offending) require further investigations.

A clear asset for future research in all areas of female sexual offending will be the development of universally agreed upon constructs, whether these are mental health issues, recidivism or even definitions of sexual offending by women. This will alleviate any misunderstandings within and across research findings and make the results more interpretable. Finally, the conduct of rigorous, empirically-based research using consistent definitions on the areas outlined above will provide the basis for the future development of verifiable multifactorial theory to explain sexual offending by women that will guide future efforts in this area.

A final caveat in our current knowledge on female sexual offenders concerns the treatment needs of juvenile females who commit sexual offences (see Chapter 4) and the factors that lead to continued offending – or desistance – in these young females. Clearly, carefully planned longitudinal research could be paramount for answering such important questions. However, until such research comes to fruition, we would advise research professionals to take special care when researching the treatment needs of these young women. Currently, treatment efforts with adolescent female sexual offenders are not empirically guided to any great degree and this situation will only be addressed if research efforts are focused on this population.

CONCLUSION

In this chapter, we have summarised the key developments that have occurred in our research and treatment efforts with female sexual offenders over the past decade. Particular developments of note appear to be the generation of gender-specific sexual offending processes of female sexual offenders, the establishment of baseline recidivism figures for this population, a proliferation of research in the area of offence-supportive cognitions and mental health and the establishment of comprehensive treatment practices for convicted female sexual offenders (notably in the UK, Canada and the USA). Nevertheless, while some substantial developments have occurred in recent years, there is still much work to do in this area and many gaps to fill. As yet, we still do not hold satisfactory answers to questions such as: 'To what extent are female sexual offenders similar to, and different from, male sexual offenders?' However, it does seem that there are many differences between female and male sexual offenders, associated with gender, that we simply must not overlook in our future research efforts. Furthermore, in asking questions about whether female sexual offenders are similar to female offenders who do not sexually offend, it seems as though there are likely to be key similarities (e.g. previous victimisation, mental health issues).

We excitedly await a time when we will be able to write about empirically-informed 'What Works' information on female sexual offenders. We believe that this day will come. In the meantime, we believe it is crucial for professionals in this area to ensure that that their research is gender-informed and treatment empirically-based whenever possible. In our view (see also Blanchette & Brown, 2006), the only way to ensure this happens is to adhere to major rehabilitative theories (i.e. the Risk-Need-Responsivity Model; Andrews & Bonta, 2007) and gain knowledge on each of these core principles as they are applied to female sexual offenders in a manner that is gender-informed. After all, gender *is* important and it must be acknowledged in our work.

REFERENCES

Adshead, G., Howett, M., & Mason, F. (1994). Women who sexually abuse children: The undiscovered country. *The Journal of Sexual Aggression*, 1, 44–56.

Allen, C. M. (1991). *Women and men who sexually abuse children: A comparative analysis*. Orwell, VT: Safer Society Press.

Andrews, D. A., & Bonta, J. (2007). *The psychology of criminal conduct* (4th ed.). Cincinnati, OH: Anderson.

Bartholomew, K. (1990). Avoidance of intimacy: An attachment perspective. *Journal of Social and Personal Relationships*, 7, 147–178.

Beckett, R. C. (1987). *The children and sex questionnaire*. Unpublished manuscript.

Beckett, R. C. (2008, October). *Female sexual abusers: A comparison with men who sexually abuse children*. Paper presented at the 27th conference for the Association for the Treatment of Sexual Abusers, Atlanta, GA.

Beckett, R. C., & Fisher, D. (1994, November). *Assessing victim empathy: A new measure*. Paper presented at the 13th Annual Conference of the Association for the Treatment of Sexual Abusers, San Francisco.

Beech, A. R., Craig, L. A., & Browne, K. D. (2009). *Assessment and treatment of sex offenders: A handbook*. Chichester, UK: Wiley-Blackwell.

Beech, A. R., Parrett, N., Ward, T., & Fisher, D. (2009). Assessing female sexual offenders' motivations and cognitions: An exploratory study. *Psychology, Crime & Law*, 15, 201–216.

Bem, S. L. (1981). Gender schema theory: A cognitive account of sex typing. *Psychological Review*, 88, 354–364.

Blanchette, K., & Brown, S. L. (2006). *The assessment and treatment of women offenders*. Chichester, UK: Wiley.

Bloom, B. E. (2004, March). *A theoretical framework for gender-responsive strategies in corrections*. Paper presented at the Annual Meeting of the American Sociological Association, San Francisco, CA. Retrieved 18th January 2009, from http://www.allacademic.com/meta/p108747_index.html.

Bowlby, J. (1969). *Attachment and loss: Vol. 1. Attachment*. New York: Basic Books.

Bowlby, J. (1973). *Attachment and loss: Vol. 2. Separation*. New York: Basic Books.

Broadhurst, R. G., & Loh, N. S. (2003). The probabilities of sex offender re-arrest. *Criminal Behaviour and Mental Health, 13*, 125–143.

Bumby, N. H., & Bumby, K. M. (1997). Adolescent female sexual offenders. In B. K. Schwartz & H. R. Cellini (Eds.), *The sex offender: Corrections, treatment, and legal practice* (pp. 10.1–10.16). Kingston, NJ: Civic Research Institute, Inc.

Chivers, M. L., Rieger, G., Latty, E., & Bailey, J. M. (2004). A sex difference in the specificity of sexual arousal. *Psychological Science, 15*, 736–744.

Cooper, A. J., Swaminath, S., Baxter, D., & Poulin, C. (1990). A female sex offender with multiple paraphilias: A psychologic, physiologic (laboratory sexual arousal) and endocrine case study. *Canadian Journal of Psychiatry, 35*, 334–337.

Cortoni, F., & Gannon, T. A. (in press). Female sexual offenders. In A. Phenix & H. M. Hoberman (Eds.), *Sexual offenders: Diagnosis, risk assessment and management*. New York: Springer.

Cortoni, F., & Hanson, R. K. (2005). *A review of the recidivism rates of adult female sexual offenders* (R-169). Ottawa: Research Branch, Correction Service of Canada. Retrieved 4th May 2007, from http://www.csc-scc.gc.ca/text/rsrch/reports/r169/r169_e.pdf.

Cortoni, F., Hanson, R. K., & Coache, M. E. (2009). *The recidivism rates of female sexual offenders: A meta-analysis*. Manuscript under review.

Cortoni, F., & Marshall, B. (2001). Sex as a coping strategy and its relationship to juvenile sexual history and intimacy in sexual offenders. *Sexual Abuse: A Journal of Research and Treatment, 13*, 27–43.

Davin, P. A. (1999). Secrets revealed: A study of female sex offenders. In P. A. Davin, J. C. R. Hislop, & T. Dunbar (Eds.), *The female sexual abuser: Three views* (pp. 1–134). Brandon, VT: Safer Society Press.

Denov, M. S., & Cortoni, F. (2006). Adult female sexual offenders. In C. Hilarski & J. Wodarski (Eds.), *Comprehensive mental health practices with sex offenders and their families* (pp. 71–99). New York: Haworth Press.

Eldridge, H., & Saradjian, J. (2000). Replacing the function of abusive behaviors for the offender: Remaking relapse prevention in working with women who sexually abuse children. In D. R. Laws, S. M. Hudson, & T. Ward (Eds.), *Remaking relapse prevention with sex offenders: A sourcebook* (pp. 402–426). Thousand Oaks, CA: Sage.

Faller, K. C. (1987). Women who sexually abuse children. Violence and Victims, 2, 263–276.

Faller, K. C. (1995). A clinical sample of women who have sexually abused children. *Journal of Child Sexual Abuse, 4*, 13–30.

Fazel, S., Sjöstedt, G., Grann, M., & Langström, N. (2008). Sexual offending in women and psychiatric disorder: A national case-control study. *Archives of Sexual Behavior*, Online May 2008.

Feelgood, S., Cortoni, F., & Thompson, A. (2005). Sexual coping, general coping and cognitive distortions in incarcerated rapists and child molesters. *Journal of Sexual Aggression, 11*, 157–170.

Fehrenbach, P. A., & Monastersky, C. (1988). Characteristics of female adolescent sexual offenders. *American Journal of Orthopsychiatry, 58*(1), 148–151.

Ford, H. (2006). *Women who sexually abuse children*. Chichester, UK: Wiley.

Ford, H., & Cortoni, F. (2008). Sexual deviance in females: Assessment and treatment. In D. R. Laws & W. O'Donohue (Eds.), *Sexual deviance* (2nd ed., pp. 508–526). New York: Guilford Press.

Freeman, N., & Sandler, J. (2008). Female and male sex offenders: A comparison of recidivism patterns and risk factors. *Journal of Interpersonal Violence, 23*, 1394–413.

Gannon, T. A., Hoare, J., Rose, M. R., & Parrett, N. (in press). A re-examination of female child molesters' implicit theories: Evidence of female specificity? *Psychology Crime and Law*.

Gannon, T. A., & Rose, M. R. (2008). Female child sexual offenders: Towards integrating theory and practice. *Aggression and Violent Behavior, 13*, 442–461.

Gannon, T. A., & Rose, M. R. (2009). Offence-related interpretative bias in female child molesters: A preliminary study. *Sexual Abuse: A Journal of Research and Treatment, 21*, 194–207.

Gannon, T. A., Rose, M. R., & Ward, T. (2008). A descriptive model of the offense process for female sexual offenders. *Sexual Abuse: A Journal of Research and Treatment, 20*, 352–374.

Gannon, T. A., Rose, M. R., & Ward, T. (2010). Pathways to female sexual offending: Approach or avoidance? *Psychology, Crime and Law*, 1–22 (iFirst).

Gannon, T. A., Rose, M. R., & Williams, S. E. (2009). Do female child molesters hold implicit associations between children and sex? A preliminary investigation. *Journal of Sexual Aggression, 15*, 55–61.

Grayston, A. D., & De Luca, R. V. (1999). Female perpetrators of child sexual abuse: A review of the clinical and empirical literature. *Aggression and Violent Behavior, 4*, 93–106.

Green, A. H., & Kaplan, M. S. (1994). Psychiatric impairment and childhood victimization experiences in female child molesters. *Journal of the American Academy of Child and Adolescent Psychiatry, 33*, 954–961.

Hanson, R. K., & Bussière, M. (1998). Predicting relapse: A meta-analysis of sexual offender recidivism studies. *Journal of Consulting and Clinical Psychology, 66*, 348–362.

Hanson, R. K., & Morton-Bourgon, K. (2004). *Predictors of sexual recidivism: An updated meta-analysis* (User Report 2004–02). Ottawa: Public Safety and Emergency Preparedness Canada.

Heil, P., & Simons, D. (2008). Multiple paraphilias: Prevalence, etiology, assessment, and treatment. In D. R. Laws & W. T. O'Donohue (Eds.), *Sexual deviance: Theory, assessment, and treatment* (2nd ed., pp. 527–556). New York: Guildford Press.

Hunter, J. A., Lexier, L. J., Goodwin, D. W., Browne, P. A., & Dennis, C. (1993). Psychosexual, attitudinal, and developmental characteristics of juvenile female perpetrators in a residential treatment setting. *Journal of Child and Family Studies, 2*, 317–326.

Hunter, J. A., & Mathews, R. (1997). Sexual deviance in females. In R. D. Laws & W. O'Donohue (Eds.), *Sexual deviance: Theory, assessment, and treatment* (pp. 465–480). New York: Guilford Press.

Johansson-Love, J., & Fremouw, W. (2006). A critique of the female sexual perpetrator research. *Aggression and Violent Behavior, 11*, 12–26.

Kubik, E. K., & Hecker, J. E. (2005). Cognitive distortions about sex and sexual offending: A comparison of sex offending girls, delinquent girls, and girls from the community. *Journal of Child Sexual Abuse, 14*, 43–69.

Lewis, C. F., & Stanley, C. R. (2000). Women accused of sexual offenses. *Behavioral Sciences and the Law, 18*, 73–81.

Linehan, M. M. (1993). *Skills training manual for treating borderline personality disorder*. New York: Guildford Press.

Mathews, R., Matthews, J. K., & Speltz, K. (1989). *Female sexual offenders: An exploratory study*. Orwell, VT: Safer Society Press.

Miccio-Fonseca, L. C. (2000). Adult and adolescent female sex offenders: Experiences compared to other female and male sex offenders. *Journal of Psychology & Human Sexuality, 11*, 75–88.

Miller, J. B. (1986). *What do we mean by relationships?* Work in Progress No. 33. Wellesley, MA: Stone Center, Working Paper Series.

Miller, H. A., Turner, K., & Henderson, C. (2009). Psychopathology of sex offenders: A comparison of males and females using latent profile analysis. *Criminal Justice and Behavior, 36*, 778–792.

Nathan, P., & Ward, T. (2001). Females who sexually abuse children: Assessment and treatment issues. *Psychiatry, Psychology and Law, 8*, 44–45.

Nathan, P., & Ward, T. (2002). Female sex offenders: Clinical and demographic features. *Journal of Sexual Aggression, 8*, 5–21.

O'Connor, A. A. (1987). Female sex offenders. *British Journal of Psychiatry, 150*, 615–620.

Peter, T. (2006). Mad, bad, or victim? Making sense of mother–daughter sexual abuse. *Feminist Criminology, 1*, 283–302.

Pothast, H. L., & Allen, C. M. (1994). Masculinity and femininity in male and female perpetrators of child sexual abuse. *Child Abuse & Neglect, 18*, 763–767.

Sandler, J. C., & Freeman, N. J. (2007). Typology of female sex offenders: A test of Vandiver and Kercher. *Sexual Abuse: A Journal of Research and Treatment, 19*, 73–89.

Sandler, J. C., & Freeman, N. J. (2009). Female sex offender recidivism: A large-scale empirical analysis. *Sexual Abuse: A Journal of Research and Treatment, 21*, 455–473.

Saradjian, J. (1996). *Women who sexually abuse children: From research to clinical practice.* Chichester, UK: Wiley.

Serran, G. A., & Marshall, L. E. (2006). Coping & mood in sexual offending. In W. L. Marshall, Y. M. Fernandez, L. E. Marshall, & G. A. Serran (Eds.), *Sexual offender treatment: Controversial issues* (pp. 109–124). Chichester, West Sussex: John Wiley & Sons.

Sheehan, R., McIvor, G., & Trotter, C. (2007). *What works with women offenders.* Cullumpton, Devon: Willan.

Simons, D., Tyler, C., & Heil, P. (2005, November). *Childhood risk factors associated with crossover offending.* Poster presented at the 24th Annual Association for the Treatment of Sexual Abusers Research and Treatment Conference in Salt Lake City, Utah.

Strauss, A., & Corbin, J. (1998). *Basics of qualitative research: Techniques and procedures for developing grounded theory* (2nd ed.). Thousand Oaks, CA: Sage.

Strickland, S. M. (2008). Female sex offenders: Exploring issues of personality, trauma, and cognitive distortions. *Journal of Interpersonal Violence, 23*, 474–489.

Suschinsky, K. D., Lalumière, M. L., & Chivers, M. L. (2009). Sex differences in patterns of genital sexual arousal: Measurement artifacts or true phenomena? *Archives of Sexual Behavior, 38*, 559–573.

Syed, F., & Williams, S. (1996). *Case studies of female sex offenders in the Correctional Service of Canada.* Ottawa: Correctional Service Canada. Retrieved 15th June 2007, from http://www.ncjrs.gov/App/publications/Abstract.aspx?id=172585.

Tardif, M., Auclair, N., Jacob, M., & Carpentier, J. (2005). Sexual abuse perpetrated by adult and juvenile females: An ultimate attempt to resolve a conflict associated with maternal identity. *Child Abuse & Neglect, 29*, 153–167.

Vandiver, D. (2007, March). *An examination of re-arrest rates of 942 male and 471 female registered sex offenders.* Academy of the Criminal Justice Sciences, Feature Panel on Sex Offenders: Seattle, WA.

Vandiver, D. M., & Kercher, G. (2004). Offender and victim characteristics of registered female sexual offenders in Texas: A proposed typology of female sexual offenders. *Sexual Abuse: A Journal of Research and Treatment, 16*, 121–137.

Vick, J., McRoy, R., & Matthews, B. M. (2002). Young female sex offenders: Assessment and treatment issues. *Journal of Child Sexual Abuse, 11*(2), 1–23.

Ward, T., & Gannon, T. A. (2006). Rehabilitation, etiology, and self-regulation: The Good Lives Model of rehabilitation for sexual offenders. *Aggression and Violent Behavior, 11*, 77–94.

Ward, T., & Hudson, S. M. (2000). A self-regulation model of relapse prevention. In D. R. Laws, S. M. Hudson, & T. Ward (Eds.), *Remaking relapse prevention with sex offenders: A sourcebook* (pp. 79–101). New York: Sage.

Ward, T., & Keenan, T. (1999). Child molesters' implicit theories. *Journal of Interpersonal Violence, 14*, 821–838.

Ward, T., Louden, K., Hudson, S. M., & Marshall, W. L. (1995). A descriptive model of the offense chain for child molesters. *Journal of Interpersonal Violence, 10*, 452–472.

Wijkman, M., & Bijleveld, C. (2008, September). *Female sex offenders: Recidivism and criminal careers.* Paper presented at the 8th Annual Conference of the European Society of Criminology, Edinburgh, Scotland.

Yates, P. M., Kingston, D., & Hall, K. (2003, October). *Pathways to sexual offending: Validity of Hudson and Ward's (1998) self-regulation model and relationship to static and dynamic risk among treated high risk sexual offenders.* Presented at the 22nd Annual Research and Treatment Conference of the Association for the Treatment of Sexual Abusers (ATSA), St. Louis, MO.

INDEX

abusive experiences 4–5, 41–9, 55–9, 62, 74–82,
  112–13, 120, 123–6, 128–31, 134–5, 143–57,
  162–77, 190, 195
  see also victimisation
adaptive lifestyle outcomes 42–9, 120, 123
adjustment disorder 61
adolescent-boys category, typologies of female
  sexual offenders 33–4
adult-abusers category, typologies of female
  sexual offenders 33, 35–6, 47–9, 183
adult-based fantasies, treatment methods 124
ages
  juvenile female sexual offenders 53–9,
    60–1
  offenders 53–9, 60–1, 144–56
  victims 16, 18, 58–9, 60–1, 76, 149–56
'aggressive homosexual offenders' 35–6
aggressive-approach category, Descriptive
  Model of Female Sexual Offending
  (Gannon *et al*) 44, 46–9
alcohol abuse 37–8, 44, 47, 73–5, 79–82, 124–6,
  129–31, 146–7
antisocial behaviours 61, 77, 93–8, 156
apology letters 134–5
Approved Premises (APs) 167–8
Ashfield, Sherry 5–6, 161–80, 192–3
assertiveness skills 65–6, 126, 127–31, 137, 168
assessment of female sexual offenders
  see also risk . . .
  concepts 1–6, 9–10, 62–8, 73, 81–2, 87–98,
    121–37, 176–7, 190–5
  existing initiatives 5, 121–37, 181–95
  introduction 1–6
  juvenile female sexual offenders 3–4, 62–8,
    189, 194
  practices 93–8, 121–38, 181–95
attention deficit hyperactivity disorder
  (ADHD) 57–8
Australia 5, 11–12, 88, 135–8, 192
avoidant personality disorder 24, 77–82,
  110–11, 152

babysitters 149
Background Factors phase, level III
  micro-theories of female sexual offending
  41–9
Beckett, Richard 129, 191
behavioural assessments, assessment of female
  sexual offenders 122–3
behavioural therapy 63, 123–6, 127–31, 133,
  175–6
bestiality 58, 149, 151–2
betrayal dynamic, victim impact assessments
  21, 23–4, 25–6
biases, research 13, 16–17, 162–3
bipolar disorder 78–82
bisexuality 22
blame factors, victims 15–16, 21–2, 40–1, 47–9,
  75, 79, 104
Blanchette, Kelley 5, 77, 80–2, 91–7, 112, 114,
  119–41, 161, 190–2, 195
borderline personality disorder (BPD) 77–8, 120
Brotherston, Sheila 5–6, 161–80, 192–3
Bumby Rape and Molest Scales 122
Burton, David 5, 62, 143–60, 186, 188–9

California treatment initiatives 5, 131, 135
Canada 5, 11–12, 14–15, 56–7, 74, 88, 91, 110,
  120, 121–6, 136–7, 190–1, 194–5
case-file analyses 10–13, 14, 16–17, 18, 19, 22–3,
  25, 186
change goals
  stories and mirroring uses 174–5
  therapeutic process issues 169–77
characteristics
  female sexual offending 3–4, 33–49, 55–61,
    67–8, 73–82, 90–8, 147–54
  juvenile female sexual offenders 3–4, 55–61,
    67–8, 156, 189, 194
child protection systems 11–12, 19
childhood victimisation 3, 4–5, 39, 80–2, 94–5,
  96, 106–8, 110, 112–13, 120, 123–6, 144–56,
  162–77, 185, 190, 195

Childline 11
children of offenders 166–7
children victims 2–6, 166–7
children-as-sexual-objects perception, cognitive
    distortions 40–1, 102–4, 185–6
clinical histories, juvenile female sexual
    offenders 57–8, 61
clinical interviews, assessment of female sexual
    offenders 122–38
co-morbidity issues 81–2
    see also mental health
co-offenders 5, 33, 34–5, 39, 47–9, 59, 92–3, 94–5,
    102–6, 107–8, 111–12, 120, 125–6, 136–7,
    143–57, 164–77, 183–95
cognitive distortions 3, 4–5, 36, 38–41, 46–9, 61,
    63–8, 79, 93, 95, 102–4, 114–15, 120, 124–6,
    129–31, 134–5, 149–56, 185–6, 194–5
    see also perceptions
cognitive-behavioural therapy (CBT) 63, 123–6,
    133, 175–6
collaborative approaches 126, 130, 131, 136, 138,
    169–77
Colorado 5, 131, 133–4, 136–7, 138, 147–8, 154,
    157, 191–2
community reintegration, therapeutic process
    issues 167–8
community-based programmes 55, 62–8, 167–8
compulsive masturbation 58, 76, 105–6, 146,
    151–6, 170–1, 186
conduct disorder 61
confidence features, therapeutic process issues
    169–77
'consensual' sexual acts 18, 23–6, 134–5
consequences for female sexual offenders
    19–20, 54, 74–5, 108, 166–7
consultation programmes 122–31
controlling personality disorder 21–2, 24, 107–8
Coping Inventory for Stressful Situations
    (CISS) 123
coping styles 4–5, 42–9, 63–8, 94–6, 108–9,
    113–14, 123, 151–6, 163–77, 185, 187–95
coprophilia 150
Correctional Services of Canada (CSC) 5, 121–6,
    190–1
Cortoni, Franca 1–7, 12, 33, 34–5, 63, 73–86,
    87–100, 104–6, 108–9, 110, 113, 115, 119,
    125, 136, 143, 156, 158, 181–98
Counseling Institute of Texas (CIT) 132–3, 192
counselling services 65–8
crime 11–12, 14, 19–20, 31–49, 53–4, 73–82, 87,
    109–10, 120–38, 144–56, 161, 162–3, 166–7
criminal justice systems 11–12, 14, 19, 87,
    120–38, 144–56, 161, 162–3, 166–7
criminal prosecutions, statistics 19–20, 53–4,
    74–5, 109–10, 162–3
crossover offending 144–56

dangerous-world perception, cognitive
    distortions 40–1, 102–4, 112, 185–6
data-collection methods, research-design issues
    16–17, 55, 77–8

definitions of sexual abuse 17–19, 53–4, 75–6,
    90
denial mechanisms, cognitive distortions 40–1,
    47–9, 93, 95, 102–4, 123, 129–31, 155–6, 175
dental health 67
Department of Correctional Services 5, 135, 138,
    192
dependent personality disorder 4–5, 24–5, 45,
    77–82, 96, 103–15, 135, 152–6, 185, 188–9,
    194
depressive disorder 77–82, 108, 110–11, 129–31,
    151–2, 166
    see also dysthymic...
Descriptive Model of Female Sexual Offending
    (DMFSO) (Gannon et al) 3, 36, 41–9, 182–3
developments in female sexual offending 6,
    181–95
diagnosis see assessment...
Diagnostic and Statistical Manual of Mental
    Disorders (DSM-IV) 10, 75–81
dialectical behaviour therapy 127–30, 191
digital vagina penetration 60
directed-avoidant pathway to offending,
    Descriptive Model of Female Sexual
    Offending (Gannon et al) 43, 46–8, 182–3
directiveness features, therapeutic process
    issues 172
disclosure dynamic
    adulthood disclosures 16
    concepts 10–12, 13, 15–20, 54, 68, 169–77
    practitioner disclosures 169, 173–7
    relationships with abusers 16, 23–4, 25–6, 68
    therapeutic process issues 169, 173–7
dissociation 24, 64–8
domestic violence 44–9, 55–9, 96, 108–9, 112,
    150–6, 164–77, 190
drug misuse 19, 22–3, 37–8, 44, 45, 47, 56, 61,
    66–7, 73–82, 92, 94, 96, 110–11, 120, 124–6,
    129–31, 137, 146–7, 150–1, 156
DSM-IV see Diagnostic and Statistical Manual of
    Mental Disorders
dynamic risk factors 90–1, 93, 97–8, 184–5,
    193–4
dysthymic disorder 77–82
    see also depressive...

early family environment 41–9, 55–61, 80–2, 94,
    106–8, 112–13, 120, 123–6, 150–6, 164–5,
    190
egocentric features 96
Eldridge, Hilary 5–6, 75, 80, 81, 94–6, 101, 103,
    105, 108, 111, 128, 138, 161–80, 185, 192–3
Elliott, Ian 5–6, 161–80, 192–3
emotional bonds, therapeutic alliance 170–1
emotional regulation 63–8, 93, 95–6, 104, 108–9,
    115, 120, 123, 127–31, 152–6, 161, 175–7,
    185, 187–8
empathy 4–5, 104–5, 106, 124–6, 128–31, 132–4,
    163–77, 185–6
employment instability 44–9
empowerment 65–8

enemas 155–6
engaged victims, theories of female sexual offending 44, 47–9, 103–4, 155–6
entitlement perception, cognitive distortions 40–1, 102–4, 185–6
evidence-based outcome studies 63–8, 87–98, 115, 194
exhibitionism 58, 156
expert witnesses 127
explicit-precise pathway to offending, Descriptive Model of Female Sexual Offending (Gannon *et al*) 43, 46–8, 183
exposure behaviours 18

family environment 41–9, 55–61, 80–2, 94, 106–8, 112–13, 120, 123–6, 150–6, 164–5, 190
family-based court systems 166–7
fantasies 75–82, 94–5, 105–6, 123–6, 128–31, 146, 151–6, 171, 186–7
female outreach projects 130–1
female sexual arousal interest inventory (FSAII) 132–3
female sexual offending
  see also assessment . . . ; theories . . . ; treatment . . .
  ages of offenders 53–9, 60–1, 148–56
  causes 31–49, 55–61, 62, 73–82, 93–6, 101–2, 119–20, 133, 134, 151–6, 164–77, 182–3, 186–7
  characteristics 3–4, 33–49, 55–61, 67–8, 73–82, 90–8, 147–54
  children of offenders 166–7
  consequences 19–20, 53–4, 74–5, 108, 166–7
  criminal prosecutions 19–20, 53–4, 74–5, 109–10, 162–3
  developments 6, 181–95
  introduction 1–6
  juvenile female sexual offenders 3–4, 53–68, 189, 194
  male sexual offenders 1–2, 3, 5, 9–10, 12, 13, 17, 19–20, 21, 31–3, 53–4, 60–1, 62–3, 66, 75–7, 79–80, 87, 90–1, 95–6, 101–15, 119–38, 143–57, 162–77, 181–95
  mental health 1, 3, 4–5, 13, 14, 42, 43, 45–9, 56, 57–8, 60, 61, 73–82, 94, 108, 109–11, 113, 120, 137, 151–6, 165–6, 185, 189–90, 194–5
  non-sexually offending females 1–2, 3, 4, 39, 61, 77–8, 87–98, 104, 110, 112–13, 121, 150–1, 164–77, 189–90, 193–4
  polygraph uses 3, 5, 132–3, 147–57, 186, 188–9, 192
  prevalence 2, 3, 9–26, 53–4, 73–6, 143, 157, 162–3
  recidivism 1, 4, 67, 87–98, 136–7, 183–4, 192, 194
  role as mother 166–7
  statistics 2, 9–12, 17, 19–21, 53–61, 62–3, 73–7, 87–90, 102–4, 109–11, 147–56, 162–3, 183–4
  typologies 1, 3, 32, 33–49, 58–9, 61, 65–6, 81–2, 90–3, 101–2, 147–57, 182–3, 194
feminism 31

file reviews 121–3
Finkelhor Model 134–5
flexibility needs, therapeutic process issues 169, 176
fondling 59, 60
Ford, Hannah 4–5, 93, 95, 96, 101–17, 162, 171, 185, 187
Forensic Mental Health Associates (FMHA) 134–5
formal studies, prevalence of female sexual offending 9–20, 73–5, 162–3
Freud, S. 10
Frey, Lisa L. 3–4, 53–71, 192
frottage 58
future research and treatments 3, 6, 48–9, 54, 67–8, 114–15, 120, 135–7, 181–95

Gannon, Theresa A. 1–7, 18, 33, 35, 36–47, 77, 93–7, 101–14, 119–20, 128, 155, 161, 164–5, 168, 181–98
gender issues, victims 10–14, 15–16, 17–18, 19–26, 53–4, 58–9, 76, 105–6, 144–56
gender-informed interventions 5, 6, 136–7, 162–3, 181–95
gender responsive therapeutic approaches 5–6, 162–77, 181–95
gender-specific initiatives 5–6, 41–9, 120–38, 162–77, 181–95
General Theory of Crime (Gottfredson and Hirschi) 45
genuineness features, therapeutic process issues 169–77
Gibb, W. Travis 10
'good decisions diary' uses 176
Good Lives Model 126, 191
grooming 42, 110, 146–7
grounded theory methodologies 41–9, 182–3
group therapy 123, 133–4, 136–7, 168, 175–7, 191–2
guilt feelings 22–3

Hamill, Richard 134
Harris, Danielle A. 3, 31–51, 182
health care systems 19–20
Heil, Peggy 1, 5, 143–60, 186–90
heterosexuality 10–12
historical evidence, prevalence of female sexual offending 9–12, 93–8, 143, 181–2
HIV 67
holistic approaches to assessment and treatment 120–1, 137, 163–77
Home Office 12
'homosexual criminals' 35–6
homosexuality 10–12, 22, 35–6
honesty focus
  polygraph uses 3, 5, 132–3, 143–57, 192
  therapeutic process issues 169, 173–7
  treatment initiatives 132–3
human trafficking 47
humiliation, Descriptive Model of Female Sexual Offending (Gannon *et al*) 43, 46, 47

Illinois treatment initiatives 5, 131, 135
impact assessments
    betrayal dynamic 21, 23–4, 25–6
    concepts 3, 13, 18, 19, 20–6
    gender issues 21–6
    mental health 21–6
    powerlessness dynamic 21, 24–6
    self-concepts 24–5
    stigmatisation dynamic 21, 22–3, 25–6
    traumatic-sexualisation dynamic 21–2, 25–6
implicit-disorganised (impulsive) pathway to
    offending, Descriptive Model of Female
    Sexual Offending (Gannon et al) 43, 46–8,
    183, 185–6
impulse control disorder 43, 46–8, 77–82
in-depth interviews, data-collection methods
    16–17
incest 10, 14–18, 23–4, 25–6, 35, 38, 55–6, 145–56
instant offence disclosure polygraph tests
    145–6, 147
Integrated Theory (Marshall and Barbaree) 41,
    45–6
intellectual disabilities 74–5, 78–9, 188
internalising/externalising behaviours 61, 75
interpersonal relationships 4–5, 39–49, 60, 63–8,
    80–2, 93–4, 95–6, 106–8, 111, 115, 120,
    122–6, 128–31, 134–5, 137, 152–6, 164–77,
    188–95
interventions 5, 87, 90–8, 110–11, 119–38, 190–5
    see also treatment . . .
interviews
    see also polygraph uses
assessment of female sexual offenders 121–38
intimacy motivations, theories of female sexual
    offending 43, 46–9, 93, 107–8, 114, 122–3,
    125–6, 129–31, 183, 185, 187
Ireland 131

juvenile female sexual offenders 3–4, 53–68,
    156, 189, 194
    adult female sexual offenders 3–4, 59–60
    ages 53–9, 60–1
    assessment 3–4, 62–8, 189, 194
    characteristics 3–4, 55–61, 67–8, 156, 189, 194
    clinical histories 57–8, 61
    comments on the current literature 3–4, 55,
    64–6, 67–8
    male sexual offenders 60–1, 62–3, 66
    other offender populations 3–4, 59–61
    other problematic sexual behaviours 58
    PTSD 57–8, 61–4
    statistics 53–61, 62–3, 76
    treatments 3–4, 54, 56–7, 62–8, 189, 194

kidnapping 88

language uses
    research-design issues 18–19
    therapeutic process issues 170–1, 175
learning difficulties 24, 74–82

level I multifactorial theories of female sexual
    offending 32, 36–8
level II single-factor theories of female sexual
    offending 3, 32, 34–5, 36, 38–41
level III micro-theories of female sexual
    offending 32, 36, 41–9
lifestyle outcomes, Descriptive Model of
    Female Sexual Offending (Gannon et al)
    41–9, 95, 96
listening skills, professionals 162–3
locus of control 129–31
'love' misconceptions 21, 107–8
LSI-R 97
Lucy Faithfull Foundation (LFF) 5, 126–31, 138,
    161–77, 190–1
'Ludic lovestyle' 107–8

maintenance polygraph tests 146–7, 156
major life stressors 41–9, 108–9, 120, 175, 188
maladaptive lifestyle outcomes 4–5, 42–9, 63–8,
    94–6, 104, 108–9, 113–14, 120, 123, 151–6,
    163–77, 185, 187–95
male sexual offenders 1–2, 3, 5, 9–10, 12, 13, 17,
    19–20, 21, 31–3, 53–4, 60–1, 62–3, 66, 75–7,
    79–80, 87, 90–1, 95–6, 101–15, 119–38,
    143–57, 162–77, 181–95
    crossover offending 144–56
    gender responsive therapeutic approaches
    5–6, 163–4
    juvenile female sexual offenders 60–1, 62–3, 66
    polygraph uses 5, 143–57
    therapeutic process issues 162–77
Marshall, W.L. 161–3, 168–75, 177
masculine identity 32–3
'masks' 171–2
masochism 10, 75–6, 150–1
masturbation 58, 76, 105–6, 146, 151–6, 170–1,
    186
maternal-approach category, Descriptive
    Model of Female Sexual Offending
    (Gannon et al) 44, 46–9, 105–6
maternal-avoidant category, Descriptive Model
    of Female Sexual Offending (Gannon et al)
    44, 46–9, 182–3
media reports 2
medications, mental health 166
mental disorders 74–82, 94, 108, 109–11, 113,
    120, 151–6, 165–6, 189–90, 194
mental health
    see also personality disorders;
    psychopathology
    female sexual offending 1, 3, 4–5, 13, 14, 42,
    43, 45–9, 56, 57–8, 60, 61, 73–82, 94, 108,
    109–11, 113, 120, 137, 151–6, 165–6, 185,
    189–90, 194–5
    medications 166
    research 73–82, 109–11, 120, 185, 189–90, 194
    statistics 73–5, 77–8, 109–11, 166
    victimisation histories 80–1, 94
    victims 21–6

mentors 66–7
meta-analyses 88–90, 136–7, 183–4
micro-level theories, level III micro-theories of female sexual offending 32, 36, 41–9
Miller Social Intimacy Scale 122
Miller's relational theory 164–5
Millon clinical multiaxial inventory 129–31
mirroring uses, therapeutic process issues 174–5
mixed-gender treatment programmes 5, 133–8, 164–77
monitoring polygraph tests 146–7
mood disorders 74–82
    see also depressive . . . ; dysthymic . . .
mothers, offender's role as mother 166–7
motivations
    intimacy motivations 43, 46–9, 93, 107–8, 114, 122–3, 125–6, 129–31, 183, 185, 187
    therapeutic process issues 171–2
MSI-II 78, 104, 107

National Offender Management Service (NOMS) 5, 135, 138, 167–8, 192
nature-of-harm perception, cognitive distortions 40–1, 93, 95, 102–4, 155–6, 185–6
'neediness' 135
    see also dependent . . .
Netherlands 56–7, 88
neutralisation techniques, cognitive distortions 40–1, 47–9
New Life Plan 127–9, 168, 171–2, 174
New South Wales 5, 135–8, 192
New York treatment initiatives 5, 131, 134–5, 137, 191–2
New Zealand 11–12, 14–15
non-sexually offending females 1–2, 3, 4, 39, 61, 77–8, 87–98, 104, 110, 112–13, 121, 150–1, 164–77, 189–90, 193–4
NSPCC 11, 16
nursery settings 17

obscene phone calls 58
obsessive compulsive disorder 24
offence approach/behaviour, Descriptive Model of Female Sexual Offending (Gannon et al) 41, 44–9
offence chain theory 3, 36, 41–9, 182–3, 188
    see also Descriptive Model of Female Sexual Offending
Offence Period phase, level III micro-theories of female sexual offending 41, 44–9
offence styles 14, 35–6, 43, 44–9, 58–60, 182–95
olfactory reconditioning 124
openness features, therapeutic process issues 169, 173–7
operational-approach category, Descriptive Model of Female Sexual Offending (Gannon et al) 44, 46–9
oral sex 14, 59

orgasmic reconditioning 124
overview of the book 2–6

paedophilia, definition 76–7
paranoid personality disorder 78–82
paraphilias 75–7, 93, 104–15, 124–6, 144–56
parenting skills 168
pathways, Descriptive Model of Female Sexual Offending (Gannon et al) 47–9, 182–3
patriarchy powerlessness pathway 37–49
Paulhus Deception Scales 123, 129
peer relationships 4–5, 39, 42, 45, 63–8, 80–2, 93–4, 95–6, 104, 106–8, 111, 115, 120, 122–6, 128–31, 134–5, 137, 152–6, 164–77, 188–95
perceptions 13–20, 21–2, 23–6, 40–1, 54, 93, 95, 102–4, 123–6, 149–56, 169–77, 185–6, 194–5
    see also cognitive distortions
    cognitive-behavioural therapy (CBT) 63, 123–6, 175–6
    'consensual' sexual acts 18, 23–6, 134–5, 155
    social/cultural construction of women 13–20, 21–2, 25–6, 54, 143, 182–3
    therapeutic alliance 169–77
personality disorders 21–5, 42, 43, 45–9, 57–8, 60, 74–82, 110–11, 120, 151–6
    see also mental health
physical abuse 10, 19–20, 21, 41–9, 59–60, 74–82, 106, 112, 144–56, 165–77, 190, 194
physical exercise 175
pilot programmes 128–31
planning, Descriptive Model of Female Sexual Offending (Gannon et al) 43, 46–9
police 14–15, 19
polygraph uses
    accuracy statistics 147
    concepts 3, 5, 132–3, 143–57, 186, 188–9, 192
    deterrent effects 146–7
    female sexual offenders 3, 5, 132–3, 147–57, 186, 188–9, 192
    male sexual offenders 5, 143–57
    overview 145–7
    recommendations 154–7
    research 5, 143–57, 186, 188–9
    test types 145–7
pornography 58, 146, 150, 151–4
positive psychology 124, 128–31, 171–2
post-traumatic stress disorder (PTSD) 57–8, 61–4, 74, 77–82, 110–11, 127–31, 151–2, 165–6, 191
powerlessness dynamic
    patriarchy powerlessness pathway 37–49
    theories of female sexual offending 3, 33–49, 106–8
    victim impact assessments 21, 24–6
    victimisation powerlessness pathway 37–49
practitioners see professionals
Pre-Offence Period phase, level III micro-theories of female sexual offending 41, 43–9
pre-verbal abuse 16

prevalence of female sexual offending 2, 3, 9–26, 53–4, 73–6, 143, 157, 162–3
  confounding establishment factors 13–20, 143
  formal studies 9–20, 143
  historical evidence 9–12, 93–8, 143, 181–2
  professional responses 13, 14–20, 157
  research-design issues 3, 16–20
  secrecy aspects 9
  social/cultural construction of women 13–20, 21–2, 25–6, 54, 62, 65–7, 143, 182–3
problem-focused solutions 128–31, 174
professionals
  concepts 1–6, 9, 13, 14–20, 65–8, 121, 126–30, 132, 137, 157, 161–77, 186–90
  flexibility needs 169, 176
  listening skills 162–3
  practitioner disclosures 169, 173–7
  responses 13, 14–20, 157
  therapeutic alliance 168–77, 190–5
  therapeutic process issues 5–6, 161–77
  training 14–15, 65–8, 121, 126–30, 132, 137, 162
progress-recognition features, therapeutic process issues 169, 175–7
promiscuous behaviour 44–9
prostitution 21–2, 35–6, 37–8, 47, 88–90, 92, 150–1, 194
proximal planning, Descriptive Model of Female Sexual Offending (Gannon et al) 43, 46–9
psychiatric disorders 74, 77–82, 109–11
psychological/psychometric tests 122–9
psychopathology 4, 55–6, 61, 73–82
  see also mental health
psychosis 25–6, 74–82, 110–11, 190
  see also schizophrenia

racial/ethnic demographic factors 55, 66–8
rapes 9, 14–20, 53–4, 122–3, 144–7, 152–6
recidivism
  concepts 1, 4, 67, 87–98, 136–7, 156, 183–4, 192, 194
  definitions 88, 184
  dynamic risk factors 90–1, 93, 97–8, 184–5, 193–4
  relative/absolute contrasts 91
  risk assessments 4, 87, 90–8, 156, 183–4
  statistics 87–90, 136, 183–4
  types 88–9
relapse prevention therapy 63, 133, 182–3
relational theory 164–5
relational-cultural model 65–8, 93, 120, 126
relationships
  interpersonal relationships 4–5, 39–49, 60, 63–8, 80–2, 93–4, 95–6, 106–8, 111, 115, 120, 122–6, 128–31, 134–5, 137, 152–6, 164–77, 188–95
  victims 16, 23–4, 25–6, 39–49, 58–9, 60, 134–5
religious beliefs 66–7
research
  see also studies

biases 13, 16–17, 162–3
concepts 1–6, 9–20, 53–68, 73–5, 119–38, 143–57, 181–95
data-collection methods 16–17, 55, 77–8
definitions of sexual abuse 17–19, 53–4
design issues 3, 16–20, 181–95
juvenile female sexual offenders 53–68, 156, 189, 194
language uses 18–19
mental health 73–82, 109–11, 120, 185, 189–90, 194
polygraph uses 5, 143–57, 186, 188–9
recidivism 87–93, 136, 183–4
target populations 17, 73–5, 87–90
residentially-based programmes 55–6, 59, 62, 67, 167–8
resistance to treatment 134, 166
resistant victims 44, 47–9
risk assessments 4, 41, 43–9, 87, 90–8, 128–37, 156, 183–95
  see also assessment . . .
risk factors 41, 43–9, 90–8, 128–31, 156, 183–4
Risk-Need-Responsivity Model 192, 195
role models 66–7
role-plays 123–6
Rose, Marianne R. 1, 2, 6, 33, 34, 35, 39, 40, 44, 93–5, 101–5, 112, 119–20, 155, 161, 164–5, 181–98
Rosenberg Self-Esteem Inventory 122
Rousseau, Myriam-Mélanie 4, 73–86, 187

sadism 21, 150–1
safety boundaries, therapeutic process issues 172
Saradjian, Jacqui 3, 9–30, 75, 78–81, 94–6, 128, 150, 164, 167–8, 170, 174–5, 185–8
Saratoga County Probation Department (SCPD) 135, 138
schema therapy 127–30, 191
schizoid 78–82
schizophrenia 78–82
  see also psychosis
school bullying 44, 61, 96, 190
school failure 44, 57, 61, 67
secrecy aspects, prevalence of female sexual offending 9
seductive touching 18, 146
self-concepts
  offenders 6, 24–5, 34, 63–8, 96, 109, 112–13, 122–3, 124–6, 127–31, 134–5, 137, 151–6, 161–77, 191–5
  victims 24–5
self-control measures 45, 48–9, 63–8, 93, 104, 120, 124–6, 191–5
self-efficacy 109, 112, 122–3
self-esteem 6, 109, 112, 122–3, 125, 127–31, 134–5, 137, 151–6, 168, 175
self-harming 22–3, 57–8, 80–2, 108–9, 175
self-management treatment 124–6, 128–31
self-medication 79

self-reported studies 13, 16–17, 54, 56, 75, 124–6, 143–57, 186–7, 188–9
sentences, statistics 19–20, 53–4, 74–5, 109–10
services, concepts 3
sexual abuse, definitions 17–19, 53–4, 75–6, 90
sexual arousal 36, 40, 44, 47, 63–8, 76–82, 94–5, 104–6, 124–6, 132–3, 137, 155–6, 185–7, 191–2
sexual coercion 4–5, 32–4, 38–49, 59, 61, 94, 103–5, 107–8, 110–12, 137, 149–56, 183–95
    see also co-offenders
sexual gratification, theories of female sexual offending 43, 46–9, 63–8
sexual history disclosure polygraph tests 144, 145–6, 151, 154–6
sexual offence histories 1, 5, 41–9, 55–61, 80–2, 90, 91–2, 93–8, 123, 132–3, 143–57
sexual trauma treatment 57–8, 61–8, 74, 77–82, 110–11, 127–31, 151–2, 165–6, 191
sexuality 10–12, 22, 35–6, 94–5, 129–31
shame 22–3, 163–77
shoplifters 37–8
Simons, Dominique 1, 2, 5, 143–60, 186–90
social learning theory 63, 123–6
social phobia 152–6
social support 4–5, 42–9, 94, 96, 106–8, 111–12, 115, 120, 125–6, 187
social/cultural construction of women 13–20, 21–2, 25–6, 54, 62, 65–7, 143, 182–3
societal attitudes 3, 9–26
solo sexual offenders 92–3, 103–4, 136–7, 149–56, 188–9
somatic complaints 80–2
specialised sexual offender assessments 122–3
specific issues polygraph tests 147
static risk factors, recidivism 90–3
STATIC-99 risk tool 97
statistics, sexual offending 2, 9–12, 17–18, 19–21, 53–61, 62–3, 73–6, 87–90, 102–4, 109–11, 144–56, 162–3, 183–4
stigmatisation dynamic, victim impact assessments 21, 22–3, 25–6
stories and mirroring uses, therapeutic process issues 174–5
strengths-based approaches, therapeutic process issues 127–9, 168
studies
    see also research
    historical evidence 9–12, 143, 181–2
    known offenders 11–12
    prevalence of female sexual offending 3, 9–26, 73–5, 143, 162–3
    recidivism 87–93, 136, 183–4
    self-reported studies 13, 16–17, 54, 56, 75, 124–6, 143–57, 186–7, 188–9
submissive victims 44, 47–9
substance abuse *see* drug misuse
suicides 22, 57, 80–1, 151
support features, therapeutic process issues 169–77

survival strategies, therapeutic process issues 167, 172, 175
Sweden 189–90

target populations, research-design issues 17, 73–5, 87–90
Taylor, Kelly N. 5, 119–41, 161, 190–2
teacher/lover female sexual offenders 34, 47–9, 154
Texas treatment initiatives 5, 131, 132–3, 136–8, 191–2
theories of female sexual offending
    concepts 1–6, 31–49, 55–9, 93–4, 101–15, 119–20, 133, 134, 149–56, 164–77, 182–95
    Descriptive Model of Female Sexual Offending (Gannon *et al*) 3, 36, 41–9, 182–3
    introduction 1–6
    level I/II/III theories 3, 32, 34–5, 36–49
therapeutic alliance
    concepts 168–77, 190–5
    emotional bonds 170–1
therapeutic process issues
    see also treatment...
    change goals 169–77
    children of offenders 166–7
    community reintegration 167–8
    concepts 5–6, 161–77, 190–5
    gender responsive therapeutic approaches 5–6, 162–77, 181–95
    honesty focus 169, 173–7
    important factors 168–77, 190–5
    language uses 170–1, 175
    motivations 171–2
    openness features 169, 173–7
    practitioner disclosures 169, 173–7
    progress-recognition features 169, 175–7
    realistic shared goals 171–2
    safety boundaries 172
    stories and mirroring uses 174–5
    strengths-based approaches 127–9, 168
    survival strategies 167, 172, 175
therapist-client relationship *see* therapeutic alliance
'throwaway services for throwaway girls' 68
training 14–15, 65–8, 121, 126–30, 132, 137, 162
trauma therapy 57–8, 61–4, 74, 77–82, 110–11, 127–31, 151–2, 165–6, 191
traumatic-sexualisation dynamic, victim impact assessments 21–2, 25–6
treatment of female sexual offenders
    see also therapeutic process issues
    community reintegration 167–8
    community-based programmes 55, 62–8, 167–8
    concepts 1–6, 17, 48–9, 54, 56–7, 62–8, 73, 77, 81–2, 87, 90–3, 96, 101–15, 119–38, 143–57, 161–77, 181–95
    critique 119–38, 161–77, 181–95
    existing initiatives 5, 121–37, 181–95

treatment of female sexual offenders (*Cont'd*)
  future research and treatments 3, 6, 48–9, 54,
    67–8, 114–15, 120, 135–7, 181–95
  gender-specific initiatives 5–6, 41–9, 120–38,
    162–77, 181–95
  goals 171–2
  group therapy 123, 133–4, 136–7, 168, 175–7,
    191–2
  introduction 1–6
  juvenile female sexual offenders 3–4, 54,
    56–7, 62–8, 189, 194
  needs 4–5, 101–15, 123–38, 161–77, 184–95
  pilot programmes 128–31
  polygraph uses 3, 5, 132–3, 143–57, 186, 188–9
  residentially-based programmes 55–6, 59, 62,
    67, 167–8
  resistance to treatment 134, 166
  review of initiatives 119–38, 190–2
  therapeutic alliance 168–77, 190–5
truancy 44–9
trust problems, victims 21–6
typologies of female sexual offenders 1, 3, 32,
    33–49, 58–9, 61, 65–6, 81–2, 90–3, 101–2,
    111–12, 120, 147–57, 182–3, 194
  adolescent-boys category 33–4
  adult-abusers category 33, 35–6, 47–9, 183
  categories 33–6, 47–9, 58–9, 102–4, 120
  co-offenders category 5, 33, 34–5, 39, 47–9, 59,
    92–5, 94–5, 102–6, 107–8, 111–12, 120,
    125–6, 136–7, 143–57, 164–77, 183–95
  concepts 1, 3, 33–49, 58–9, 90–3, 101–2, 182–3
  level I/II/III theories 3, 32, 34–5, 36–49
  violence 34–6, 44–9, 59, 61, 65–6, 81–2, 96,
    110, 122–6, 150–6, 164–77, 183–4
  young-children category 33–4, 47–9, 58–9,
    102–15, 151–6, 161–77, 182–95

U.C.L.A. Loneliness Scale 122, 129
UK 5, 11–12, 15, 88, 120, 126–31, 135–8, 161–77,
    190–1, 192, 194–5
uncontrollability perception, cognitive
    distortions 40–1, 102–4, 112, 185–6
unstable lifestyle with negative affect 41, 43–9,
    95, 96, 182–3
urophilia 150
USA 5, 11–12, 19–20, 53–4, 73–4, 87, 88, 91, 108,
    120, 131–5, 136–7, 147–8, 154, 157, 163–4,
    190–1, 194–5

vaginal inspections 155–6
vaginal photoplethysmography 106
victimisation
  see also abusive experiences
  histories 3, 4–5, 39, 80–2, 94–5, 96, 106–8, 110,
    112–13, 120, 123–6, 128–33, 143–57, 162–77,
    185, 190, 195
  powerlessness pathway 37–49
victims 2–6, 9–26, 40–9, 53–4, 58–9, 68, 102,
    104–5, 106, 124–6, 128–38, 144–56
  see also impact assessments
  ages 16, 18, 58–9, 60–1, 76, 149–56
  blame factors 15–16, 21–2, 40–1, 47–9, 75, 79,
    104
  Descriptive Model of Female Sexual
    Offending (Gannon *et al*) 41, 44–9, 182–3
  disclosure dynamic 10–12, 13, 15–20, 54, 68
  empathy 4–5, 104–5, 106, 124–6, 128–31,
    132–3, 163–77, 185–6
  gender issues 10–14, 15–16, 17–18, 19–26,
    53–4, 58–9, 76, 105–6, 144–56
  mental health impacts 21–6
  relationships with abusers 16, 23–4, 25–6,
    58–9, 60, 104, 134–5
  self-concepts 24–5
  therapy 16, 17, 24–6
  trust problems 21–6
violence
  domestic violence 44–9, 55–9, 96, 108–9, 112,
    150–6, 164–77, 190
  typologies of female sexual offenders 34–6,
    44–9, 59, 61, 65–6, 81–2, 88–90–2, 96, 110,
    122–6, 150–6, 164–77, 183–4
violent recidivism, statistics 88–90, 183–4
visualisation techniques 175
voyeurism 18, 58, 146, 155–6
vulnerability factors 41–9

Warren County Probation of New York 134–5,
    137, 138
Wells, Ruth 68
'What Works' information 192, 195
Wisdom Works Counseling Services (WWCS)
    133–4, 190–2

young-children category, typologies of female
    sexual offenders 33–4, 58–9, 102–15, 151–6,
    161–77, 182–95

Index Compiled by Terry Halliday